eSports Yearbook

Editors: Julia Hiltscher and Tobias M. Scholz
Layout: Tobias M. Scholz
Cover Photo: Tobias M. Scholz
Copyright © 2024 by the Authors of the Articles or Pictures.
ISBN: 978-3-7597-5071-6
Production and publishing: BoD – Books on Demand, Norderstedt
Printed in Germany 2024
www.esportsyearbook.com

eSports Yearbook 2021-23

Editors: Julia Hiltscher and Tobias M. Scholz

Contributors:
Kamelia Bankova, Guillermo Benito-Corps, Adrián Martín Castellanos, Despoina Farmaki, Bruno Duarte Abreu Freitas, Iván Bonilla Gorrindo, Kim S. Johnson, Cora Kennedy, Andrés Chamarro Lusar, Brian McCauley, Amelia Nablsi, Manuel Barba Ruíz, Eric Gargallo Serrano, Brett Shelton, Chareen Snelson, Diego Muriarte Solana, Jesus H. Trespalacios, Ziqi Wang

Content

Summer is Coming   **8**
By Julia Hiltscher and Tobias M. Scholz

Effective eSports Sponsoring Must Be Planned Long-Term   **10**
By Bruno Duarte Abreu Freitas

What is the difference between the Major and the regional leagues?
Comparisons between the demands of European teams.   **20**
By Adrián Martín-Castellanos, Iván Bonilla Gorrindo, Guillermo Benito-Corps,
Andrés Chamarro Lusar, Manuel Barba Ruíz, Diego Muriarte Solana

"Old-School" is now too cool! Exploring motivations for attending a
LAN from a U&G perspective   **32**
By Kamelia Bankova and Amelia Nablsi

Traditional sports organizations' expansion to eSports   **59**
By Eric Gargallo Serrano

The Electric Brain: New Intelligent Agents in eSports   **101**
By Ziqi Wang

Balancing Acts: Copyright, Expression, and the Nintendo Paradigm in Esports Streaming 112
By Despoina Farmaki

Gaming Their Way to Success: Esports and the Crucial Skills for Tomorrow's Workforce 120
By Tobias M. Scholz

Startup Culture Shouldn't Last Forever 123
By Cora Kennedy

CS:GO to Valorant: Informal Reflections on an Ongoing Auto-Netnographic Journey in Esports 133
By Brian McCauley

Exploring Women's Experiences in Collegiate Esports Leadership 143
By Kim S. Johnson, Jesus H. Trespalacios, Brett Shelton, Chareen Snelson

Summer is Coming

By Julia Hiltscher and Tobias M. Scholz

As we open the pages of this edition of the eSports Yearbook, we find ourselves at a pivotal juncture, reminiscent of the thawing transition from the starkness of winter to the promise of summer. The preceding 'eSports winter' has been a crucible, testing the mettle of the community, businesses, and athletes alike, with its harsh economic downturns and the forced introspection and recalibration of strategies within the industry. This period, however challenging, has been instrumental in fostering innovation, resilience, and a renewed sense of unity across the eSports landscape. Now, as we stand on the cusp of 'Summer is Coming,' this edition aims to encapsulate the burgeoning optimism and the collective yearning for renewal. It serves as both a reflection on the trials overcome, and a forward-looking anticipation of the vibrant growth poised to redefine the future of eSports.

However, just as winter gives way to spring and then summer, the world of eSports is beginning to see the first signs of thawing, heralding the onset of a new era. This edition, aptly titled 'Summer is Coming', captures the essence of resilience and adaptability that has become the hallmark of eSports.

Our contributors, hailing from diverse backgrounds and expertise, offer insights into the multifaceted nature of eSports, from technological innovations to cultural shifts, legal challenges, and beyond. Let's take a closer look at the rich tapestry of topics covered in our chapters:

Innovation and Evolution in eSports: The digital battlegrounds of eSports are constantly reshaped by technological advancements and strategic foresight. Bruno Duarte Abreu Freitas unravels the complexities of long-term eSports sponsorship, while Ziqi Wang peers into the future with intelligent agents revolutionizing the industry. These chapters underscore the importance of innovation in sustaining the growth and excitement of eSports.

Comparative Analyses and Insights: The structure and impact of competitions vary significantly across the globe. A. Martín Castellanos and colleagues provide a detailed comparison between Major leagues and regional leagues, offering a lens through which to understand the strategic and operational nuances of eSports organizations.

Cultural Shifts and Community Engagement: The eSports community thrives on its vibrant culture and engaged fan base. Kamelia Bankova and Amelia Nablsi revisit the charm of 'Old-School' LAN events, while Eric Gargallo Serrano explores traditional sports organizations' foray into the digital arena, highlighting the ongoing cultural exchange between traditional sports and eSports.

Legal and Economic Perspectives: The rapid expansion of eSports encounters a complex web of legal and economic challenges. Despoina Farmaki delves into copyright issues in streaming, and Cora Kennedy critically examines the startup culture within eSports organizations, advocating for a more sustainable approach to growth and development.

Personal and Professional Development: Beyond entertainment, eSports offers pathways for personal and professional growth. Tobias Scholz links eSports with skill development for future careers, and Brian McCauley shares his personal journey through different gaming communities, emphasizing the learning and adaptation within the eSports ecosystem. Kim S. Johnson, Jesus H. Trespalacios, Brett Shelton, Chareen Snelson are investigating the experiences of women in collegiate esports leadership.

Each chapter, contributed by a variety of authors, enriches our understanding of eSports, painting a picture of an industry at the cusp of a new dawn. As we delve into this year's

Yearbook, we celebrate the resilience, creativity, and spirit of the eSports community, looking forward to the sunny days ahead in the realm of competitive gaming.

In this moment of reflection and anticipation, 'Summer is Coming' transcends the literal change of seasons, embodying the resurgence and revitalization within the eSports community. This Yearbook, rich with the contributions of visionaries and pioneers, not only chronicles the journey through the eSports winter but also heralds the advent of a new era marked by innovation, inclusivity, and unprecedented growth. As you navigate through the chapters, let them inspire you with the stories of resilience, the strategic insights, and the shared dreams that bind the eSports community. This collection is a beacon of hope and a testament to the indefatigable spirit that drives the industry forward. Together, we embark on this journey into the summer of eSports, ready to embrace the challenges and opportunities that await, and to celebrate the endless possibilities that the future holds.

Yours,

Julia Hiltscher (Christophers) &

Tobias M. Scholz

... keep on gaming!

P.S. Although there is seemingly a consensus to write esports and not eSports, we will stay with the path we chose over a decade ago with the first eSports Yearbook. More importantly, Julia's and Tobias's first project together in 2004 was also writing eSports, so for us, it is tradition.

Effective eSports Sponsoring Must Be Planned Long-Term

By Bruno Duarte Abreu Freitas

In 2019, when I was doing my PhD, I interviewed 22 experts in eSports sponsoring from 22 different companies. Seven worked at endemic brands (i.e. brands whose business and products are directly connected to eSports) that sponsored eSports (hereinafter referred to as *EES*), eight at non-endemic brands (i.e. brands whose business and products are not related to eSports) that sponsored eSports (hereinafter referred to as *NEES*), and seven at marketing agencies with expertise in eSports sponsoring (hereinafter referred to as *MA*). Unfortunately, I do not have permission to disclose the real names of these brands or of the individuals I interviewed (which is very unfortunate because I am so proud of being able to reach and talk with these amazing and extremely knowledgeable human beings). An online survey for eSports fans was also created on Google Forms and conducted on Reddit (i.e. on 1,155 subreddits) and Discord (i.e. on 78 Discord Channels), with 5,638 fans filling out the survey.

The research had three objectives: to identify the main (1) benefits, (2) risks, and (3) strategies of sponsoring eSports. Fortunately, the interviewees answered all the questions presented to them (as did the fans), which allowed all these objectives to be reached and the PhD to be successfully finished. But one of the most interesting things when conducting interviews for scientific research, is the things people say without being asked about. These sequences of grammatically constructed words pronounced out of the sheer will to freely express oneself (or maybe a desire to stress a point that the interviewee failed to see as relevant) should be seen as central and vital pieces of information for most research. Anyone who conducted interviews has most likely had the feeling that they are being an inconvenience or taking precious time from the interviewee, so why should the person being interviewed take extra time to add something without being directly asked? The reason is that they are passionate and knowledgeable about the subject and want to make sure the interviewer clearly understands the most important points. Unfortunately, these extra answers are usually set aside or just briefly mentioned in the final paper. But not this time. This entire article is dedicated to one particularly important strategy that 10 eSports experts decided to mention without being asked about it. Bearing in mind that these interviews did not happen at the same time (and the interviewees did not know who else was being interviewed), it is evident that, instead of a simple coincidence, this is an indicator that this is likely a very important strategy for eSports sponsors. Oh, and five eSports fans also mentioned this strategy without being asked about it.

The online interviews with the eSports experts happened between 15 August 2019 and 12 December 2019. A structured questionnaire with 45 questions was used to guide the interviews. At the end of each interview, it was always asked "Would you like to add anything else about the main benefits, risks, and strategies of eSports sponsorships?". Similarly, the online survey with 37 questions for eSports fans occurred between 29 June 2019 and 3 December 2019, and, the last question asked "Would you like to add anything else about what was addressed in this survey? (Optional)". Given the large number of questions, it is even more remarkable that participants dedicated even more time to provide additional information (in fact, most interviews lasted between one and three hours).

Results and Discussion

In total, 45.5% (i.e. $n = 10/22$) of the sample of experts and 0.08% (i.e. $n = 5/5,638$) of the sample of eSports fans provided comments directly stating, or alluding, that eSports sponsors should enter competitive gaming with a long-term sponsoring strategy. Despite the miniscule number of eSports fans, the fact that almost half of the sample of experts indicated this (and without being asked about it) proves the high relevance of the provided information. It is believed that the reason why so few eSports fans added this information is because their survey did not directly ask them to indicate, or grade, the importance of strategies for successful eSports sponsoring. By contrast, experts were directly asked to indicate how much they agreed (or disagreed) with statements indicating strategies for sponsoring eSports.

"If you're in it for the long term, then it's a sustainable investment"

As stated by all 10 experts, overall, brands that are sponsoring competitive gaming for the long-term are the most likely to be happy and have positive return-on-investments: *"Those who are patient and are willing to wait it out will receive a return on their investment. […] If you are in it for the long-term, you will be happy with your investment"* (EES1); *"In the long-term those generate sales"* (EES2); *"Sponsorships should always be long-term activations or a long-term marketing tool […] It should be something long-term"* (NEES1); *"I think this is less about the problems and more about educating brands about the benefits here and the long-term benefits here"* (NEES2); *"Commit to a longer sponsorship agreement"* (MA2); *"On the long term, yes"* (MA3); *"Plan long-term"* (MA4); *"Don't expect to lead to a large increase in sales in the short-term"* (MA5); and *"Sponsoring in eSports is a long run"* (MA6). Some eSports fans also stated a desire for long-term sponsorships: *"Sponsor things for the long run"*

(Fan ID 66) and *"Continued interest in current and future generations of the player base is what everyone wants for the games they love"* (Fan ID 107). This is in sync with Korpimies (2017), Renard and Sitz (2011), and Söderman and Dolles (2010), who indicate that sponsorships must be long-term. Interestingly, MA1 points out that brands should not perceive eSports as a passing trend nor as something solely targeted at teenagers (probably because, as we have already discussed, these teenagers will grow and have needs and wishes, so it is better to start fostering brand preference from this tender age): *"This is not a trend, this is not something for teenagers, this is a part of your marketing strategy for the next years"* (MA1).

According to several experts, eSports sponsorships are only sustainable in the long-term: *"If you're in it for the long term, then it's a sustainable investment"* (EES1); *"If you pursue a long-term strategy in eSports then it's a sustainable investment"* (NEES1); and *"The market is growing so I'd say on the long term it's a sustainable investment"* (MA3). EES1 explicitly pointed out that companies hunting for "a quick ROI" with short-term eSports sponsorships may be disappointed and will be better off in other industries because competitive gaming does not provide good short-term returns. Specifically: *"Those who are investing now, for the short term, may be disappointed in their investment, if they pull out too soon. […] if they're looking for a quick ROI, if you're just looking to get in and get out, I don't think eSports is right for you"* (EES1). EES2 even stressed that simple things, like gathering a social media following, take time and that, only after that long-term commitment, they might notice an increase in sales: *"Most of the time we increase followings in our social media accounts that maybe in the long-term those generate sales"* (EES2).

Interestingly, MA3, MA5, and MA6 provided the example of expensive car brands, like Porsche or Mercedes that sponsor competitive gaming with the clear objective of firstly creating awareness, then promoting preference and, only after all that, fostering a purchase intent and, finally, making the sale:

"On the long term, yes, because if you look at the traditional brand objectives, most of the non-endemic brands like car manufacturers, insurances, etc., they are just entering eSports so first they are trying to build awareness among the target audience, and then preference, and then latter on purchase intent and try to drive sales" (MA3); *"Mercedes has been sponsoring eSports, a relatively expensive car brand, those I don't expect to lead to a large increase in sales in the short-term"* (MA5); and *"Sometimes sponsoring in eSports is a long run, and you see, for example, Mercedes or Porsche, they're not sponsoring eSports because they expect to get things sold tomorrow"* (MA6). These companies have this well-established long-term commitment because they are aware that the competitive gaming fans' demographic is, in general, young and, thus, will only have the necessary monetary means to afford these high-priced luxury cars in the next five or 15 years: *"When a car manufacturer, like Mercedes is communicating in eSports, today they probably know that the people who watch eSports are around 25, they won't be the ones buying the Mercedes car the next day but maybe in 10 or 15 years they will"* (MA3) and *"They definitely understand that the core audience of eSports will not buy the Mercedes tomorrow. However, they understand that the audience of eSports might be able to buy a Mercedes in 5 or 7 years from now"* (MA6). So why sponsor so early? MA6 clearly states that the young age eSports fans are at is the perfect age to begin investing in these potential clients: *"This is the prime time to start investing in this audience"* (MA6). This is a great example of effective long-term sponsoring and is very interesting because, since car brands are non-endemic to eSports, it is often assumed that these will be the ones to be the least in-tune with competitive gaming and, thus, the ones less aware of the importance of a carefully calculated long-term sponsorship in eSports. These data are in accordance with Butcher, Tang, and Phau (2017) and Wesley and Barczak (2010), who defend that sponsors must target consumers from the youngest possible age to foster brand loyalty from early on and promote sales as these individuals grow older. The empirical data also comply with Edeling, Hattula, and Bornemann (2017),

Vance, Raciti, and Lawley (2016), and Vashisht and Sreejesh (2015), who report that long-term sponsoring is much better at building brand awareness.

Besides the importance of the long-term aspect, the example of the car brands sheds light on another vital element: A carefully crafted sponsoring plan. The importance of this component is further highlighted by the several other experts who stressed the relevance of planification. For example, EES1 pointed out the importance of a detailed evaluation prior to investing: *"If you get a good evaluation on your investments […] then it's a sustainable investment"* (EES1). As stated, if companies do not thoroughly evaluate the eSports market, and the eSports entity they wish to sponsor, the sponsorship will not be sustainable even if it is long-term. EES1 also noted that, if you do not perform this careful and detailed analysis before sponsoring, you will not obtain the best deal and may pay too much, which means you will not maximize your ROIs: *"I do think people who don't do their homework, they end up paying too much"* (EES1). NEES1 explicitly put together the best of both worlds by stressing, not only the relevance of a sponsoring strategy, but the relevance of a long-term sponsoring strategy: *"The sponsorship itself will probably not increase your brand awareness on the long-term unless you have a long-term marketing strategy"* (NEES1). It will probably not work if you are on the long-term with a short-term strategy that simply repeats itself. Both the commitment and the strategy must be long-term.

Fan ID 390 provided a very complex comment that connects with a lot of what was covered up to this point: *"For eSports to grow a step further, I think it's fundamental for well-established brands to sign up long-term contracts once they have tested the waters, so all the other parts can increase their investment/commitment as well and increase the overall stability and interest, getting also better long-term structures and a potential increase in the spectators' fidelity to this form of entertainment and to the brands involved"* (Fan ID 390). After deconstructing this elaborate statement, we can observe that, just like some experts have mentioned, this eSports fan also urges brands to commit to long-term sponsorships. But this fan goes into more detail here. He seems to allude that well-established brands should commit to long-term sponsorships even more than lesser-known companies (this makes sense since, when compared to smaller brands, in general, well-established brands have much higher capital to invest and their survivability is not that much damaged when a sponsorship does not live up to expectations). Fan ID 390 also makes the smart remark that brands should only commit to long-term sponsoring after they have tested the waters. That is, after making a detailed analysis of the eSports market, carefully selecting which entity to sponsor, and making some short-term sponsorships to gain experience in this new and unknown industry and to obtain a first insight of what ROIs may be obtained by sponsoring eSports. Fan ID 390 then indicates that the implementation of long-term sponsorships will allow all other agents of the eSports sphere to increase their commitment and investment in eSports (this is probably because long-term sponsoring means the certainty of long-term revenue) which, in turn, will create a more stable eSports market. This will then generate more interest from all eSports entities (because the market is more stable). Lastly, Fan ID 390 makes the ingenious observation that long-term sponsoring will lead to higher spectator loyalty, which may then translate into increased brand loyalty for the long-term sponsors.

> *"Yeah, welcome to eSports I hope you stay'. So that helps a lot because they create the narrative, they give us mainstream coverage, etc. [...] Longer time commitment".*

Still, it is true that some short-term sponsorships may reap positive ROIs. But, like NEES2 cleverly alludes, long-term ROIs will be much greater than short-term ROIs: *"There's immediate short-term gain and then there's long-term gain"* (NEES2). This information is in sync with Korpimies (2017), Nicholls, Roslow, and Dublish (1999), Pitkänen (2015), Portlock and Rose (2009), Quester and Farrelly (1998), Renard and Sitz (2011), Ströh (2017), and Yang, Sparks, and Li (2008), who point out that long-term sponsoring provides much higher ROIs in comparison to short-term. Even one eSports fan indicated that sponsors should look beyond immediate gains and understand, not only the better gains they may have on the long term, but also the positive impact that they can have on the eSports market: *"It could be good to think about -- not only what action will bring you the most apparent benefit now, but also what impact your brand can have on the scene in the long term"* (Fan ID 215).

One of the most mentioned added benefits of committing to long-term sponsorships seems to be improved brand image and increased loyalty. As NEES1 states, as long as brands commit to long-term sponsorships, they will benefit from increased loyalty: *"Another one I think has to do with brand loyalty and customer loyalty, provided that you pursue a long-term strategy"* (NEES1). The reason for improved brand image seems to be connected to most brands only committing to short-term strategies. According to MA2, eSports fans are tired of new sponsors coming in and out of eSports. This, in turn, creates a storytelling opportunity for the new sponsor to use the narrative of a brand that is truly committed to sponsoring eSports in the long-term: *"Every brand that first comes in is celebrated like 'Yeah, welcome to eSports I hope you stay'. So that helps a lot because they create the narrative, they give us mainstream coverage, etc. [...] Longer time commitment"* (MA2). Similarly, MA4 states that brands should do their best to be perceived as an entity that is benefiting the eSports' fans: *"Try to be seen as a supporter of the community"* (MA4). This is in line with Quester and Farrelly (1998), Ströh (2017), and Yang et al. (2008), who state that those who chose to sponsor for the long-term eventually start being perceived as organic and integral elements of the events or entities that they are partnered with. These data are also in accordance with Korpimies (2017) and Vance et al. (2016), who mention that long-term sponsoring is much more efficient at improving brand image than short-term sponsorships.

Unfortunately, there is more evidence that most sponsors commit to a short-term presence in eSports. As stated by Fan ID 299, brands usually sponsor competitive gaming for six months or less: "*We see multiple sponsors come and go in less 6 months*" (Fan ID 299). This is in line with Franke (2015), who states that, regrettably, many companies choose short-term sponsorships. According to Fan ID 215 this creates frustration among the fanbase: "*It's very frustrating to see some sponsors basically sign on to teams that make big events, without really ever supporting any one team long-term*" (Fan ID 215). It seems that fans are tired of brands not perceiving competitive gaming as a serious long-term investment.

Besides frustrating fans, the implementation of short-term sponsorships may also damage the brand in other ways. Like many will know, companies gain momentum as they continue sponsoring an entity, so ending the sponsorship early will kill that momentum and will prevent the brand from maximizing their ROIs. This was clearly exemplified by NEES1: "*If you do something very short-term just to serve short-term marketing KPIs, I think you are losing momentum*" (NEES1). EES1 went even further by alluding that brands should not end their sponsorships even if ROIs are below what was expected. They must be patient because they will only

know the real success in the long-term: "*Some people will get out and not have a good experience with their investment, but those who are patient and are willing to wait it out will receive a return on their investment*" (EES1). The tendency for short-term eSports sponsoring is worrying since, according to a plethora of authors, the eSports economy is dependent on sponsor (Callus & Potter, 2017; Holden, Kaburakis, & Rodenberg, 2017; Nichols, 2017; ONTIER, 2018; Ströh, 2017; Winnan, 2016) and cannot survive without them (AEVI, 2018; Lokhman, Karashchuk, & Kornilova, 2018; Mooney, 2018; Nichols, 2017; ONTIER, 2018; Shabir, 2017; Ströh, 2017; SuperData, 2015, 2017, 2018; TEO, 2018; Winnan, 2016). Despite the strong success of eSports, it requires sponsors to ensure the sustainability and growth of its market (Nichols, 2017; Shabir, 2017).

The Process of Long-Term eSports Sponsoring

Bearing in mind the inferences that were drawn from the discussion, we propose the model present in Figure 1. This model was adapted from Collett and Fenton (2011). While the original was created for any type of sponsorship, we must understand that eSports are a new phenomenon, with a new audience from a newer generation, so the data from this research was used to adapt the previous model to the eSports market. This new model describes how the ideal long-term sponsoring process should be in competitive gaming.

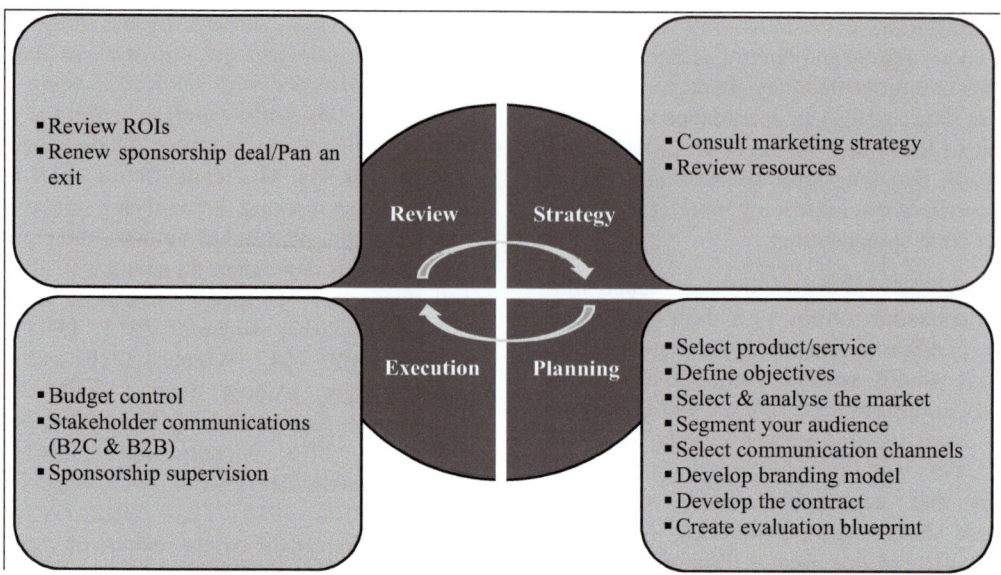

Figure 1: The long-term sponsoring process in eSports

As Figure 1 shows, the long-term sponsorship process must be composed of four main phases: (1) Strategy, (2) Planning, (3) Execution, and (4) Review. While short-term sponsoring will either neglect the last phase or give it very little attention, for a long-term commitment, it is one of the most crucial stages. In phase 1, Strategy, brands must firstly analyse the overall marketing strategy of the company to know if sponsorships adequately align with the company's business objectives. Afterwards, the brand must calculate the company's resources to understand how much it can invest on the sponsorship.

While sales and viewership on certain digital channels may be easily counted, things like brand awareness, brand image, brand loyalty and prefer-

ence are almost impossible to measure with an adequate degree of certainty.

In phase 2, Planning, the brand must first select which product or service (or set of products and services) it wishes to promote in its sponsorship. Subsequently, the brand must establish what it expects to obtain through the sponsorship by creating clear and verifiable objectives. Then, a market must be selected and, above all, thoroughly analysed. Esports are a new and vastly unknown market, so this part is vital for success and sustainability. After understanding the market and its audience, the target-public must be selected. Although the eSports fanbase is generally young, it still is very heterogeneous. Brands must decide if they wish to target a global or a local audience, with high or low-income, the age group, gender, etc. Only after answering all of these questions can the brand choose which communication channels will be more suitable to reach this segment of the eSports audience. After that, the brand must develop a branding model, a contract, and an evaluation blueprint. This last one will later allow the brand to measure the

ROIs, identify if the objectives were reached, and analyse the overall success of the sponsorship. If an evaluation blueprint is not created now, it will be almost impossible to keep track of how the sponsorship is doing and if any corrective measures are necessary.

Phase 3, Execution, is arguably the most straightforward one. Here, brands must follow the plan that was created on the previous phase, while performing a continuous supervision of the sponsorship. The investment budget must also be closely controlled and the brand must continuously communicate with its eSports fans and business partners.

Although phase 4, Review, seems short and simple, it is far from it. Here, the brand must perform a careful and thorough review of the ROIs and evaluate if they justify the investment that was made. The brand must also bear in mind that not all marketing elements can be easily measured. While sales and viewership on certain digital channels may be easily counted, things like brand awareness, brand image, brand loyalty and preference are almost impossible to measure with an adequate degree of certainty. Fortunately, when compared to other forms of entertainment, eSports are an online phenomenon and its online audience can be easily reached through various digital platforms, which facilitates the distribution and implementation of surveys to analyse several of these elements. The high vocality of the eSports fans also allows brands to easily access social channels like Twitter, Facebook, Reddit, Instagram, etc. to analyse if the discourse around their brand and its eSports sponsorship have been positively received. After careful consideration the brand must decide to either renew the sponsorship or end it. On the one hand, if they wish to terminate it, they must elaborate a careful communication strategy with both its business partners and public audience of the sponsorship (brands are usually not well-perceived when they simply end a sponsorship without saying a thing). On the other hand, if the brand wishes to renew the sponsorship it should firstly analyse how the eSports market has been evolving (as well as the sponsored entity) to ensure that it is safe to renew the sponsorship. If the

answer if positive, then the cycle begins again.

Implications

The implications from the empirical findings obtained from these added answers are quite relevant. Although short-term eSports sponsoring may lead to some benefits, brands must become aware of the much more attractive ROIs of sponsoring competitive gaming for the long-term. Still, it is obvious that most brands' first attempt at sponsoring eSports should be short-term so that they can better understand the market and gain experience, which will allow them to develop a much more efficient long-term sponsorship strategy. Also, eSports are not just a passing trend. Ergo, brands must perceive competitive gaming sponsorships as an integral element of their marketing strategies for the next years, and be committed to that long-term partnership. The fanbase is showing several signs of frustration towards sponsors that perceive eSports just as a tool to obtain quick ROIs and leave as quickly as they entered. This has led fans and experts to advise companies to commit to long-term sponsoring.

This is very important to avoid brands from sponsoring, then taking some time off eSports, and then coming back again when they have already angered both the eSports fanbase and the sponsored entities.

Fans want sponsors to show a continued interest in the videogames that they love as this is likely increase the stability of the eSports market. This means that the brands that commit to long-term sponsoring, and implement efficient and clever activations, will be celebrated by eSports fans as true and authentic supporters of this new market that is in dire need of sponsors. Ultimately, these long-term eSports supporters are likely to reap the largest ROIs of all.

Another strong reason to sponsor eSports for the long-term is so that the sponsoring brand can stay in continuous contact with the young eSports fans and accompany them from their teens throughout their 20s, 30s, and the rest of their adult life. Brands that are able to gain the attention and preference of customers from a tender age are generally able to maintain them as loyal customers throughout their entire life. MacDonalds has been doing this for a long time and they own a large portion of their success to that simple yet astonishingly effective strategy.

Still, just sponsoring eSports for the long-run does not guarantee long-term ROIs, like increased customer loyalty or awareness. For that to happen, brands must implement a carefully crafted and thorough long-term sponsoring strategy. This will provide sponsors with the opportunity to develop a narrative of their long-time involvement with this market and better engage with fans.

The creation of the long-term eSports sponsoring model provided a process that is adapted for both large and small-scale brands with various degrees of economic power. It is also adapted for first and long-time sponsors. The strategy and planning phases allow all brands to carefully calculate how much they may invest (and if they should). Also, the implementation of the review phase allows every brand to analyse if the sponsorship should be immediately renewed or terminated. This is very important to avoid brands from sponsoring, then taking some time off eSports, and then coming back again when they have already angered both the eSports fanbase and the sponsored entities.

References

AEVI. (2018). *Libro blanco de los esports en España*. In. Retrieved from http://www.aevi.org.es/web/wp-content/uploads/2018/05/ES_libroblanco_online.pdf

Butcher, L., Tang, Y., & Phau, I. (2017). Pawning n00bs: Insights into perceptions of brand extensions of the video game industry. *Australasian Marketing Journal, 25*(3), 215-224. doi:https://doi.org/10.1016/j.ausmj.2016.11.008

Callus, P., & Potter, C. (2017). Michezo Video: Nairobi's gamers and the developers who are promoting local content. *Critical African Studies, 9*(3), 302–326. doi:https://doi.org/10.1080/21681392.2017.1371620

Collett, P., & Fenton, W. (2011). *The Sponsorship Handbook: Essential Tools, Tips and Techniques for Sponsors and Sponsorship Seekers*. San Francisco, CA: Jossey-Bass.

Edeling, A., Hattula, S., & Bornemann, T. (2017). Over, out, but present: recalling former sponsorships. *European Journal of Marketing, 51*(7/8), 1286-1307. doi:https://doi.org/10.1108/EJM-05-2015-0263

Franke, T. (2015). The Perception of eSports - Mainstream Culture, Real Sport and Marketisation. In J. Hiltscher & T. M. Scholz (Eds.), *eSports Yearbook 2013/14* (pp. 111-144). Norderstedt: Books on Demand GmbH.

Holden, J. T., Kaburakis, A., & Rodenberg, R. (2017). The Future Is Now: Esports Policy Considerations and Potential Litigation. *Journal of Legal Aspects of Sport, 27*(1), 46-78. doi:https://doi.org/10.1123/jlas.2016-0018

Korpimies, S. (2017). *Sponsorships in eSports*. (Bachelor thesis), Aalto University, Espoo. Retrieved from http://urn.fi/URN:NBN:fi:aalto-201705114490

Lokhman, N., Karashchuk, O., & Kornilova, O. (2018). Analysis of eSports as a commercial activity. *Problems and Perspectives in Management,* *16*(1), 207-213. doi:http://dx.doi.org/10.21511/ppm.16(1).2 018.20

Mooney, C. (2018). *Inside the E-Sports Industry.* North Mankato, MN: Norwood House Press.

Nicholls, J. A. F., Roslow, S., & Dublish, S. (1999). Brand recall and brand preference at sponsored golf and tennis tournaments. *European Journal of Marketing, 33*(3/4), 365-387. doi:https://doi.org/10.1108/0309056991025 3198

Nichols, M. (2017). Endemics vs Non-Endemics: eSports expanding its sponsorship horizons. *European Sponsorship Association.* http://sponsorship.org/wp-content/uploads/2017/08/Sportcals-Endemics-vs-Non-Endemics-eSports-expanding-its-sponsorship-horizons.pdf

ONTIER. (2018). *Guía legal sobre e-Sports: Presente y futuro de la regulación de los esports en España.* In. Retrieved from https://es.ontier.net/ia/guialegalesports-2018web.pdf

Pitkänen, J. (2015). *Value creation through sponsorship in electronic sports.* (Master Thesis), Lappeenranta University of Technology, Lappeenranta. Retrieved from http://www.doria.fi/handle/10024/104883

Portlock, A., & Rose, S. (2009). Effects of ambush marketing: UK consumer brand recall and attitudes to official sponsors and non-sponsors associated with the FIFA World Cup 2006. *International Journal of Sports Marketing and Sponsorship, 10*(4), 2-17. doi:https://doi.org/10.1108/IJSMS-10-04-2009-B002

Quester, P., & Farrelly, F. (1998). Brand association and memory decay effects of sponsorship: the case of the Australian Formula One Grand Prix. *Journal of Product & Brand Management,* *7*(6), 539-556. doi:https://doi.org/10.1108/1061042981024 4693

Renard, N., & Sitz, L. (2011). Maximising sponsorship opportunities: a brand model approach. *Journal of Product & Brand Management,* *20*(2), 121-129. doi:https://doi.org/10.1108/1061042111112 1116

Shabir, N. (2017). *Esports: The Complete Guide 17/18: A guide for gamers, teams, organisations and other entities in, or looking to get into the space.* Wroclaw: Independently published.

Söderman, S., & Dolles, H. (2010). Sponsoring the Beijing Olympic Games: Patterns of sponsor advertising. *Asia Pacific Journal of Marketing and Logistics, 22*(1), 8-24. doi:https://doi.org/10.1108/1355585101101 3128

Ströh, J. H. A. (2017). *The eSports Market and eSports Sponsoring.* Marburg: Tectum Verlag.

SuperData. (2015, May). eSports: The market brief 2015. Retrieved from https://pt.scribd.com/document/269675603/ESports-Market-Brief-2015-SuperData-Research

SuperData. (2017, February). European eSports Conference Brief. Retrieved from http://strivesponsorship.com/wp-content/uploads/2017/04/Superdata-2017-esports-market-brief.pdf

SuperData. (2018). 2017 Year in Review: Digital Games and Interactive Media. Retrieved from https://www.super-dataresearch.com/market-data/market-brief-year-in-review/

TEO. (2018, February 25). An Introduction to the Esports Ecosystem. *The Esports Observer.* Retrieved from https://esportsobserver.com/the-esports-eco-system/

Vance, L., Raciti, M. M., & Lawley, M. (2016). Beyond brand exposure: measuring the sponsorship halo effect. *Measuring Business Excellence,* *20*(3), 1-14. doi:https://doi.org/10.1108/MBE-07-2015-0037

Vashisht, D., & Sreejesh, S. (2015). Effects of brand placement strength, prior game playing experience and game involvement on brand recall in advergames. *Journal of Indian Business Research, 7*(3), 292-312. doi:https://doi.org/10.1108/JIBR-11-2014-0082

Wesley, D., & Barczak, G. (2010). *Innovation and Marketing in the Video Game Industry: Avoiding the Performance Trap.* Farnham: Gower Publishing Limited.

Winnan, C. D. (2016). *An Entrepreneur's Guide to the Exploding World of eSports: Understanding the Commercial Significance of*

Counter-Strike, League of Legends and DotA 2. Kindle eBook: The Borderland Press.

Yang, X. S., Sparks, R., & Li, M. (2008). Sports sponsorship as a strategic investment in China: perceived risks and benefits by corporate sponsors prior to the Beijing 2008 Olympics. *International Journal of Sports Marketing and Sponsorship, 10*(1), 57-72. doi:http://dx.doi.org/10.1108/IJSMS-10-01-2008-B008

What is the Difference Between the Major and the Regional Leagues? Comparisons Between the Demands of European Teams.

By Adrián Martín-Castellanos, Iván Bonilla Gorrindo, Guillermo Benito-Corps, Andrés Chamarro Lusar, Manuel Barba Ruíz, Diego Muriarte Solana

Esports can be defined as 'organised video game competitions that pit players around the world for prize money' (Himmelstein et al. 2017). Its primary aspect is facilitated through electronic systems where teams or players compete using computers or consoles. In common sense, esports refers to competition through coordinated video games in leagues and tournaments where players belong to organised teams, which may be sponsored by various companies (Hamari & Sjöblom, 2017). Although this is a relatively new concept, it is experiencing a boom in popularity, having a great impact on an economic and social level (Nagorsky & Wiemeyer, 2020; Sainz et al., 2020). One of the most popular esports is League of Legends (LoL), a space-based multiplayer online battlefield game developed and published by RiotGames, where two teams composed of five players must coordinate and face each other. In this way, players control a character (called "champion") to achieve this objective, trying to control the vision around the map, minion armies (named "waves"), and demolishing the enemy structures in a competition to destroy the opponent's Nexus, based on enemy spawn zone (Hrabec, 2017; Reitman, 2018). Currently, LoL is one of the most popular video games, with more than 100 million monthly active players (Thomas et al., 2019).

Most of the existing scientific literature has examined esports performance by focussing on expertise and development within the game (Fanfarelli, 2018; Hodge et al., 2017), the strategy before game development (Ong

et al., 2015), and use of mental abilities (Himmelstein et al., 2017). However, there is a gap in the literature on the differences between competitions by major leagues and minor leagues that occur within this area, with a few studies in this area. The studies carried out have focused on comparisons with other leagues (i.e. [Bulckaen, 2021; Kho et al., 2020]), although they have not compared the major leagues with the minor in the European region, as they have done in other research areas, such as traditional sports (Carvalho et al., 2020; Fontana et al., 2015). In the European scenario, the most important competition is the League of Legends European Championship (LEC), considered a major league. It is organised as a structured league where ten teams from different regions of this continent are confronted. Nevertheless, several minor leagues can be found, named as European Regional Leagues, such as SuperLiga (SL), in Spain; La Ligue Française League of Legends (LFL), in France; Ultraliga (UL), in Poland; or Prime League (PL), which is composed by Germany, Austria and Switzerland squads. These leagues follow a similar framework, nevertheless, teams belong to specific countries.

These types of study can determine whether there are differences in strategies, priorities, or styles of play (Alharthi et al., 2018; Hrabec, 2017) adopted by teams in their approach to matches, assessing the influence of different elements to increase the probability of winning. For example, Martín-Castellanos & Benito-Corps (2021) observed the most important game variables to achieve victory in international professional LoL matches. The variables included in this study were several that refer to elements of game development: interaction with the enemy team, the elements of the field, or neutral elements. Regarding the interactions with the enemy team, the first blood and kills can be found, which team kills first. About the map structures, the towers destroyed by the teams and the inhibitors were analysed, finding at this point that the number of towers destroyed could be a good predictor of the winner. Finally, as far as neutral elements are concerned, neutral objectives which can provide buffs or advantages, such as the rift herald, the elimination of Baron Nashor, and dragons of different types, were also studied. These elements are accessible to both teams, being an interesting point in the strategy to be developed within the game (Novak et al., 2019b).

This information could be interesting to know if the teams of the major and minor leagues seek to prioritise the same elements within the game or if this strategic base differs according to the region and its playing style.

Additionally, several authors (Gaina & Nordmoen, 2018; Todeschini de Souza & Nogueira Cortimiglia, 2017; Yang et al., 2020) point out the importance of gold earned in the game, which can be crucial to improve the players' stats; the elements related with a vision to control rival movements around the structures, lanes, or neutral monsters (Pedrassoli Chitayat et al., 2020), or even the creep score, based on the number of minions killed by teams, as a way to improve the gold obtained and giving to the team another strategy to scale and gain an advantage (Do Nascimento et al., 2017).

At a strategic level, the work carried out by do Nascimento (2015) is interesting in an attempt to approximate the game models and the strategic aspect within it through influence maps and the interaction of team members. Subsequently, Ani et al. (2019) tried to establish these models within the game that lead us to predict victory based on the variables that make up the game. Along these same lines, Edmondson (2021) develops his work, which tries to attend to the different strategies that can be developed during the game and its corresponding victory condition when carried out.

However, there can be found other performance variables used for this kind of analysis in different esports, such as DotA 2 or Honour of Kings. For example, Aryanata et al. (2017) used the experience gained per minute, previous match results, and gold per minute to establish a victory estimation model for matches in DotA 2, another multiplayer online battle arena as LoL. In the same lane and esport, several authors (Aung et al., 2018; Hodge et al., 2017, 2019; Y. Yang et al., 2016) consider among differences from pre – match, in game or post-match elements (Wang, 2018), as the characteristics of the champions or heroes selected (Ong et al., 2015), the interaction between them in different teams, and the win ratio of each one. Most of them have used this information to develop a model to obtain the best possible system for victory forecast; however, this is not the objective of this research.

The main purpose of this research is to establish a comparison of the performance variables based on the competition between the major league (LEC) and the minor regions (ERL) and to compare between them considering the outcome of the matches. This information could be interesting to know if the teams of the major and minor leagues seek to prioritise the same elements within the game or if this strategic base differs according to the region and its playing style. and could point to differences in the determining variables that could help players make a quality leap.

Methods

Sample

The inclusion criteria followed in this study considered (i) completed games (no missing data), and (ii) the games had to be related to the first competitive period of the session (Spring split), excluding the schedule of the playoffs.

A total of 386 games played in the Spring regular season were collected by different competitions. 90 of those games were related to LEC, 92 with SL, 91 with LFL, 57 in LPLOL and 56 for UL. Some competitions had a higher number of matches than expected due to a draw in the final ranking of the team, which required a tie break to clarify the position and the playoffs. From these 386 games, the performance of both teams was recorded, giving a final number of 772 entries in the database. Although a larger number of registered ERLs can be found, the selected ERLs have a larger number of places available to play in the European Master, a competition that pits the best teams from each ERL against each other, and this is the selection criterion taken into account.

These data were extracted from RIOT Developer Web, an official source for obtaining match reports from amateur and professional games, and can be found provided by Sevenhuysen (2021).

Process

To avoid the influence of win-loss matches, all games were divided into loser and winner teams, to establish an equal analysis. This fact could bias performance analysis, as has been observed in other studies (Martín-Castellanos & Corps, 2021).

In addition, to specify the values per minute and relativise them, the total time of the games was rounded considering the seconds: if the number was higher than 30, towards the greater, and if were less than or equal to 30, toward the lesser. This fact is important for the area (Wang, 2016) due to as large is the match played, as higher will be the gold, kills or neutral objectives obtained (Martín-Castellanos & Corps, 2021).

Variables

Different variables were recorded in similar ways to other studies (Gaina & Nordmoen, 2018; Jiménez Toribio, 2019; Martín-Castellanos & Corps, 2021; Novak et al., 2019a, 2019b; Pedrassoli Chitayat et al., 2020; Todeschini de Souza & Nogueira Cortimiglia, 2017; Yang et al., 2020), considering kills, deaths, assistances, neutral monsters, structures (turrets and inhibitors) and vision ward scores as key variables for this research.

Table 1. Definition of variables examined in the study

Variable	Description
Game length	Total time spent to finish the match in minutes: seconds
Kills	Total number of enemy kills achieved by the team
Deaths	Total number of deaths by team
Assists	Total number of assistances by team
Double-kills	Number of total double kills (2 kills in a short time managed by the same player) achieved in the match by team
Triple-kills	Number of total triple kills (3 kills in a short time managed by the same player) achieved in the match by team
Quadra-kills	Number of total Quadra kills (4 kills in a short time managed by the same player) achieved in the match by team
Penta-kills	Number of total Penta kills (5 kills in a short time managed by the same player) achieved in the match by team
Dragons	Number of drakes managed by a team
Elder dragons	Number of elder drakes managed by a team
Heralds	Number of Heralds (neutral monster) managed by a team
Baron Nashor	Number of Baron Nashors (neutral monster) managed by a team
Towers	Number of total turrets destroyed by the team
Inhibitors	Number of total Inhibitors destroyed by the team
Gold spent	Number of total amounts of gold used to obtain artefacts, potions or improvements during the game.
Damage to champions	Damage done to enemy champions by the team per minute
Wards placed	Total number of vision wards placed by the team per minute
Wards killed	Total number of vision wards cleaned by the team per minute
Control wards bought	Total number of control wards placed by the team per minute
Vision score	Value that indicates how much vision has influenced in the game by team per minute, considering vision provided and denied
Total gold	Gold earned by the team per minute

Statistical analysis

The collected data were studied using the software Statistical Package for the Social Science (SPSS, IBM Corporation; Armonk, New York, USA) 25.0. version. The level of significance was set at 0.05. The normal distribution of the variables was studied using the Kolmogorov–Smirnov, and the homogeneity of variance was tested using Levene's test. Due to the results in these tests, a Kruskal Wallis test was performed to compare performance variables among leagues, split by result. The effect size (*ES*) was calculated using Eta squared ($\eta2$) (Morse, 1999), and interpreted as: small effects (<0.06); moderate effects ($\geq$0.06 to <0.14); and large effects ($\geq$0.14) (Cohen, 1988). The post hoc comparison was carried out using the Bonferroni adjustment.

Results

Starting with winners' analysis, it could be observed in Table 2 significative differences in dragons for league ($\chi^2_{(4)}$ = 14.1; p = .007; $\eta2$ = 0.03; *ES* = small), scoring higher for SL (p = .017) than LEC, and pentakills obtained ($\chi^2_{(4)}$ = 10.4; p = .034; $\eta2$ = 0.02; *ES* = small), were significatively greater in case of LPLOL compared to LEC (p = .044) and LFL (p = .043).

In addition, the relative variables showed significative differences in all cases. Damage to champions per minute ($\chi^2_{(4)}$ = 13.9; p = .002; $\eta2$ = 0.04; *ES* = small) were lower in SL (p = .031) and UL (p = .014) compared to LFL. Regarding to the vision control across the map, wards placed ($\chi^2_{(4)}$ = 29.7; p < .001; $\eta2$ = 0.05; *ES* = small) and killed ($\chi^2_{(4)}$ = 24.5; p < .001; $\eta2$ = 0.10; *ES* = moderate) showed differences between groups; LPLOL and UL performed poorly in comparison to LEC (p = .008; p = .002, respectively), SL (p = .007; p = .002) and LFL (p = .004; p = 001) to set wards. UL presented worse results cleaning wards for several comparisons (LEC, p = .025; SL, p = <.001; LFL, p = .037), and SL performance was better than LPLOL in this area (p = .005). Furthermore, SL got higher results for control wards bought per minute ($\chi^2_{(4)}$ = 38.7; p < .001; $\eta2$ = 0.06; *ES* = moderate) than LEC (p = .001), LPLOL (p = .001) and UL (p = <.001). Ultra-league also presented differences with LFL (p = <.001), with a worse performance.

Additionally, LPLOL and UL obtained worse numbers in vision score per minute ($\chi^2_{(4)}$ = 20.4; p < .001; $\eta2$ = 0.07; *ES* = moderate) than SL (p = .013 and p = .008) or LFL (p = .044 and p = .029) and total gold per minute ($\chi^2_{(4)}$ = 16.5; p = .008; $\eta2$ = 0.03; *ES* = small) had worse values in SL victorious teams than LEC (p = .009) or LFL (p = .020).

No significative differences were found in rest of variables (p >.05)

In losers' team scenarios, Table 3 showed differences between leagues, with a higher number of towers ($\chi^2_{(4)}$ =12.9; p = .012; $\eta2$ = 0.03; *ES* = small) in SL than UL (p = .011).

Further, variables that were relative to the time played showed significative differences. The damage to champions ($\chi^2_{(4)}$ = 15.6; p = .004; $\eta2$ = 0.04; *ES* = small) was higher in LFL than UL (p = .001); also, UL obtained a worse performance than LEC (p = .002) and SL (p = .044) in total gold per minute ($\chi^2_{(4)}$ = 16.3; p = .003; $\eta2$ = 0.04; *ES* = small).

Related to vision around map, wards placed ($\chi^2_{(4)}$ = 28.3; p < .001; $\eta2$ = 0.07; *ES* = moderate) presented differences between UL and LEC (p < .001), SL (p = .001) and LFL (p = .012), scoring lower for the Poland ERL; additionally, LEC obtained higher values than LPLOL (p = .006). For wards killed ($\chi^2_{(4)}$ = 37.5; p < .001; $\eta2$ = 0.09; *ES* = moderate), UL and LPLOL showed worse values than LEC (p = .002 and p = .041, respectively) and SL (p < .001, and p < .001). Moreover, UL scored poorly than LFL (p = .038). Similarly, same differences were found for vision score per minute ($\chi^2_{(4)}$ = 25.9; p < .001; $\eta2$ = 0.06; *ES* = moderate), where UL and LPLOL got lower values than LEC (p = .002 and p = .042, respectively) and SL (p < .001, p = .010), even LFL scored higher than UL (p = .022). Finally, LEC (p = .001), SL (p < .001) and LFL (p =. 013) averaged higher number of control wards bought than UL ($\chi^2_{(4)}$ = 38.2; p < .001; $\eta2$ = 0.09; *ES* = moderate); SL also presented greater results in this variable than LPLOL (p < .001). No significative differences were found in the rest of the variables related to lost games (p >.05).

Table 2. Mean values for performance variables by league in winners' scenario

Performances variables	LEC (90) M	SD	SL (92) M	SD	LFL (91) M	SD	LPLOL (57) M	SD	UL (56) M	SD	p	ε²	INT
Game length	33:02	5:09	33:41	4:46	32:09	06:02	31:58	4:54	32:19	5:47	.142		
Kills	18.38	5.46	17.78	4.39	19.33	4.64	19.11	5.03	17.43	4.80	.053		
Deaths	8.70	4.60	7.93	4.28	8.78	5.44	9.26	5.73	7.57	4.63	.328		
Assists	43.26	12.38	41.85	10.48	44.41	13.43	45.07	11.84	40.48	11.04	.183		
Double kills	2.44	1.49	2.23	1.33	2.40	1.41	2.56	1.51	2.38	1.32	.545		
Triple kills	0.51	0.66	0.46	0.70	0.56	0.62	0.65	0.81	0.48	0.66	.448		
Quadra kills	0.06	0.23	0.08	0.27	0.05	0.23	0.19	0.44	0.09	0.35	.070		
Penta kills	0.01	0.11	0.02	0.15	0.01	0.10	$0.09^{A*, C*}$	0.29	0.02	0.13	.034	0.02	S
Dragons	3.00	1.14	3.49^{A*}	0.96	3.31	0.99	3.42	0.84	3.04	1.03	.007	0.03	S
Elder dragons	0.12	0.33	0.12	0.36	0.12	0.36	0.05	0.23	0.09	0.29	.709		
Heralds	1.16	0.75	1.07	0.80	1.37	0.78	1.18	0.83	1.32	0.72	.053		
Baron Nashor	1.19	0.65	1.23	0.56	1.11	0.64	1.14	0.55	1.07	0.63	.474		
Towers	9.30	1.35	9.10	1.34	9.20	1.35	9.07	1.39	9.07	1.32	.779		
Inhibitors	1.83	0.99	1.61	0.76	1.74	0.83	1.72	0.92	1.80	0.92	.666		
Gold spent	57167.72	8500.53	57200.08	7700.44	55856.54	9590.41	54308.33	8903.65	54530.68	7943.57	.120		
Damage to champions (/min)	2077.20	394.24	2016.18	346.50	$2181.99^{B*,E*}$	353.99	2047.50	368.24	2003.33	395.49	.002	0.04	S
Wards placed (/min)	3.28	0.42	3.31	0.49	3.30	0.43	$3.05^{A**,B*,C**}$	0.42	$3.01^{A**,B*,C**}$	0.43	<.001	0.05	S
Wards killed (/min)	1.40	0.28	1.45	0.27	1.38	0.27	1.28^{B**}	0.31	$1.25^{A*,B***,C*}$	0.29	<.001	0.10	M
Control wards bought (/min)	1.23	0.22	$1.35^{A**,D*,E***}$	0.18	1.31	0.18	1.21	0.20	1.16^{C***}	0.21	<.001	0.06	M
Vision score (/min)	7.65	0.78	7.71	0.85	7.65	0.76	$7.25^{B**,C*}$	0.92	$7.27^{B***,C***}$	0.82	<.001	0.07	M
Total gold (/min)	1942.72	100.42	$1898.91^{A**,C*}$	87.48	1941.41	93.88	1907.89	110.90	1909.24	129.04	.008	0.03	S

Note: M = Mean, SD = Standard deviation, LEC = League of Legends European Championship, SL = SuperLiga, LFL = La Ligue Française League of Legends, LPLOL = Prime League, UL = Ultraliga. Significative differences are illustrated as: A = significative differences with LEC, B = significative differences with SL, C = significative differences with LFL, D = significative differences with LPLOL, E = significative differences with UL. ε² = Eta squared. INT = Effect Size Interpretation. S = Small effect size; M = Moderate; L = Large. Post hoc comparisons are highlighted: * p < .05; ** p < .01; *** p < .001

Table 3. Mean values for performance variables by league in losers´ scenario

Performances variables	LEC (90)		SL (92)		LFL (91)		LPLOL (57)		UL (56)		p	ε²	INT
	M	SD	M	SD	M	SD	M	SD	M	SD			
Kills	8.68	4.55	7.89	4.33	8.74	5.43	9.25	5.72	7.54	4.64	.305		
Deaths	18.39	5.46	17.80	4.41	19.34	4.65	19.14	5.05	17.43	4.80	.052		
Assists	18.62	10.14	17.05	10.40	18.79	12.39	20.96	15.00	17.37	11.46	.665		
Double kills	0.46	0.74	0.61	0.84	0.55	0.95	0.65	1.03	0.57	1.04	.642		
Triple kills	0.04	0.21	0.09	0.32	0.08	0.31	0.05	0.23	0.11	0.31	.652		
Quadra kills	0.01	0.11	0.00	0.00	0.00	0.00	0.02	0.13	0.00	0.00	.472		
Penta kills	0.00	0.00	0.00	0.00	0.00	0.00	0.00	0.00	0.00	0.00	NaN		
Dragons	1.58	1.24	1.50	1.15	1.41	1.11	1.35	1.01	1.70	1.24	.625		
Elder dragons	0.01	0.11	0.03	0.18	0.01	0.11	0.02	0.13	0.02	0.13	.811		
Heralds	0.72	0.72	0.92	0.79	0.62	0.77	0.77	0.80	0.64	0.70	.062		
Baron Nashor	0.28	0.60	0.32	0.65	0.26	0.59	0.23	0.46	0.21	0.49	.968		
Towers	2.79	1.97	3.18	1.92	2.59	2.29	2.67	2.18	2.14 [B*]	1.71	.012	0.03	S
Inhibitors	0.09	0.36	0.11	0.35	0.16	0.64	0.14	0.48	0.09	0.29	.933		
Gold spent	52095.47	10296.69	52576.77	9889.47	50055.73	11787.21	49160.04	10693.83	48707.43	10997.36	.105		
Damage to champions (/min)	1691.57	445.79	1657.56	371.70	1791.17	409.07	1670.49	492.98	1509.10 [C**]	367.85	.004	0.04	S
Wards placed (/min)	3.25	0.41	3.16	0.43	3.20	0.40	2.97 [A**]	0.48	2.89 [A***, B**, C*]	0.50	< .001	0.07	M
Wards killed (/min)	1.26	0.30	1.36	0.33	1.23	0.37	1.12 [A*, B***]	0.29	1.05 [A**, B***, C*]	0.28	< .001	0.09	M
Control wards bought (/min)	1.26	0.19	1.32	0.20	1.23	0.20	1.16 [B***]	0.20	1.10 [A**, B***, C*]	0.23	< .001	0.09	M
Vision score (/min)	6.96	0.90	6.97	0.92	6.79	1.17	6.39 [A*, B**]	0.95	6.19 [A**, B***, C*]	1.13	< .001	0.06	M
Total gold (/min)	1628.35	89.70	1611.71	93.28	1608.95	98.91	1586.33	109.51	1554.15 [A**, B*]	106.44	.003	0.04	S

Note: M = Mean, SD = Standard deviation, LEC = League of Legends European Championship, SL = SuperLiga, LFL = La Ligue Française League of Legends, LPLOL = Prime League, UL = Ultraliga. Significative differences are illustrated as: A = significative differences with LEC, B = significative differences with SL, C = significative differences with LFL, D = significative differences with LPLOL, E = significative differences with UL. ε² = Eta squared. INT = Effect Size Interpretation. S = Small effect size; M = Moderate; L = Large. Post hoc comparisons are highlighted: * p < .05; ** p < .01; *** p < .001. NaN = Not a Number; it can not been considered due to lack of pentakills in the sample.

Discussion

The main aim of this study was to compare performance variables based on the competition between major leagues (LECs) and small leagues (ERLs) and to compare them according to the results of matches.

In this way, the main finding of the research was that principal differences between the leagues were found in the variables related to match time. However, there were no major differences in the rest of the variables between teams belonging to the European region (LEC) and teams in regional leagues (SL in this case).This fact is striking due to, taking as a reference other studies on behaviours in professional leagues (Bulckaen, 2021) it can be observed that in general the upper regions (such as the LEC) are more similar to other upper regions than when compared to lower regions (such as the ERL).

It has been pointed out that LFL was the only league that did not show significant differences in any comparison with LEC (the benchmark league), in victory or defeat scenarios, as can be observed in Table 4. This could determine that it was the league closest in performance to this major division, considering the dominance it has had in the European Master, winning the last 3 editions played (Summer and Spring split in 2021, Spring split in 2022). This should be taken with caution and further research, as the data in this analysis pertain to the 2021 Spring split.

Table 4. Summary of differences between LEC and ERLs

Performances variables	Winners´ scenario				Losers´ scenario			
	SL	LFL	LPLOL	UL	SL	LFL	LPLOL	UL
Penta kills			↑*					
Dragons	↑*							
Wards placed (/min)			↓**	↓**			↓**	↓***
Wards killed (/min)				↓*			↓*	↓**
Control wards bought (/min)	↑**							↓**
Vision score (/min)							↓*	↓**
Total gold (/min)	↓**							↓**

Note: ↑ = Higher values; ↓ = Lower values. Differences in post hoc comparisons are highlighted: * p < .05; ** p < .01; *** p < .001

Furthermore, it is interesting to note that, although there are favourable and unfavourable variations in the comparison of different leagues with LEC in victorious situations, in the case of defeats, the differences presented are always negative, indicating a worse performance of the losing teams in these leagues (mainly LPLOL and UL). Gold obtained per minute should be noted because it is considered an important variable for both modelling and performance in different studies (Gaina & Nordmoen, 2018; Todeschini de Souza & Nogueira Cortimiglia, 2017) and is related to neutral infrastructures (Martín-Castellanos & Corps, 2021), which are important when comparing performance (Novak et al.,

2019b). Surprisingly, SL showed the lowest level of gold per minute, differing significantly from LEC and LFL in the victory scenario. In the rest of the variables a similar behaviour to these two leagues had prevailed, however, finding differences in such an important variable could signal that there is a small step difference in performance in these leagues, placing it currently between the LEC and LFL (which showed no differences between them) and the LPLOL and UL (which generally performed worse).

Between the analysis of the variables, vision seems to be one of the most discriminating factors in differentiating these types of leagues according to the outcome. The UL presented a poor performance compared to

LEC, SL and LFL in wards placed, killed, control wards bought, and vision score in defeat matches. LFL also showed a lower value compared to LEC (wards placed), SL (control wards bought) or both (wards killed and vision score) in the same scenario. In the case of victory, UL underperformed overall with LFL and SL; that was a leading league in the purchase of control vision guards. These differences would highlight the importance of wards and the resarch published by Pedrassoli Chitayat et al. (2020), which also showed better use of this item by professional players when compared to average players. In this case, all leagues are professional, but considering the results of this study and the previous bibliography, the wards could be determined as a key element to differentiate performance between professional levels.

> ## *These leagues can become showcases for professional teams that allow them to generate players adapted to a specific style of play.*

When a comparison is carried out between leagues in performance variables without considering the relative ones, solely a small difference can be observed between pentakills and the number of dragons obtained in victorious cases. It could be highlighted that both had differences with LEC (LPLOL and SL, respectively), although LPLOL also had differences with LFL. In defeat scenarios, the towers showed a difference between UL and SL, although these differences do not appear in the victories. Taking into account the importance of the towers in the victories according to previous literature, is the key to distinguishing between winning and non-winning teams (Kho et al., 2020; Martín-Castellanos & Corps, 2021; Novak et al., 2019b), it could be considered that the winning strategy about this variable was similar. However, the small or moderate differences found in the other comparisons could determine the styles of play or the focus of the team match

planning efforts. Perhaps the principal component analysis or other types of statistical analysis could characterise these styles of play, as has been done in other research areas (Zhou et al., 2021; Martín-Castellanos et al., 2023).

Finally, the behaviour of the teams in the leagues does not tend to vary much over the seasons (Bulckaen, 2021), so one would expect the LEC to tend to emphasise early play compared to other leagues (Kho et al., 2020). It may be that the style of play in these minor leagues is influenced by the top league and, therefore, no significant differences were found in the other variables. It would be interesting to make this comparison considering ERLs from other regions of the world.

Conclusion

These results illustrate that, although there may be differences between teams in higher and lower divisions, ERLs teams are not that far apart from LEC teams in terms of neutral goals achieved per game. However, variables related to vision around the map seem to be crucial in establishing differences between leagues.

At this time, and considering the results, it could be said that LEC and LFL were very similar. Arguably, the SL is close to LEC and LFL, although it varies in different elements (i.e. gold per minute in the win). Finally, UL and LPLOL are the leagues that differed the most from LEC, with the lowest performance in the differences found.

Practical Applications

The findings of this study can encourage the promotion and regulation of ERLs, as well as the recruitment of rookie players to the LEC who could perform close to the level of players competing at the international level. These leagues can become showcases for professional teams that allow them to generate players adapted to a specific style of play.

Also, these results could be interesting for scrims or pre- split matches knowing that in this type of league you can find competent teams that can stand up to the LEC. In fact, they could even change the franchise structure currently imposed, providing a place in this major league for those winners of the European Master, being aware that they can meet the level required for these leagues.

Study Limitations

The main limitations in this study are determined by the lack of comparative studies that present a similar situation in the field of esports, although it may be one of the advantages of this study, the innovation field.

Another factor to consider would be the patches in which the competition has been developed, ranging from 11.01 to 11.05, which must be considered in others analysis. Although those that involve big changes are usually those of preseason or change of season, as this is the first competition of the year, the players could be in an adaptation process.

For future studies, it is interesting to relate certain variables to time, as these will be positively or negatively related to playing time. For example, in LoL, the amount of gold earned will increase over time, as there is a certain amount that is earned passively. However, in our opinion, not all variables should be relativised because they could lose the context in which they are explained (i.e. the number of towers per minute or quadra/pentakills per minute would make less sense than the value without relativising). This should be taken with care, as there could be a risk of bias when taking time-relativised variables, facilitating the emergence of significant differences. In this research, the length of the game did not show any differences between leagues.

Finally, future studies could include a greater number of ERLs to obtain cross-sectional information on the statistics of the region or develop a factorial analysis by teams to specify the styles of play based on the final statistics and/or those obtained in the middle of the game (15 minutes).

Declaration of interest statement

The authors report that there is no conflict of interest. This research was partially funded by the XVI Convocatoria de ayudas para el development of Research Projects FUAX-Santander 2023 through the project "Rendimiento y Salud en Esports (RYSE)" with the project code: 1.016.010 and has the approval of the ethical committee of the University Alfonso X el Sabio.

References

Alharthi, S. A., Dolgov, I., Raptis, G. E., Nacke, L. E., Katsini, C., & Toups, Z. O. (2018). Toward understanding the effects of cognitive styles on collaboration in multiplayer games. *CSCW '18: Companion of the 2018 ACM Conference on Computer Supported Cooperative Work and Social Computing*, 3–7. https://doi.org/10.1145/3272973.3274047

Ani, R., Harikumar, V., Devan, A. K., & Deepa, O. S. (2019). Victory prediction in a league of legends using feature selection and ensemble methods. *International Conference on Intelligent Computing and Control Systems, ICCS 2019*, 74–77. https://doi.org/10.1109/ICCS45141.2019.9065758

Aryanata, G. A., Rahadi, P. S. A. D., & Sudarmojo, Y. P. (2017). Prediction of DOTA 2 Match Result by Using Analytical Hierarchy Process Method. *International Journal of Engineering and Emerging Technology*, 2(1), 22. https://doi.org/10.24843/ijeet.2017.v02.i01.p05

Aung, M., Bonometti, V., Drachen, A., Cowling, P., Kokkinakis, A. V., Yoder, C., & Wade, A. (2018). Predicting skill learning in a large, longitudinal MOBA dataset. *IEEE Conference on Computatonal Intelligence and Games (CIG), 1–7. https://doi.org/10.1109/CIG.2018.8490431

Bulckaen, J. (2021). *Uncovering differences between League of Legends competitions*. Ghent university.

Carvalho, A., Roriz, P., & Duarte, D. (2020). Comparison of morphological profiles and performance variables between female volleyball players of the first and second division in Portugal. *Journal of Human Kinetics*, *71*(2020), 109–117. https://doi.org/10.2478/hukin-2019-0076

Cohen, J. (1988). *Statistical power analysis of the behavioral sciences*. (2nd edition). Academic Press.

Do Nascimento, F. F., Da Costa, I. B., Da Costa Melo, A. S., & Marinho, L. B. (2017). Profiling successful team behaviors in League of Legends. In *Proceedings of the 23rd Brazillian Symposium on Multimedia and the Web* (Issue iii, pp. 261–268). https://doi.org/10.1145/3126858.3126886

Do Nascimento Silva, V., & Chaimowicz, L. (2015). On the development of intelligent agents for MOBA games. *Brazilian Symposium on Games and Digital Entertainment, SBGAMES*, *0*, 142–151. https://doi.org/10.1109/SBGAMES.2015.33

Edmondson, L. (2021). *Identifying strategies of esports players at various proficiency: The case of League of Legends*. Northeastern University.

Fanfarelli, J. R. (2018). Expertise in professional overwatch play. *International Journal of Gaming and Computer-Mediated Simulations*, *10*(1), 1–22. https://doi.org/10.4018/IJGCMS.20180101 01

Fontana, F. Y., Colosio, A. L., De Roia, G., Da Lozzo, G., & Pogliaghi, S. (2015). Anthropometrics of Italian senior male rugby union players: from elite to second division. *Int J Sports Physiol Perform*, *10*(6), 674–680. https://doi.org/10.1123/ijspp.2015-0014

Gaina, R., & Nordmoen, C. (2018). *League of Legends: A Study of Early Game Impact*.

Hamari, J., & Sjöblom, M. (2017). What is eSports and why do people watch it? *Internet Research*, *27*(2), 211–232. https://doi.org/10.1108/IntR-04-2016-0085

Himmelstein, D., Liu, Y., & Shapiro, J. L. (2017). An exploration of mental skills among competitive league of legend players. *International Journal of Gaming and Computer-Mediated Simulations*, *9*(2), 1–21. https://doi.org/10.4018/IJGCMS.20170401 01

Hodge, V., Devlin, S., Sephton, N., Block, F., Cowling, P., & Drachen, A. (2019). Win Prediction in Multi-Player Esports: Live Professional Match Prediction. *IEEE Transactions on Games*, *PP*, 1–1. https://doi.org/10.1109/tg.2019.2948469

Hodge, V., Devlin, S., Sephton, N., Block, F., Drachen, A., & Cowling, P. (2017). Win prediction in esports: Mixed-rank match prediction in multi-player online battle arena games. *ArXiv, 2015*.

Hrabec, O. (2017). Categorizing play styles in competitive gaming. *International Journal of Gaming and Computer-Mediated Simulations*, *9*(4), 62–88. https://doi.org/10.4018/IJGCMS.20171001 04

Jiménez Toribio, M. (2019). Videojuegos violentos, violencia y variables relacionadas: estado del debate. *Revista de Psicología Aplicada Al Deporte y Al Ejercicio Físico*, *4*(4), 1–12.

Kho, L. C., Kasihmuddin, M. S. M., Mansor, M. A., & Sathasivam, S. (2020). Logic mining in League of Legends. *Pertanika J. Sci. & Technol*, *28*(1), 211–225.

Martín-Castellanos, A., Flores, M. R., Solana, D. M., Del Campo, R. L., Garrosa, F. N., & Mon-López, D. (2023). How do the football teams play in LaLiga? Analysis and comparison of playing styles according to the outcome. *International Journal of Performance Analysis in Sport*, 1-13.

Martín-Castellanos, A., & Corps, G. B. (2021). Variables related to the outcome of an eSports professional tournament: case study of 2019 League of Legends World Championship Series. *International Journal of Esports*, *2*(2), 1–14.

Morse, D. . (1999). Minsize2: a computer program for determining effect size and minimum sample size for statistical significance for univariate, multivariate, and nonparametric tests. *Journals.Sagepub.Com*, *59*(3), 518–531.

https://doi.org/10.1177/0013164992196990 1

Nagorsky, E., & Wiemeyer, J. (2020). The structure of performance and training in esports. In *PLoS ONE* (Vol. 15, Issue 8 August 2020). https://doi.org/10.1371/journal.pone.0237584

Novak, A. R., Bennett, K. J. M., Pluss, M. A., & Fransen, J. (2019a). Performance analysis in esports: part 1 - the validity and reliability of match statistics and notational analysis in League of Legends. *SportRxiv, October.* https://doi.org/10.31236/osf.io/sm3nj

Novak, A. R., Bennett, K. J. M., Pluss, M. A., & Fransen, J. (2019b). Performance analysis in esports: part 2 – modelling performance at the 2018 League of Legends World Championship. *SportRxiv, October.* https://doi.org/10.31236/osf.io/84fmy

Ong, H. Y., Deolalikar, S., & Peng, M. (2015). *Player Behavior and Optimal Team Composition for Online Multiplayer Games.* http://arxiv.org/abs/1503.02230

Pedrassoli Chitayat, A., Kokkinakis, A., Patra, S., Demediuk, S., Robertson, J., Olarewaju, O., Ursu, M., Kirmann, B., Hook, J., Block, F., & Drachen, A. (2020). WARDS: Modelling the Worth of Vision in MOBA's. In K. Arai, S. Kapoor, & R. Bhatia (Eds.), *Intelligent Computing. Proceedings of the 2020 Computing Conference* (Vol. 2, pp. 63–81). Springer International Publishing. https://doi.org/10.1007/978-3-030-52246-9_5

Reitman, J. G. (2018). Distributed cognition and temporal knowledge in league of legends. *International Journal of Gaming and Computer-Mediated Simulations, 10*(1), 23–41. https://doi.org/10.4018/IJGCMS.2018010102

Sainz, I., Collado-Mateo, D., & Coso, J. Del. (2020). Effect of acute caffeine intake on hit accuracy and reaction time in professional e-sports players. *Physiology and Behavior, 224*(April). https://doi.org/10.1016/j.physbeh.2020.113031

Sevenhuysen, T. (2021). *Oracle's Elixir: League of Legends esports stats.* Https://Oracleselixir.Com/Tools/Downloads.

Thomas, C. J., Rothschild, J., Earnest, C. P., & Blaisdell, A. (2019). The effects of energy drink consumption on cognitive and physical performance in elite League of Legends players. *Sports, 7*(9), 1–10. https://doi.org/https://doi.org/10.3390/sports7090196

Todeschini de Souza, R., & Nogueira Cortimiglia, M. (2017). *Aplicação de algoritmos classificadores para previsão de vitória em uma partida de League of Legends* (pp. 1–21).

Wang, T. (2018). *Predictive Analysis on eSports Games – A Case Study on League of Legends (LoL) eSports Tournaments.*

Wang, W. (2016). *Predicting Multiplayer Online Battle Arena (MOBA) game outcome based on hero draft data.*

Yang, Y., Qin, T., & Lei, Y. H. (2016). Real-time eSports Match Result Prediction. *ArXiv, Nips,* 1–9.

Yang, Z., Pan, Z., Wang, Y., Cai, D., Shi, S., Huang, S., & Liu, X. (2020). Interpretable Real-Time Win Prediction for Honor of Kings, a Popular Mobile MOBA Esport. *ArXiv,* 1–8. http://arxiv.org/abs/2008.06313

Zhou, C., Lago-Peñas, C., Lorenzo, A., & Gómez, M. Á. (2021). Long-Term Trend Analysis of Playing Styles in the Chinese Soccer Super League. *Journal of Human Kinetics, 79*(1), 237–247. https://doi.org/10.2478/hukin-2021-0077

"Old-School" is Now Too Cool! Exploring Motivations for Attending a LAN from a U&G Perspective

By Kamelia Bankova and Amelia Nablsi

The full thesis paper: https://www.diva-portal.org/smash/record.jsf?pid=diva2%3A1673491&dswid=-9936

Esports has been around since 1972, and it has been developing ever since (Tuting, 2020). Esports is a form of sports but takes place on different virtual platforms with other real or automated players, also referred to as "Gamebot" (Kaminka et al., 2002) in a digital and global sphere, where gamers compete (Jenny et al., 2017; Candela & Jakee, 2018; Pizzo et al., 2018; Scholz, 2019). Esports is expanding and becoming meaningful because people are becoming more appreciative of their leisure time (Seo, 2016). Additionally, esports is regarded as an escape from daily routine, which is why gamers take part in esports, whether online or offline. However, a player's experience with a game encounter is heavily influenced by the game's setting (Seo, 2013; Wang et al., 2021).

Esports is an electronic form of sport in media that implies that gamers are connected through the internet and play with other gamers worldwide by a technical interface (Hutchins, 2008; Seo, 2013; Hamari & Sjöblom, 2017; Yu et al., 2018). Esports can occur online and offline (Seo & Green, 2008; Seo, 2013). In an online setting, esports can be a connecting point between amateur and professional gamers (Seo, 2013; Hamari & Sjöblom, 2017; Yu et al., 2018). The gamers who engage in online esports desire high-quality performance, live streaming, and being part of the action (Neus et al., 2019).

On the other hand, in a LAN, gamers come physically together in big arenas to play and compete with other gamers. A LAN provides a unique setting where gamers can gain a greater experience of esports beyond the digital realm and establish deeper bonds and relationships with other gamers (Hamari & Sjöblom, 2017). There is a potential for

knowledge sharing through online streaming platforms in the context of online media consumption. Online gamers are more likely to have a closer perspective on the action than visitors attending LANs. Due to streaming platforms such as Twitch, Facebook Gaming, and other similar ones, online users can follow the game's action, learn the strategy, employ tactics, and learn about the game (Hamilton et al., 2014). However, it has been argued that online gaming creates less of an escape from the surrounding environment for gamers, especially when they play from home (Neus et al., 2019).

LANs have shifted competitive video games from player-vs-machine to the physical player-vs-player in a local area network connection. Computers are connected locally to the same network; usually, a high-speed connection and gamers are gathered physically to interact and play competitive games (Griffiths et al., 2003; Taylor & Witkowski, 2010). LANs are popular due to the unique social features where gamers share the same passion, meet, and compete with like-minded gamers (Jansz & Martens, 2005; Taylor & Witkowski, 2010; Eklund, 2015; Taylor, 2006). Furthermore, offline communication is essential for gamers to build bonds and achieve high performance (Tang, 2018). Therefore, LANs are crucial for establishing bonds between gamers (Seo, 2013; McCauley et al., 2020). In addition, they are interested in emotional connection and social interaction with other gamers (Neus et al., 2019). Online, gamers can chat and interact on streaming platforms. However, it is argued that online chatting can never substitute for authentic human interaction that a LAN can provide. Nevertheless, the LAN environment forms new and unexplored feelings and impressions for gamers; therefore, it should be further explored (Neus et al., 2019).

Problem

From a gamers' perspective, esports online and at a LAN cannot be considered a replacement for each other (Neus et al., 2019). Gamers who attend and play at a LAN anticipate certain gratifications that an online game will not satisfy (Ruggiero, 2000).

LANs have shifted competitive video games from player-vs-machine to the physical player-vs-player in a local area network connection.

There is extensive research on gamers' motivations when playing online such as Fetscherin et al. (2005), Jansz & Martens (2005), Pöyhtäri (2016) and McCauley et al. (2019). However, Michailidis (2019) and Lui (2020) indicated that there is little research done on the motivations to attend LANs. Furthermore, Taylor & Witkowski (2010) proposes that LANs carry vital qualities not yet explored. Further, a gap in the literature has not been adequately addressed when it comes to LANs (Neus et al., 2019). As a result, exploring the different elements that can affect gamers' motivation to attend LANs is crucial to utilise (Jansz & Martens, 2005; Scheibe et al., 2016; Bründl et al., 2017; Hilvert-Bruce et al., 2018; Neus et al., 2019). As a result, the esports literature was reviewed to analyse motivations observed in online contexts and apply them to LAN contexts. Lastly, the study does not compare online and LAN gaming but instead explores the motivations for attending LANs, since a deeper understanding is needed to gain a richer perspective.

Theoretical Framework

The U&G theory is used to examine and analyse the reasons behind using interactive media and what gratifications it might give to people using it (Katz et al., 1973; Ruggiero, 2000). In a world where media technology proliferates rapidly, research on the U&G theory has become more relevant than ever in exploring and understanding people's motivations for interactive media use and their gratifications (Ruggiero, 2000; Neus, 2020; Sundar & Limperos, 2013).

Katz et al. (1974) set the basic five assumptions of the U&G theory as the following:

1. Users are active and use mass media for a specific goal.

2. Users choose media in connection to a previous experience and expectations.

3. Selecting and using media are purposive and motivating where users want to satisfy needs and desires.

4. Media compete with other sources of communication to satisfy needs.

5. Users judge the value and importance of mass communication they use on their terms of understanding and views.

U&G theory argues that people want to use media to satisfy certain needs and desires (Rubin, 2002; Cummings, 2008). Contrary to many other media theories which describe users as passive, the U&G theory describes users as active and interacting which allows them to have control over their media usage (Katz et al., 1973; Severin & Tankard, 1997; Ruggiero, 2000; Rubin, 2002; Neus, 2020). People consume media because they desire essential gratifications such as the need to improve knowledge, relax, social interactions, diversion, or escape (McQuail, 2010), which can be satisfied by using various media (Cummings, 2008; McQuail, 2010).

Two principles govern how media consumers use media. The first one characterises users as active in their choice of media consumption. This perspective implies that people do not just passively consume media but are engaged and motivated in their media selection process (Lowery & De Fleur, 1988). The second one states that people are aware of the reasons for selecting a particular media format and rely on their knowledge of motivations to make a media choice that meets their specific needs and wants (Ruggiero, 2000).

The U&G theory has been used within the research of online contexts (Whiting and Williams, 2013), Facebook and esports (Sjöblom and Hamari, 2017). The U&G theory is considered proper to explore and acquire insights into the uses and motivations of using video games and esports (Katz et al., 1973; Stafford et al., 2004; Sundar & Limperos, 2013; Hamari & Sjöblom, 2017). Researchers used the U&G theory to examine and understand the motives of why and how people consume esports and what needs esports as a media can gratify (Qian et al., 2020).

Due to the nature of electronic computer mediation, esports is considered a form of media and communication, so many researchers have used the U&G theory to better understand specific media consumption (Hamari & Sjöblom, 2017). Video games are played to satisfy certain needs. Due to their interactive nature, gamers find video games fascinating and appealing (Jansz & Martens, 2005). Further, video games allow gamers to be active rather than passive in selecting and customising the game according to their needs, which from a U&G perspective will contribute to understanding the motivations for gamers to consume esports and the gratification they get because of that interaction (Jansz & Martens, 2005; Kim & Ross, 2006; Sherry et al., 2006; Qian et al., 2020).

Today, media providers or companies are seen as public and media-based communication organisers providing content and operating platforms in hybrid forms valid online and offline (Hess, 2014). Esport has been defined in the literature as a media provider where information, media, and events are integrated materially in a social field, which is a product of social relations in hybrid forms (Hutchins, 2008; Lash, 2002). Nowadays, human activities intersect with ICTs (Information and communications technology). As a result, a LAN is the social form of esports

that integrates the physical (offline) and technological (online) basis of competition which is considered a form of media. Therefore, we argue that a LAN is a media provider in an offline form, and that is why it is relevant to explore the motivations to attend a LAN using the U&G theory (Hess, 2014; Hutchins, 2008; Lash, 2002).

Motivations and Benefits

The following part will present ten motivations chosen to explore gamers' motivations. The chosen motivations are adapted from the pool of already existing knowledge in the field of esports and modified due to the intertwinement in the articles. Thus said, in some articles, the motivations are presented as submotivations and vice versa. The chosen motivations were deemed fit for the purpose of the research based on the availability of information and comprehensive description in the literature. Further, the chosen motivations are described in studies using U&G theory, which makes it applicable for this study to explore the motivations to attend a LAN from a U&G perspective. The explored motivations revealed critical benefits participants get out of their attendance at a LAN. The explored motivations are the input that influences gamers to attend a LAN. However, the perceived benefits are the output gamers get from their LAN attendance and experience. The benefits are tied to motivation and vice versa, meaning there is an interrelated connection. Therefore, defining and understanding gratifications is challenging because they are user-centred (Becker, 1979).

#1 Competition

Competition is identified as the urge to compete with others in a game, where winning can satisfy the need to be competitive and bring a sense of power (Barnett et al., 1997; Jansz & Martens, 2005; Yee, 2006). Thus, gamers always expect esports, in general, to have a competitive nature in the games which is perceived by gamers as a possibility to gain and achieve power and capability in the games (Sherry et al., 2006; Yee, 2006; Taylor, 2006; Jansz & Tanis, 2007; Weiss, 2011; Wang et al., 2021).

Competition can be seen as a major reason why gamers play video games (Kim & Ross, 2006; Sepehr & Head, 2018). LANs are usually organised around multiplayer competitive games between different teams attending, and often, there are rewards for the winning team. Therefore, gamers who attend LANs regularly desire to compete in games and win to enhance their image and position among the other gamers (Jansz & Martens, 2005; Chang et al., 2021).

The presence of adequate game skills is an important factor influencing gamers to compete in LANs. Skill improvement is a motivation specifically applicable in the esports context. Gamers compete in various games driven by the need to advance, and that need reinforces the motivation to acquire competent skills (Qian et al., 2020).

#2 Skills

This motivation is considered important for gamers who want to learn and advance their gameplay and therefore watch how the professionals do it. Barney (2021) identifies skills as one of the reasons why people watch esports. Skill motivation is highly valued by spectators of esports thanks to the visual presentation provided online and the skilled gameplay of gamers. By comparing the virtual and physical game settings, a study by Neus et al. (2019) explored the motivations of esports audiences to engage in and spectate esports. The study's findings suggest a difference in the appreciation of skills between online game spectators and game spectators at a LAN. Online spectators have a better position to watch the esports event because they are usually streamed online and have the option to watch at home on a big screen or their PC.

On the contrary, the spectators at a LAN who watch the esports event are at a disadvantage in appreciating the gaming skills because the screens are far away, and there is a high chance of missing out on parts due to the fast pace of the game (Neus et al., 2019). The enjoyment of the skillset states that the availability for users to enjoy the event entirely is somewhat limited. Thus, the online spectators' enjoyment and immersion are higher due to the option of switching through channels and following a certain gamer at a slower pace, where all the detailed tactics are more visible and clearer (Hamari & Sjöblom, 2017; Neus et al., 2019). The skillset of gamers is more beneficial to online users due to the difference in the online and offline dimensions of experience (Neus et al., 2019). The motivation behind the skillset category is rooted in the human need for prosperity, capability, and the ability to be competent (Ryan & Deci, 2000).

Skill improvement is a motivation specifically applicable in the esports context. Gamers compete in various games driven by the need to advance, and that need reinforces the motivation to acquire competent skills.

Qian et al. (2020) outlined two types of skills in their research. Skill Improvement is described as the range of acquiring new knowledge regarding various skills, tactics, and strategies while watching esports. On the other hand, skill appreciation is the ability to acknowledge other gamers' skills, tactics, and strategies while watching esports. Qian et al. (2020) suggest that skill improvement is the main motivation for spectators involved in gaming themselves who want to learn and improve their gameplay. However, skill appreciation was a new motivation in the esports context, already known in traditional sports. This motivation is a valuable one prone to influencing spectators into committing to the game (Qian et al., 2020). Gaming skills are a vital factor for gamers, as Barney (2021) discussed. His research focuses on how competitive gamers who retired from their gaming careers of pro gamers have instead turned to a streaming career where they can still show off their gaming skills to the people watching their streams. Those streams by professional gamers are highly appreciated by spectators who want to learn and turn for information from gamers with knowledge and experience in the esports field (Barney, 2021). Skills are an important gameplay component for gamers as they try to mimic the tactics and strategies they see on streams. Therefore, the appreciation of skills is an important motivation for spectators and gamers who want to acquire relevant knowledge (Wang et al., 2019). The findings of Barney (2021) show that people who have skill-based motivations to spectate esports did not have specific preferences for online or offline presence mode.

#3 Escape

Escape has shown to be a strong motive for gamers within previous research on motivations and gratification related to esports and gaming (Trail & James, 2001; Hamari & Sjöblom, 2017; Neus et al., 2019).

Escapism refers to how media provides an escape and distraction from daily routines and ordinary activities, responsibilities, or problems (Gantz & Wenner, 1995: Yee, 2006). The escape motivation for gamers is not dependent on the game outcome; whether they win or lose, it is more about the sense of escape from real life (Wann et al., 2008; Neus et al., 2019). Since gamers need a sense of escapism, esports events, in general, should make it possible for gamers to feel the escapism experience. However, it is argued that the settings of esports can influence the escapism experience (Seo & Green, 2008; Seo, 2013). Hence, playing games or watching streams at home, e.g., using the same computer or television in the same room, which is considered a daily routine, will not create the same escape experience as attending events or changing the surroundings. The

gamer's environment will give more of an escape experience and deliver unexplored feelings (Neus et al., 2019).

#4 Entertainment

Entertainment is essential to gamers because they expect that they will enjoy the game and its results, such as winning, which will cheer them up and entertain them (Griffiths & Wood, 2000; Jansz & Martens, 2005; Tang, 2018; Gan & Li, 2018; Qian et al., 2020). In addition, gamers play games because it provides entertainment and enjoyment, specifically when regularly playing with peers and friends (Whiting & Williams, 2013). Therefore, we argue that gamers at a LAN will play games to entertain esports spectators on social networking events (Ko et al., 2005; Pons et al., 2006; Kerr & May, 2011; Hamari & Sjöblom, 2017).

In the context of LANs, information and communication technology is an important factor contributing to gamers' entertainment. A quality LAN is when computers are connected to a local area network without internet connection troubles (lag). It gives the internet a high speed, which allows the gamers to enjoy their game and communicate within the game. As a result, LANs can be pleasing and entertaining for gamers because they can enjoy high-speed Internet access to engage in other activities like updating their games or watching streams (Jansz & Martens, 2005). It is argued that even watching esports activities is a form of entertainment where it can also contribute to learning new skills because it provides information (Hamari & Sjöblom, 2017; Hilvert-Bruce et al., 2018; Qian et al., 2020).

#5 Information

Information is important due to the availability to access data and the opportunity to find and learn a wide range of information to keep one updated with the current events in their area of interest (Seo & Green, 2008). Whiting & Williams (2013) identified two aspects of information: seeking and sharing of information. Information seeking is referred to as a way to improve by learning new information ("*self-educate*") or gaining new knowledge by seeking information (Whiting & Williams, 2013). Chang (2019) conducted a study exploring the motivations of esports audiences and found that information seeking is done online rather than using traditional information channels such as TV or radio. The main reason for that is the convenience factor. The esports audience prefers to seek information online by using Twitch, YouTube, and smartphone applications that automatically send notifications when there is news in the esports field and update all the news to keep the information source up to date.

According to Whiting & Williams (2013), seeking information is considered a facilitator in managing communication and initiating socialisation with others. Information is further explored as motivation and the main reason why gamers engage and spend time on the Twitch streaming platform. The results found that the desire to learn more and gain knowledge leads gamers to spend more time engaging on Twitch (Hilvert-Bruce et al., 2018).

Information sharing was described as how "*interpersonal communication*" is achieved (Whiting & Williams, 2013). Gamers acquire their information by interacting with friends. The importance of information sharing is particularly evident in the esports field. It is a fundamental part of the esports culture and is highly valued by gamers, encouraging them to continue engaging in esports (Chang, 2019). Furthermore, it is argued that events are a great source of information for gamers. A LAN is perceived to be a platform to exchange information where gamers expect other professional gamers to attend the LAN to seek information about new gaming tactics and new gaming updates to learn new things (Jansz & Martens, 2005; Neus et al., 2019).

#6 Achievement

Yee (2006) describes achievement as a personal motivation that gamers are driven to play games to advance in the game and improve their character. However, the achievement is also described as a socialising motivation tied up to the subcategory of teamwork. Achievement as a social motivation is when one thinks about achievements as a group and works together in collaboration to attain the goal (Laal & Ghodsi, 2012).

Achievement motivation is often cited in relation to competitive offline gaming and frequently attributed motivation that refers to the gamers accomplishing goals within their chosen game (Weiss, 2011). Achievement is one of the major motivations for gamers to play video games, along with social interaction and escapism. Yee (2006) has suggested that those motivations with a combination of prolonged hours playing can cause online game addiction. However, Wang et al. (2021, p.1) suggest a coping strategy for the online gaming addiction and propose that gamers susceptible to this addiction engage in "*outdoor activities, such as sports competitions and offline cosplay games to address the need for achievement and escapism*". Furthermore, Yee et al. (2012) found that gamers driven by achievement motivations are not interested in-game activities that do not provide instant or direct rewards and therefore suggest better tailoring of games to the users' needs and interests.

The esports audience prefers to seek information online by using Twitch, YouTube, and smartphone applications that automatically send notifications when there is news in the esports field and update all the news to keep the information source up to date.

Moreover, there is a share of experience when a favourite sports athlete wins a game and shares the achievement online and offline. The satisfaction of observing a favourite gamer's success and celebrating a triumph is considered a key motivating factor for all esports spectators and thus suggested to have the same value in the online and offline esports context (Neus et al., 2019).

#7 Community

Hilvert-Bruce et al. (2018) researched the community as a motivation in the context of Twitch and the engagement of live streams. During a LAN, gamers like to watch live streams together in a group (Scholz, 2012). The results concluded that a sense of community in the users of Twitch is one of the main drivers gamers engage with the streaming platform and the driver that engages users to continue their usage and consumption of the live-streaming content. Users are highly appreciative when they have a sense of belonging to a community "*live-stream viewers are attracted to channels where they feel noticed, important, and influential*" (Hilvert-Bruce et al., 2018, p.59). Spectators of live streams are subscribing to channels on Twitch to expand their social circle, improve connections and integrate themselves within the community. The sense of community is maintained by continued participation and engagement from both spectators and streamers. Smaller channels are more likely to provide spectators with attention (being noticed), acknowledgement (reward participation), and engagement (creation and preservation). All those benefits a small channel provides are necessary to maintain the sense of community and provide a sense of belonging to the community, which is very important for spectators (Hilvert-Bruce et al., 2018).

According to Eklund (2015), members of online communities tend to connect with other members in the offline setting because offline connections are crucial for online interaction. Further, online interactions are an extension of offline social relations (Castells, 2001).

When it comes to establishing offline connections, a LAN allows gamers to connect with like-minded people while engaging in video game play and building a community (Jansz & Martens, 2005). The practice of gaming with other like-minded individuals creates a strong social bond for the community. Those communities are called gaming communities formed around a specific video game where people engage with other members to enhance their playing experience (Gee, 2008).

The connections established in a community are based on common characteristics to enhance the gameplay in the community, create norms and regulations and bolster the companionship within the community. Therefore, as a result, online and offline relationships become interconnected (Eklund, 2015). Thus, a sense of community is fostered by engaging the gamers within the gaming community's experiences, engaging with streamers, participating in chat discussions, and socialising (Hilvert-Bruce et al., 2018).

#8 Social Interaction

Socialising with peers is of great importance within esports (Whiting & Williams, 2013; Hamilton et al., 2014; Sjöblom & Hamari, 2017). The multiplayer option in games can be gratifying to sociality, where gamers need to play together (Jansz & Martens, 2005). Multiplayer games can occur when peers get together to play and achieve (Orleans & Laney, 2000) or when other unknown gamers compete with others online (Griffiths et al., 2004). Maslow's hierarchy of needs implies that social interaction between individuals can satisfy the needs of belonging and love (Maslow, 1943).

Social interaction is an experience created by playing games with others. Consequently, one achieves a sense of understanding as it revolves around an interest and shared experiences (Eklund, 2015). Socialising can be seen as a major part of attending events. People usually go to events to socialise and interact with people who often have the same interest or share something in common. Therefore, they attend the same event in the first place and use that interest or common things to interact and keep up with each other socially (Ko et al., 2005; Pons et al., 2006;

Kerr & May, 2011; Hamari & Sjöblom, 2017). However, in esports, gamers can still interact online through streaming platforms, not only in events which means gamers can interact online or offline (Scheibe et al., 2016; Bründl et al., 2017). Regardless, attending LANs provides a higher sense of social interaction because gamers can physically come together (Neus et al., 2019). Moreover, it is argued that digital interaction can never replace authentic real-life social experience and interaction (Scheibe et al., 2016; Bründl et al., 2017; Hilvert-Bruce et al., 2018). Socialising is also a key factor impacting gamers' engagement and continuous usage of games (Chen et al., 2006; Hamari & Koivisto, 2015).

#9 Relationship

Some studies contradict the importance of socialisation while spectating esports, even though communication tools are available to initiate socialisation in the virtual space. Not all research supports the relevance of relationships as a motivation in the gaming literature (Weiss, 2011). This contradiction comes from the fact that online communication is not considered as effective as communication and relationship formation in a real-life context (Hamari & Sjöblom, 2017; Xiao, 2020).

Gamers can be highly motivated to watch esports because of socialising, engaging with others and the feeling of connection with specific teams or gamers.

However, relationships are part of the social motivation category. According to Wang et al. (2021), it is related to building and maintaining relationships with others which further includes helping and supporting. In online games, relationships help gamers further improve in games and continue the game storyline (Przybylski et al., 2010; Wang et al., 2021). Relationships are based on collaboration between individuals. However, establishing this connection can satisfy the need for belongingness and love (Maslow, 1943). Gamers with the best game performance are the ones that cooperate and communicate (Badatala et al., 2016). The presence of a relationship provides them with better ideas, more knowledge, and consequently, best game results. In situations where there are challenges in the game, gamers tend to put in a team effort to pass the obstacles and hardships (Chang et al., 2018).

Gamers can be highly motivated to watch esports because of socialising, engaging with others and the feeling of connection with specific teams or gamers. Those aspects can influence spectators to continue engaging in esports (Qian et al., 2020). In addition, esports can be regarded as a social activity that creates a feeling of belonging to a group or being part of a community. Chang et al. (2021) describes social relationships as a need to relate with people, feel part of a group, need for belonging, or engage, connect, and socialise with others. The importance of building and maintaining long-lasting relationships in the gaming world is discussed by Trepte et al. (2012), describing cases in which gamers leave a game. The prior built relationship in the online game provides a greater chance for the gamer to maintain a strong relationship offline. Furthermore, Chang et al. (2021) suggests that long-term relationships in online games may be able to transform into offline relationships in the offline world. The ability to socialise and communicate with others is valued highly by people, with a particular emphasis on ones that engage in LANs (Sjöblom et al., 2019). Social relationships drive gamers to engage in video games to gain social recognition regarding social interactions and build long-term relationships. Barney (2021) explored gamers with relationship-based motivations and found that people driven by that motivation prefer to watch esports in person rather than online.

#10 Teamwork

Teamwork is a social activity acquired by actively cooperating with other teammates (Yee, 2006). Teamwork is used to describe a group effort sharing the same collective purpose, where gamers collaborate to help each other, team up, or learn new skills to help the team reach in-game goals and win the game (Decortis et al., 2010; Kang et al., 2013; Chang et al., 2021). At its core, gamers interact and communicate with others to achieve goals such as winning a game or completing a task successfully. In the hierarchy of needs, Maslow proposes that interactivity between people serves as a course of action that satisfies individuals' need for love and belonging (Maslow, 1943; Wang et al., 2021). The presence of good teamwork is described as when the team sets common rules, tactics, and strategies to be followed in the game by everyone in the team, which is built on communications and collaboration (Decortis et al., 2010). There are diverse stages in gaming where teammates provide help and support for their alliances to mutually achieve goals within a game, such as levelling up characters, finding treasures, fulfilling quests, entering dungeons, and fighting bosses (Teng & Chen, 2014; Chang et al., 2021). The effort done by the team collaboration and the group achievement will make teammates satisfied (Yee, 2006). Becoming part of a team in-game provides gamers with benefits such as connecting with like-minded people who have similar interests and building loyal relationships with other gamers. Teamwork helps gamers build long-lasting relationships that can be held and continued in the offline setting (Kang et al., 2013; Chang et al., 2021).

Method

This study uses an **abductive approach** to explore a phenomenon that has not been explored well. Previous research has been examined and used to collect empirical data, resulting in new assumptions or unexplored theories (Kovács & Spens, 2005; Saunders et al., 2016). There is a scarcity of qualitative studies about gamers' motivation in esports; most of the available studies have been done quantitatively. Consequently, conducting a qualitative study can provide a better understanding of a phenomenon and can be beneficial for the research area of esports (Hamari & Sjöblom, 2017; Neus et al., 2019). Qualitative research is involved in understanding individuals more profoundly by capturing their thoughts and views due to the lack of qualitative research on gamers' motivations in relation to LANs. In-depth knowledge is required to understand the phenomenon that quantitative methods cannot achieve (Bryman & Bell, 2011; Barnham, 2015; Hamari & Sjöblom, 2017; Michailidis, 2019). Therefore, qualitative research was used to reach gamers who have attended a LAN, to explore their motivations and thus help understand the phenomena of LANs (Saunders et al., 2016; Michailidis, 2019).

Empirical Findings

The findings represent the motivations and the benefits of attending a LAN. The study initially started with ten motivations which were presented in **Chapter 2**. However, after conducting all interviews, there was evident intertwining between the motivations based on the answers participants provided. Therefore, the authors have merged the motivations due to the similarity of answers provided for different motivations. As a result, the ten motivations are categorised into either first-level codes, second-level codes, or themes resulting in five final themes. To better illustrate the findings and due to intertwinement, **Table 1** presents the data structure of thematic analysis where the left column shows the first-level codes originated from participants' statements. Then they were further developed to connect the same set of concepts, presented as second-level codes. Both theory and second-level codes contributed to the emergence of themes.

Table 1. Data structure of thematic analysis

First Level Codes	Second Level Codes	Themes
Urge to compete	Competitive Nature	Competition
Win/lose emotions		
Tangible rewards	Rewards	
Intangible rewards		
LAN competence	Improvement	Skills
Competitive skills		
Refine abilities	Team Composition	
Collective skills		
Individual skills		
Positive feelings	Escape	Diversion
Negative feelings		
LAN experience		
Home experience		
Enjoyment	Entertainment	
Network benefits		
Technical issues		
Game META	Learning	Information
Esports updates		
Share & exchange	Sharing	
Sense of belonging	Community	Social Interaction
Motivation to attend		
Socialising	Relationships	
teammates		
Team dynamics		

Competition

Competitive Nature

The **urge to compete** at a LAN differs among participants. The minority go to a LAN to compete because they find it an important and more pleasing experience than competing from home. Playing competitive games at a LAN is more entertaining and cooler because the participants are around other people who share the same interest. On the other hand, the majority think it is not important to compete at a LAN and prefer to do other activities instead because they are casual gamers who do not invest much in certain games and do not have the urge to compete. Therefore, they do not want to carry their PC to the LAN. Those participants prefer to socialise instead when going to a LAN.

Participants expressed their **emotions about winning or losing** at a LAN. The majority feel lucky and happy to win when they celebrate in groups and have fun together. However, some referred to losing as a happy feeling. However, the minority feel unlucky, sad, annoyed, and disappointed when losing at a LAN as it affects participants' mood. Those feelings were described as irritation, mentally crushing, overall anger and physical anger. After much effort put into training in a game, it is frustrating and disappointing when faced with a loss.

Rewards

Participants expressed how **getting rewards** affects their motivation to attend a LAN again. The minority said that **tangible rewards would** affect their motivation to attend a LAN again. These rewards can be free merchandise (t-shirts, graphic cards, headsets, keyboards, mouses, computers, underwear, hoodies, keychains, bags). In addition, items they get from giveaways (DreamHack tickets), food and beverages (limited-edition Monster). There are also monetary rewards or discounts in hardware stores. Moreover, the size of the LAN and the amount of money spent on tickets affect participants' expectations of receiving tangible rewards. Those participants who received these rewards expressed that it made them feel lucky and awesome.

The majority shared that the **intangible rewards** affect their motivation to go to a LAN. These rewards were expressed as meeting new people, socialising, building relationships, finding new teammates, doing your hobbies, playing video games, competing, and advancing gameplay. Furthermore, they appreciate the pleasant memories and experiences created from the enjoyment a LAN brings.

Skills

Improvement

Many participants think a LAN is a place to learn and improve social skills to gain **LAN competence.** Examples of those skills are communication, socialisation with others,

and exchanging knowledge. Some participants shared that going to a LAN helps them become more extroverted by socialising. Other participants think a LAN is a place to learn new skills by getting tips from coaches and ideas from other gamers by learning how they play, which improves overall skills. However, participants also think a LAN can teach important skills but not improve them. A new perspective was presented, where gamers go to a LAN to demonstrate their skills instead of learning new skills.

When it comes to being a successful **competitive** gamer, specific **skills** are needed. The majority of participants emphasised the importance of having sportsmanship conduct, good communication within the team, risk-taking, and encouraging others. Further, being a good person, having patience, logical thinking, handling distractions, learning from mistakes and ignoring ego. Additionally, they believe that having steady emotions, calmness, determination, and acknowledgement of their mistakes will help one focus during competition and manage the emotions whether the outcome (winning or losing). Besides, participants outlined other important competitive skills such as practice, good decision-making, map awareness, good reflexes (fast adaptation), target aim, ahead planning, knowing game technique and mechanics.

The majority of participants emphasised the importance of having sportsmanship conduct, good communication within the team, risk-taking, and encouraging others.

When it comes to **refining abilities** is not as important for all participants. Some participants want to improve their gaming skills, keep getting better in games and feel comfortable in a social setting around people. Refining abilities provides satisfaction, enjoyment, and pleasure for the gamers. However, there were interviewees who were satisfied with their current skills level and did not want to improve them because they are not competitive gamers. Nevertheless, the minority wanted to improve their skills but had certain obstacles preventing them. Examples mentioned by participants are that improving skills is time-consuming and for many work and studies are a priority, so they cannot spend enough time playing their game. Further, an interviewee shared her experience being faced with toxicity in the gaming community and how that prevented her from improving her skills.

Team Composition

Participants indicated whether they preferred to play single-player or multiplayer games. The majority shared that they play both types of games with multiplayer as the main one. However, some interviewees shared that they switch game types based on their current mood.

The ones who listed multiplayer as the type of game they play were asked what **collective skills** are needed to have a strong team composition. According to respondents, having a clear structure in a team, knowing your position in the game, and determining responsibilities were the most common answers. Further, having a leader who calls out the big shots in the game (shot caller) and support is important for the team to have a strong composition. Participants shared that anticipating and counteracting the other teams' actions is a necessary skill for the team to learn to be successful.

Finally, participants were asked to name **individual skills** that make a strong team composition. The most common answers were knowing game tactics, having map awareness, execution of strategies, having dexterity, good reflexes, and being able to multitask. Participants shared other good individual skills, such as restraining yourself from blaming others, taking criticism, not being toxic, arrogant, narcissistic, egoistic, or micromanaging when playing along with having the same goals. Respect, communication,

teamwork, emotional stability, patience, positivity, calmness, and lack of ego are viewed as skills necessary for fostering good synergy in a team by most participants.

Diversion

Escape

A mix of **positive and negative feelings** was reported regarding playing games at a LAN. The majority associated attending a LAN with positive feelings such as excitement, happiness, and relaxation. LANs can be enjoyable if you find a group of people to play and spend time with. An interviewee expressed other special feelings that a LAN brings that brings back happy memories and makes one feel happy and engaged by simply being part of a LAN. Nevertheless, a minority of participants expressed negative feelings when playing games at a LAN. A challenging situation can arise due to the unpleasant conditions (screaming, loud noise), lack of personal social skills, long distances and in line waiting for essentials (drinks, food, toilets) because there are many people at a LAN.

Participants discussed how their experiences vary at LANs or home. Most participants described their **experiences at LANs** as out of the ordinary, magical, and cosy. They perceived it as a vacation from daily life. At a LAN, gamers get together with other people sharing the same interest where they can have interesting conversations on a deeper level of interaction. The social atmosphere motivates gamers to play, and thus a sense of community is fostered. Moreover, a couple of participants connected the experience of a LAN as nostalgic, bringing back their childhood memories of Internet cafés. Nevertheless, participants mentioned that going to a LAN is not only about playing games but doing other activities too. These activities are table tennis, retro gaming, old-time consoles, cooking/getting food together, going for fresh air walks, and watching streams together. Finally, participants said that a LAN is a connection point where people get to know each other.

The other half of the participants described their game **experience at home** as more relaxed, focused on playing the game (watching streams to learn), more comfortable (better utilities at home - bathroom, food, beverages,) and having no physical interaction or background noises. However, playing online at home was described as a feeling of a chore that forces gamers to engage in gameplay. Further, some participants said that being at a big LAN such as DreamHack, it is hard to focus on playing games because there are many people around.

Entertainment

The majority of participants listed **enjoyment** would make them come back to a LAN. Reasons for that are meeting new people or friends that share the same interests, doing something different from daily life or staying at home. Therefore, participants go to a LAN to unwind, chill and relax as it is found to be a fun and cool activity that gathers people together. Other activities beyond gaming are liked to be seen by participants, such as offline activities, watching streams, movies, live events, attending a concert at the LAN, having cosplayers, and participating in tournaments and challenges. Brands related to games are highly appreciated when at a LAN, where participants can learn what is new in the game, buy rare game edition products, get free merchandise, food and beverages. Game related decorations make a LAN more enjoyable and pleasing to the eye.

The majority see many **network benefits** from the local area network as they can do multiple things at a time faster than at home. Those benefits are sharing data, transferring files faster, streaming, watching, and chatting with other people using interactive platforms. Participants explained that games have more possibilities when playing at a high-speed local area network because internet cables are connected directly to computers than a wireless connection at home.

When it comes to **technical issues** at a LAN, participants described how the occurrence of internet lag would make them feel. They expressed that they trust the local area network and assume it should have a stable and fast connection because the cables and routers are nearby and connected directly to computers. However, if a lag occurred, it would negatively affect their LAN experience, and they would label the LAN as poorly organised. The emotions described were frustration, disappointment, and annoyance because lags could affect the game, causing participants to have a negative mood.

However, the majority feel that the internet is not the main thing on a LAN. However, in case of any technical issues, participants will have a backup plan of playing offline games, while the technicians' team is fixing the internet issue quickly.

Information

Learning

For competitive gamers, **META** is one of the most important factors that gamers need to consider. There are different types of learning and adapting to the META as shared by the participants. The participants have shared different ways of learning and adapting to the META. Half of the participants described themselves as self-learners because they like to try out various things in the game by trial and error. Because they are driven to compete on a higher level, they put a lot of time and effort into game practice and are determined to adapt fast and usually take part in pre-beta releases of games to see the changes made and learn first-hand.

The other half shared that they learn by watching others and like being inspired by others. They watch streams online or at a LAN. While some participants find detailed information in books, forums, and websites, others look to professional or casual gamers for advanced game knowledge. They can also become acquainted with the revised META by looking at specific game information such as nerf, buff, patch notes, and theorycrafting.

Multiple channels keep participants **updated about esports** and upcoming LANs. In addition to social media (Facebook, Twitter, Instagram, TikTok), streaming platforms

(Youtube and Twitch), word-of-mouth (friends and family), online game communities (Discord groups), websites (game publishers), examples are given of forums (read patch notes, Reddit), and newsletters (emails and notifications). Furthermore, participants learn about game discounts through gameplay, on Steam, online shops' wish lists, Googling information, watching and following top streamers, or physical advertisements (street posters and flyers). The ticket price, however, plays an important role for some of whether they will attend an upcoming LAN or watch a stream on Twitch instead.

Sharing

At LANs, most participants consider **information sharing** essential because they want to improve their gameplay (become better at a game) by learning new skills and tactics. As a result of **exchanging information**, participants can hear other opinions and perspectives, which is beneficial in a dynamic game environment where keeping up with everything yourself is challenging. Participants who are competitive gamers actively look for better gamers and professionals at LANs to learn from them. Furthermore, LANs facilitate the development of relationships and build strong bonds by sharing information about new games and events. At a larger LAN, participants also value safety information to be shared, such as exit locations (for emergency) and the layout of facilities (entrances, exits, bathrooms).

Conversely, the minority do not see sharing information at a LAN as essential. They think sharing information at a LAN is time-consuming because people will have many questions, and when provided with the answers, there is a chance they will not fully understand the information. Some do not like to share information such as personalised strategies because of the risk of stealing.

Social

Community

Participants varied in answers to whether they belonged to a gaming community in three different ways. Participants who belong to communities have distinguished between different types of gaming communities. Some communities are clubs where members play various games, and game communities are based on a particular game (Dota2, Counter-Strike, League of Legends, World of Warcraft). Participants expressed that **belonging to a community** could be a rewarding experience because of the presence of veteran gamers (experts) and the fact that everyone is focused on the game. Several participants consider the group of friends they play with as their gaming community. In contrast, some participants said they have been part of gaming communities before but are no longer active due to a lack of time. Nevertheless, there were a few participants who had not been part of any communities since they switched games frequently, played occasionally, or preferred to speak with friends via Discord.

They can also become acquainted with the revised META by looking at specific game information such as nerf, buff, patch notes, and theorycrafting.

The majority of participants shared that being part of a community affects their **motivation to attend** a LAN. Therefore, going with other community members to a LAN is more motivating for them than going alone. However, the minority do not go with a community because they are not part of any, instead, they go with their friends to LANs. Going to a LAN with friends is a motivation to attend a LAN rather than one going alone. Some participants expressed a desire to attend a LAN with other gaming community members. However, they cannot do so due to the distance between the gamers who are part of the gaming community but are not situated within the same country or city. Participants indicated that they would be motivated to attend LANs if their gaming community was local. Nevertheless, LANs such as Dream-Hack offer gamers from around the world to meet IRL for the first time. Due to the magnitude of such events worldwide, many gamers have expressed their willingness to attend.

Relationship

Socialising with others affected participants' motivation to attend LANs. **Socialising** enables gamers to have good communication and understanding, which leads to sharing tactics, contributing to better teamwork, fostering a bond between gamers, helping and motivating each other, resulting in better game outcomes. However, the minority said that if everyone at a LAN is communicating, they will lose focus and become distracted. Furthermore, participants' willingness to return to a LAN was negatively affected by **socialising** with rude, toxic, and negative gamers. At a LAN, there is the chance to interact with different people, so it would be unpleasant if the communication is poor, therefore everyone in the team needs to be on the same page.

Participants expressed that being physically present with their teammates at a LAN is an advantage to their gameplay since they have better map awareness (thanks to communication with their teammates) and they are more relaxed (since they see facial expressions, moods, body language of their teammates) as well as being more focused on enjoying the game rather than winning, so they are less likely to get mad and they mind their language when speaking to each other. In addition, attending a LAN with teammates is considered more fun and efficient because it provides a stimulating environment where participants become more engaged in the game and think deeply about their actions. On the other hand, being physically together at a LAN affects participants' experience. A participant found it restraining because he could not use insulting language as usual. Another participant shared his unpleasant experience at a LAN when playing with less skilled people because they drag the whole team down. Furthermore, being at a LAN was described

as frustrating and nervous because of the distraction and the people watching you play. Hence, one needs a strong mentality to avoid that. However, some participants expressed that being physically together or having good or poor communication and collaboration will not affect them or their focus.

Participants shared their **team dynamics** and if they had met a new team member at a LAN. Most participants stated that they had never met anyone at a LAN who became part of their team because of Covid-19 or did not need more teammates. Regardless, participants said it was highly probable to meet a new team member at a LAN who might join the team, especially in lower-ranking or professional competitive teams where gamers want to advance in the game rank, become better gamers, and find better teams to compete with. Participants shared if their teams changed over time. Some participants shared a different team dynamics perspective where professional gamers change teams depending on their contracts and game performance. The minority of participants play with the same people and have not experienced any changes within the team. However, the majority have experienced a change in their team over a certain period.

Discussion

Competition

The relevance of competition as a **motivation** differs between casual and competitive gamers because they are aware of the reasons to attend a LAN to satisfy specific needs and wants (Ruggiero, 2000). From a U&G perspective, this can be seen as casual gamers have other needs to satisfy so they do not have the urge to compete but have other needs and wants to satisfy and therefore they attend a LAN (Lowery & De Fleur, 1988; Ruggiero, 2000).

From the findings, the urge to compete was the main reason competitive gamers attend a LAN, where they can compete with others who share the same interests and competitive needs (Kim & Ross, 2006; Sepehr & Head, 2018). They put much effort into the game to satisfy their competitive needs (Rubin, 2002;

Cummings, 2008). Certain types of skills are needed when one competes at a LAN such as emotional stability (without projecting negative emotions onto others), sportsmanship conduct and being responsible for your actions. As a result, the gamers with this skill set are motivated by the urge to compete at a LAN to enhance their reputation and position among their peers (Barnett et al., 1997; Jansz & Martens, 2005; Sherry et al., 2006; Yee, 2006; Taylor, 2006; Jansz & Tanis, 2007; Weiss, 2011; Chang et al., 2021; Wang et al., 2021). Nevertheless, when experiencing a loss, feelings of annoyance and disappointment occur because of the time and effort invested into practising the game. Whether a participant is a casual or competitive gamer, the motivations differ. Therefore, they judge the value and importance of competing at a LAN through their own perception (Katz et al., 1974).

The benefits gamers gain from attending a LAN connected to diversion motive are, escape and entertainment.

Attended LANs were regarded as **beneficial** if a reward was available when competing because it satisfied the needs of achievement (Yee et al., 2012). Therefore, most participants expected **intangible rewards** as a benefit of attending a LAN which influenced participants' motivation to attend. Social inclusion, video gameplay and new memory formation were the most common intangible rewards. Another benefit of competing is showing off game skills in front of other gamers at a LAN (Qian et al., 2020).

In contrast, few shared that **tangible rewards** are expected at a LAN among the participants. As a result, their expectation of rewards as payback for attending a LAN increase when they pay a high-priced ticket to a big LAN. In addition, they will expect rewards such as free merchandise, giveaways, discounts in hardware stores, food and beverages. From the findings, it can be assumed that if participants spend much money on a

LAN ticket and end up getting no rewards, there is a high chance their motivation to attend a LAN will decrease because they are not getting their desired benefit. Therefore, they might find an alternative solution, such as going to CoreHack or a free LAN.

However, it was evident that the casual gamers did not find competition a motivation to go to a LAN because they were motivated by social interaction (Lowery & De Fleur, 1988; Ruggiero, 2000). They also expressed that winning or losing will not affect their motivation to go to a LAN, but if they win, happiness will follow. Nevertheless, there was an outstanding opinion pointing out that some gamers possess little or no competitive game skills but are good players solely because they possess mathematical and statistical knowledge which allow them to compete in games such as League of Legends.

Diversion

The findings indicated that diversion is a strong motive to attend a LAN because it can gratify the needs to relax, escape stress, and responsibilities (Sherry et al., 2006; Sun et al., 2006; Yee, 2006). Instead of playing games or chatting at home, gamers are motivated to attend LANs based on the diversion they will get there, and all the experiences associated with it, which include people not isolated at home (Seo & Green, 2008; Seo, 2013; Neus et al., 2019). It is argued that gamers seek diversion from life which can be satisfied by attending a LAN and being around people, and this motivation is not about the diversion from people (Sherry et al., 2006). From a U&G perspective it is argued that gamers are motivated and actively seeking to attend a LAN because it can gratify the need to relax and escape (Katz et al., 1973; Severin & Tankard, 1997; Ruggiero, 2000; Rubin, 2002; Cummings, 2008; McQuail, 2010).

The **benefits** gamers gain from attending a LAN connected to diversion motive are, **escape** and **entertainment**. Where **escape** is about experiencing excitement, happiness, and relaxation. Unique exciting feelings are being explored, such as weird happiness when gamers turn into children while being at a LAN, giving nostalgia by bringing back their childhood memories of Internet cafés (Neus et al., 2019). The experience can be enjoyable and bring happiness because they can find a group of people sharing the same interest to spend time with and have engaging conversations on a deeper level of interaction. Happiness and satisfaction were also tied to LANs as it is a place to meet role models and idols because it acts as a social connecting point (Neus et al., 2019).

Gamers feel relaxed at LANs and connect it to being extraordinary, magical, and cosy experiences where they feel that they are on vacation from daily life. They can also do more activities beyond gaming that will allow them to relax and escape all daily routines, such as engaging in retro gaming, playing on old-time consoles, or even cooking/getting food together, going for fresh air walks, and watching streams (Wann et al., 2008; Neus et al., 2019).

The other benefit is **entertainment** which is essential to gamers, and they expect that a LAN should give them enjoyment and entertainment (Griffiths & Wood, 2000; Jansz & Martens, 2005; Whiting & Williams, 2013; Tang, 2018; Gan & Li, 2018; Qian et al., 2020). Since they do many things with people, such as watching streams together, movies, live events or even attending a concert at a LAN, where it is a more enjoyable and entertaining environment than doing all of that from home (Hamari & Sjöblom, 2017; Hilvert-Bruce et al., 2018; Qian et al., 2020). On top of that, gamers enjoy all the offline activities a LAN provides, such as having cosplayers, participating in tournaments and challenges, which allow them to experience joy while doing new things due to the social networking nature of the event (Ko et al., 2005; Pons et al., 2006; Kerr & May, 2011; Hamari & Sjöblom, 2017).

Moreover, gamers enjoy being at a LAN where their favourite gaming brands are present either to buy rare game edition products, get new and unique news and updates about their games from the brand itself before it is even announced, which can contribute to learning new skills because it provides information (Hamari & Sjöblom, 2017; Hilvert-Bruce et al., 2018; Qian et al., 2020).

Gamers can also get a chance to get free merchandise that is highly appreciated and make them enjoy the LAN and take something back home to remind them of the enjoyable experience and memories. Furthermore, many gamers can satisfy their need for enjoyment when they are surrounded by their favourite game-related decorations found eye pleasing. Finally, free food and beverages add a lot to the enjoyment experiences at a LAN for a gamer, especially when they get a game-related product such as (limited-edition Monster).

One of the major benefits of a LAN is enjoying the high-speed local area network (Jansz & Martens, 2005). Even with the technologies and internet access everywhere, gamers highly appreciate the local area network because they trust and assume that it will provide them with high quality experience without any technical issues compared to the home network. The **network benefits** can be seen as doing multiple things faster than at home, such as sharing data, transferring files, streaming, watching, playing and chatting with other people using interactive platforms, all can be done at the same time and faster. What is interesting about the high-speed local area network is that it brings more possibilities to the games because it is fast and provides equal opportunity for all gamers by having the same ping which becomes more evident in shooter games. However, gamers trust that in case of any technical issues, the technician team is highly qualified and will be there to fix that problem. While that is happening, gamers can still do other activities, so even if an issue occurs, it will not affect the enjoyment because of the other things to do and enjoy such as offline activities rather than being at home and not being able to fix anything or do anything else to enjoy which might make them angry or bored (Jansz & Martens, 2005).

However, a minority of participants expressed frustration when playing games at a LAN because many people there can create unpleasant conditions for those who lack social skills, so they cannot be around so many people. Also, there are loud noises and long queues to get essentials (drinks, food, toilets). Moreover, if a lag occurs, they will be disappointed and annoyed because it will affect the game. Therefore, they prefer to play games from home because they can focus on the game without distractions, watch streams to learn, chat and feel relaxed. Nevertheless, they already know that staying at home will not give the same benefits as escape and entertainment, but they value focusing on playing games rather than getting those benefits. This agrees with Neus et al. (2019) that gamers who value their gameplay will have more desire to stay home and not be motivated to go to a LAN and get benefits such as escape. One of the opinions stood out, pointing out that the price of LANs is too high thus preventing a participant from even considering attending. However, if the price of the LAN tickets was reduced, he might be more inclined to consider attending LANs.

Social Interaction

Social interaction is the main and most influential **motivation** to attend a LAN. It was evident that participants go to a LAN to socially interact with other people who share the same interest (Ko et al., 2005; Pons et al., 2006; Kerr & May, 2011; Whiting & Williams, 2013; Hamilton et al., 2014; Sjöblom & Hamari, 2017). It is argued that gamers are motivated to attend a LAN because it can gratify the need for social interactions (Cummings, 2008; McQuail, 2010). Further, because gamers are motivated by social interaction to attend a LAN a U&G perspective argues that gamers active because of the interaction at a LAN which is the media in this context (Jansz & Martens, 2005; Kim & Ross, 2006; Sherry et al., 2006; Qian et al., 2020).

The benefits gained from social interaction with others at a LAN are, **feeling acknowledged, building relationships, acquiring information, socialisation** and **finding new teammates.**

Feeling acknowledged by a group of people can satisfy the needs of belonging and love allowing gamers to have good communication and understanding which can foster relationships (Maslow, 1943; Wang et al., 2021; Chang et al., 2021). Supporting the results of

Weiss (2011), It was evident that a relationship is not a motivation to attend a LAN, however, it is found to be a benefit of the social interaction with others. When a **relationship** is established out of social interaction it leads to gaining benefits such as, **sharing experiences and information** to help and support each other, which is a fundamental part of the esports culture and is highly valued by gamers, encouraging them to continue engaging in esports and resulting in better game outcomes (Przybylski et al., 2010; Whiting & Williams, 2013; Eklund, 2015; Badatala et al., 2016; Chang et al., 2018; Tang, 2018; Chang, 2019; Wang et al., 2021). Those relationships can help **keep gamers updated** with esports related information such as upcoming events and game updates (Seo & Green, 2008).

Participants gain benefits when interacting with journalists, brand representatives and professional or better gamers than them. By interacting with experts, one is able to **acquire** first-hand **information** such as sharing their tactics, techniques, and new developments in gaming to become better gamers (Whiting & Williams, 2013). Where U&G argue that gamers seek to gratify the need for improving knowledge (Cummings, 2008; McQuail, 2010).

Socialisation with team or community members at a LAN can be beneficial because players can interact physically with each other and have fun (Neus et al., 2019). This interaction will advantage the gameplay of the whole team because members can communicate better (Eklund, 2015; Chang et al., 2018) and read each other's body language, which helps them stay relaxed and keep things under control. This will also lower the chances of getting mad at each other because they understand the situation since they are physically together rather than online and do not understand it. The results confirm that digital interaction can never replace authentic real-life social experience, interactions, communications and relationships because gamers become more understanding when physically together and mind their language and care about each other's emotions (Scheibe et al., 2016; Bründl et al., 2017; Hamari & Sjöblom, 2017; Hilvert-Bruce et al.,

2018; Xiao, 2020). Moreover, big LANs such as DreamHack offer gamers from around the world (who are part of the same team or community but in different countries) to meet IRL and socially interact for the first time.

Finding new teammates to join the team or the community is another benefit, where social interaction allows to find like-minded people who share the same passion and interest, which results in finding suitable teammates who share the same goals (Jansz & Martens, 2005; Yee, 2006; Decortis et al., 2010; Kang et al., 2013; Chang et al., 2021). Further, the findings show that team dynamics are constantly changing because gamers might have work or studies, so they change their priorities, pushing gaming back on their list. As a result, teams will be looking for a replacement. Therefore, a LAN is seen as a suitable place to find new teammates because social interaction can help gamers connect with like-minded people who have similar interests and build long-lasting loyal relationships with other gamers that can extend to the online setting (Jansz & Martens, 2005; Gee, 2008; Taylor & Witkowski, 2010; Kang et al., 2013; Eklund, 2015; Taylor, 2006; Chang et al., 2021).

> *Achievement was not seen as a motivation but rather as a benefit where gamers get rewards from achieving something in relation to competition.*

However, social interactions at a LAN affect the minority, making the experience unpleasant. If everyone is socialising and communicating, those participants will lose focus on the game and will be nervous that everyone is watching them. They also prefer to get information online because of its convenience and availability of more comprehensive information (Hilvert-Bruce et al., 2018; Chang, 2019). They improve their skills by watching professional gamers, or rewatching their mistakes which can advance their gameplay skills since a LAN does not provide enough time for that (Qian et al., 2020; Barney, 2021). Further, a LAN is not a place to learn or improve. This could be justified by Neus et al. (2019), that at a LAN, screens are distant, and it is a challenge to watch tournaments between professional gamers. There is a risk of missing out on important aspects of the gameplay, therefore, watching professionals at a LAN and learning from them is not optimal for the participants. Participants prefer to watch from home, where they have access to multiple screens and better visual images, as confirmed by Hamari & Sjöblom (2017) and Neus et al. (2019), to appreciate the skill set of professionals.

Also, if participants are socially interacting with rude, toxic, and negative players, which can discourage their urge and willingness to refine abilities. It could be restrained because of the inability to use insulting language as usual. Nevertheless, some desire to be at a LAN with their team or community to benefit from social interactions but cannot do it because they lack time to be part of one or the long distance between the gamers (not situated within the same country or city).

Revised Model

From the findings it was evident that competition, diversion, and social interaction are the motivations for attending a LAN. Further, the gained benefits from attending a LAN are **rewards, information, skills, escape, entertainment, relationships, socialisation and finding new teammates.**

Achievement was not seen as a motivation but rather as a benefit where gamers get **rewards** from achieving something in relation to competition.

This study found **information** as a benefit gained from attending a LAN rather than a motivation which contradicts Jansz & Martens (2005) and Neus et al. (2019) findings that see information as a motivation to attend a LAN. It was evident that **skills** is a benefit gained from attending a LAN rather than a motivation contradicting Barney (2021) findings.

The findings showed that **escape and entertainment** are not a motivation for gamers to attend a LAN, but it is a benefit they get out of diversion, this finding contradicts with (Trail & James, 2001; Hamari & Sjöblom, 2017; Ncus et al., 2019). Instead, LANs benefit gamers by giving them an escape and distraction from daily routines and ordinary activities, responsibilities, or problems. And it also entertains them (Gantz & Wenner, 1995: Yee, 2006). This research supports Weiss's (2011) results that **relationship** is not a motivation. However, socialising and finding new teammates were benefits that emerged from the findings and were coded into the theme.

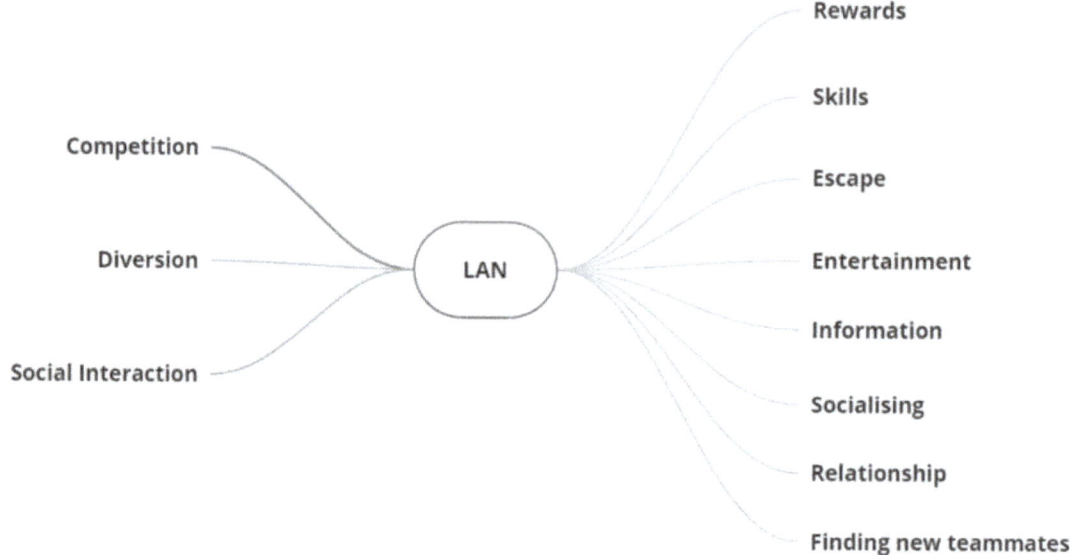

Figure 1: Revised model of the motivations to attend a LAN and the gained benefits out of it

Conclusion and Implications

Theoretical Implications and Contribution

This study has explored the motivations to attend a LAN and found the benefits gained from it. Using a small sample of gamers, following a qualitative exploratory approach that contributes to the adequate exploration of the motivations to attend a LAN where the results contribute to filling the gaps and provide novel insights in the research area where a little research was done on the topic suggested by Jansz & Martens (2005), Scheibe et al. (2016), Bründl et al. (2017), Hilvert-Bruce et al. (2018), Neus et al. (2019), Michailidis (2019) and Lui (2020). Considering the importance of this topic, there is a need for theoretical exploration.

First, this study found three motivations to attend a LAN from a U&G perspective: competition, diversion and social interactions driving gamers to attend a LAN to gratify their needs. Where rewards, information, skills, escape, entertainment, socialising, and relationships are discovered to be benefits in this context and with specific this sample. This is the contribution to the theory.

Secondly, this study explored the LAN's vital qualities, unexplored feelings and impressions for gamers suggested by Taylor & Witkowski (2010) and Neus et al. (2019), where the benefits gained from attending a LAN are the vital qualities, unexplored feelings and impressions.

Thirdly, this study adds to the literature on U&G and gamers' motivations to attend a LAN by identifying and clearing the ambiguity between motivations and benefits.

This study noticed two types of gamers (casuals and competitive), and their motivations to attend a LAN and the benefits they gain vary from a U&G perspective where gamers judge the value and importance of LAN on their terms of understanding and views. (Katz et al.,1974).

The study further contributes to the U&G theory and fills gaps in a unique context (LANs) this further adds a conceptualisation and specified distinction where it shows that needs drive the motivation to attend a LAN and therefore gain benefits where this contradicts the criticism of the theory by (Ruggiero, 2000; Krcmar & Strizhakova, 2009). We argue that gamers are active users who purposely select, engage and consume media, LANs in this context. We did an interview study rather than a self-report, resulting in rich and accurate descriptions adding to U&G literature (Katz, 1987; Ruggiero, 2000; Sherry, 2001; Williams et al., 2008; Lee et al., 2009).

The findings confirm that certain aspects of LAN cannot be substituted by online gaming and vice versa. However, both provide certain gratifications that are distinct from one another. Further, participants anticipate certain gratifications to be satisfied at a LAN that an online game will not satisfy (Ruggiero, 2000; Neus et al., 2019). Consequently, evaluating the factors that affect gamers' motivation to attend LANs is essential (Jansz & Martens, 2005; Scheibe et al., 2016; Bründl et al., 2017; Hilvert-Bruce et al., 2018; Neus et al., 2019).

Lastly, a revised model is presented to clarify and present the new contribution and serve as a base for further knowledge extension to explore or test the model further. Therefore, this study can be an initial groundwork for exploring the motivations to attend a LAN and the benefits gained.

Managerial Implications and Contribution

The study can assist LAN organisers as it provides valuable insights regarding the motivations to attend a LAN. Thus, the results of this study provide suggestions to the LAN organisers regarding how they can combine online and offline activities during the event to create greater value for the attendees of their events. The study can further provide insights useful for LAN organisers as it can inspire them to create new activities that can

become part of the event itself. The study could be used as a foundation to build onto ideas for activities gamers value from the online setting and be practically applied to a LAN.

The authors suggest the study is reviewed by LAN organisers and perhaps by event organisers as it could be found relevant for both. The attendees judge the quality of a LAN, and thus meeting their expectations as a LAN organiser or event organiser would undoubtedly increase the perceived value of the LAN. Thus affecting the motivations of gamers to attend the LAN. Meeting customer expectations increases the chance of gamers/LAN attendees coming back.

The findings confirm that certain aspects of LAN cannot be substituted by online gaming and vice versa. However, both provide certain gratifications that are distinct from one another.

It was evident from the findings that the motivations and benefits (gratifications) were intertwined, meaning there is an interconnection between them. On the other hand, LAN organisers can focus on the benefits gamers derive from their time and money investment to increase gamers' motivation to attend LAN events. This suggestion was inspired by the findings where some participants were motivated to get their money's worth back in merchandise. However, providing small tokens or merchandise is beneficial for the sponsoring brands represented on the LAN. It increases brand awareness and further creates a sense of appreciation gamers feel when provided with the freebies.

We suggest dividing the gaming areas at LANs into smaller sections, where each section consists of people playing the same game. This would make the opportunity for people to find like-minded gamers, find new teammates, and exchange information about game tactics more efficient, time-saving (since you would not need to shuffle between LAN rooms looking for gamers who play your game), and stress-free (since you would be in the same game section with like-minded people). People who play different game genres might have different personality traits, thus, some can be found incompatible as some gamers are more relaxed and easy-going, whereas others are tense and rigid. An example would be Arcade versus Shooter game players or The Sims and Call of Duty players. It can be speculated that providing an area or section dividing the players of each game genre (where all arcade players are sitting together in one section and all shooter game players in another) would increase the enjoyment gamers get from attending a LAN. Moreover, it will prevent gamers from experiencing awkward situations where they find themselves at a LAN in a group talking about a game, but they cannot participate in the discussion due to lack of knowledge or prior experience with the game. Further, sectioning the outlay of the LAN provides gamers with a better opportunity of finding teammates, socialising, and gaining information from others who might be more knowledgeable and experienced. The sections might further increase the sense of community and belonging to gamers as their preferred choice of the game puts them in a section with like-minded people who share the same interests and thus can create a sense of community within the community.

6.3 Societal Implications and Ethical Considerations

This research respects all different people in society and protects all participants' opinions and thoughts by being anonymous concerning their privacy to prevent any harm or damage to them (Oliver, 2010; Bryman & Bell, 2011).

This study is interested in understanding people who are part of society. The results might affect or change individuals' behaviours and attitudes towards esports in general, leading to a societal issue (Bryman & Bell, 2011).

Some downfalls of video game playing are discussed by Yee (2006), where gamers exposed to long hours of video gameplay can become easily susceptible to developing game addiction. However, Wang et al. (2021) suggest a coping strategy/mechanism and propose a shift in actions for gamers. Moving from an online gaming environment to an offline one, where gamers can engage in other activities such as cosplay and still be related to the gamers' interest (cosplaying their favourite game character). Also, esports is more inclusive for everyone in society and not limited to age like sports, where professional gamers can reach 76 years old (Tuting, 2020).

Anticipating how individuals might use the results of this study is tricky and can be problematic, however, this study is interested in understanding the phenomenon and producing new knowledge without the purpose of harming anyone in society. Also, this study is not aiming to encourage people to spend more or less time playing video games.

References

Badatala, A., Leddo, J., Islam, A., Patel, K., & Surapaneni, P. (2016). The effects of playing cooperative and competitive video games on teamwork and team performance. *International Journal of Humanities and Social Science Research*, 2(12), 24-28.

Barnett, M.A., Vitaglione, G. D., Harper, K. K. G., Quackenbush, S. W., Steadman, L. A., & Valdez, B. S. (1997). Late Adolescents' Experiences With and Attitudes Toward Videogames1. *Journal of Applied Social Psychology*, 27(15), 1316–1334. https://doi.org/10.1111/j.1559-1816.1997.tb01808.x

Barney, J. (2021). *Understanding the Motivations of Esports Fans: The Relationship Between Esports Spectator Motivations and Esports Fandom Engagement* [Master Thesis, University of Nevada]. University Libraries.

https://digitalscholar-ship.unlv.edu/cgi/viewcontent.cgi?article=5123&context=thesesdissertations

Barnham, C. (2015). Quantitative and qualitative research: Perceptual foundations. *International Journal of Market Research*, 57(6), 837-854. https://doi.org/10.2501/IJMR-2015-070

Becker, L. B. (1979). Measurement of Gratifications. *Communication Research*, 6(1), 54–73. https://doi.org/10.1177/009365027900600104

Bryman, A. (2016). *Social research methods*. Oxford University Press.

Bryman, A. & Bell, E. (2011). *Business Research Methods* (3. ed.). Oxford University Press.

Bründl, S., Matt, C., & Hess, T. (2017). Consumer use of social live streaming services: The influence of co-experience and effectance on enjoyment. *ECIS*.

Castells, M. (2002). *The Internet galaxy: Reflections on the Internet, business, and society*. Oxford University Press on Demand.

Chang, S. M., Hsieh, G. M., & Lin, S. S. (2018). The mediation effects of gaming motives between game involvement and problematic Internet use: Escapism, advancement and socialising. *Computers & Education*, *122*, 43-53. https://doi.org/10.1016/j.compedu.2018.03.007

Chang, W. L., Chen, L. M., & Hsieh, Y. H. (2021). Online to offline social interaction on gaming motivations. Kybernetes. https://doi.org/10.1108/K-02-2021-0156

Chang, Z. (2019). *What's the hype about esports?": a qualitative study about esports consumer motivation*. [Bachelor Thesis, Luleå University of Technology]. https://www.diva-portal.org/smash/get/diva2:1328029/FULLTEXT01.pdf

Chen, K. T., Huang, P., & Lei, C. L. (2006). Game traffic analysis: An MMORPG perspective. *Computer Networks*, 50(16), 3002-3023. https://doi.org/10.1016/j.comnet.2005.11.005

Chen, V.-H.-H., Duh, H. B.-L., Phuah, P. S. K., & Lam, D. Z. Y. (2006). Enjoyment or engagement? role of social interaction in playing massively multiplayer online role-playing games (MMORPGS). *In International Conference on Entertainment Computing* (pp. 262–267). Springer. https://doi.org/10.1007/11872320_31

Cummings, N. M. (2008). *The uses and gratifications of communication in virtual spaces: media depictions of Second Life, 2002-2008* [Bachelor Thesis, University Of Oregon]. https://scholarsbank.uoregon.edu/xmlui/bitstream/handle/1794/8987/Cumming_Nicholas_Michael_BA2008.pdf?sequence=1

Decortis, F., Lentini, L., & Meurice, D. (2010). Toward a competency model of video games effective players. In *IDC 2010 Digital Technologies and Marginalized Youth Workshop*. https://doi.org/10.1145/1810543.1810614

Eklund, L. (2015). Bridging the online/offline divide: The example of digital gaming. *Computers in Human Behavior*, 53, 527-535. https://doi.org/10.1016/j.chb.2014.06.018

Fetscherin, M., Kaskiris, C. & Wallenberg, F. (2005). Gaming or sharing at LAN- parties-what is going on?. *First International Conference on Automated Production of Cross Media Content for Multi-Channel Distribution*, 1-8.

Gan, C., & Li, H. (2018). Understanding the effects of gratifications on the continuance intention to use WeChat in China: A perspective on uses and gratifications. *Computers in Human Behavior*, *78*, 306-315. https://doi.org/10.1016/j.chb.2017.10.003

Gantz, W., & Wenner, L. A. (1995). Fanship and the television sports viewing experience. *Sociology of Sport Journal*, 12(1), 56-74. https://doi.org/10.1123/ssj.12.1.56

Gee, J. P. (2008). *Learning and games*. MacArthur Foundation Digital Media and Learning Initiative.

Griffiths, M., & Wood, R. T. (2000). Risk Factors in Adolescence: The Case of Gambling, Videogame Playing, and the Internet. *Journal of Gambling Studies*, *16*(2), 199–225. https://doi.org/10.1023/A:1009433014881

Griffiths, M., Davies, M., & Chappell, D. (2004). Online computer gaming: a comparison of adolescent and adult gamers. *Journal of Adolescence*, *27*(1), 87–96. https://doi.org/10.1016/j.adolescence.2003.10.007

Hamari, J., & Koivisto, J. (2015). "Working out for likes": An empirical study on social influence in exercise gamification. *Computers in Human Behavior*, 50, 333–347. doi:10.1016/j.chb.2015.04.018

Hamari, J., & Sjöblom, M. (2017). What is eSports and why do people watch it?. *Internet Research*, 27(2), 211-232. https://doi.org/10.1108/IntR-04-2016-0085

Hamilton, W. A., Garretson, O., & Kerne, A. (2014). "Streaming on twitch": fostering participatory communities of play within live mixed media. In *Proceedings of the SIGCHI conference on human factors in computing systems* (pp. 1315-1324). https://doi.org/10.1145/2556288.2557048

Hess, T. (2014). What is a Media Company? A Reconceptualization for the Online World. *International Journal on Media Management*, 16(1), 3-8. https://doi.org/10.1080/14241277.2014.906993

Hilvert-Bruce, Z., Neill, J., Sjöblom, M., & Hamari, J. (2018). Social motivations of livestreaming viewer engagement on twitch. *Computers in Human Behavior*, 84, 58-67. doi: 10.1016/j.chb.2018.02.013

Hutchins, B. (2008). Signs of meta-change in second modernity: the growth of e-sport and the World Cyber Games. *New Media & Society*, 10(6), 851-869. https://doi.org/10.1177/1461444808096248

Jang, W., & Byon, K. K. (2020). Antecedents of esports gameplay intention: Genre as a moderator. *Computers in Human Behavior*, 109 (106336). https://doi.org/10.1016/j.chb.2020.106336

Jansz, J., & Martens, L. (2005). Gaming at a LAN event: the social context of playing video games. New media & society, 7(3), 333-355. https://doi.org/10.1177/1461444805052280

Jansz, J. & Tanis, M. (2007). Appeal of playing online first person shooter games. *Cyberpsychology and Behavior*. 10 (1), 133-136. DOI: 10.1089/cpb.2006.9981.

Kang, A. R., Park, J., & Kim, H. K. (2013). Loyalty or profit? early evolutionary dynamics of online game groups. In *2013 12th Annual Workshop on Network and Systems Support for Games (NetGames)* (pp. 1-6). IEEE. DOI: 10.1109/NetGames.2013.6820602

Kerr, A. & D. May. (2011). An exploratory study looking at the relationship marketing techniques used in the music festival industry. *Journal of Retail & Leisure Property*, 9(5), pp. 451–464. https://doi.org/10.1057/rlp.2011.8

Katz, E. (1987). Communications research since Lazarsfeld. *The Public Opinion Quarterly*, 51(4), S25-S45.https://doi.org/10.1093/poq/51.4_PART_2.S25

Katz, E., Blumler, J., & Gurevitch, M. (1974). Utilization of mass communication by the individual. *In J.Blumler & E. Katz (Eds.), The Uses of Mass Communication: Current Perspectives on Gratifications Research* (pp. 19–34). Beverly Hills, CA: Sage.

Katz, E., Blumler, J. G., & Gurevitch, M. (1973). Uses and gratifications research. *The public opinion quarterly*, *37*(4), 509-523. http://www.jstor.org/stable/2747854

Kim, Y., & Ross, S. D. (2006). An exploration of motives in sport video gaming. *International Journal of Sports Marketing & Sponsorship*, 8(1), 28–40. https://doi.org/10.1108/IJSMS-08-01-2006-B006

Ko, H., Cho, C.H. and Roberts, M.S. (2005), "Internet uses and gratifications: a structural equation model of interactive advertising", Journal of Advertising, Vol. 34 No. 2, pp. 57-70. https://doi.org/10.1080/00913367.2005.10639191

Kovács, G. & Spens, K.M. (2005). Abductive reasoning in logistics research. *International Journal of Physical Distribution & Logistics Management*, *35*(2), 132–144. https://doi.org/10.1108/09600030510590318

Krcmar, M., & Strizhakova, Y. (2009). Uses and gratifications as media choice. In *Media Choice: A Theoretical and Empirical Overview* (pp. 53-69). https://doi.org/10.4324/9780203938652

Laal, M., & Ghodsi, S. M. (2012). Benefits of collaborative learning. *Procedia-Social and Behavioral Sciences*, 31, 486-490. https://doi.org/10.1016/j.sbspro.2011.12.091

Lash, S. (2002). *Critique of information*. Sage.

Lee, K. M., Peng, W., & Park, N. (2009). Effects of computer/video games and beyond. In *Media Effects* (pp. 567-582). Routledge.

Lowery, S., & DeFleur, M. L. (1988). *Milestones in mass communication research: Media effects*. Addison-Wesley Longman Ltd.

Lui, Y. C. A. (2020). *Rationalization and Modern Play in Local Esports Events* [Master Thesis, Tampere University]. https://trepo.tuni.fi/bitstream/handle/10024/120652/LuiYuk.pdf?sequence=2

Maslow, A. H. (1943). A theory of human motivation. *Psychological Review, 50*(4), 370–396. https://doi.org/10.1037/h0054346

McCauley, B., Tierney, K. D., Holmströmm, M., & Andersson, K. (2019). Understanding co-creation of value in LAN parties. In *ANZMAC 2019, 2nd-4th December 2019, Wellington, New Zealand* (pp. 200-203).

McCauley, B., Tierney, K., & Tokbaeva, D. (2020). Shaping a Regional Offline eSports Market: Understanding How Jönköping, the 'City of DreamHack', Takes URL to IRL. *JMM International Journal on Media Management, 22*(1), 30–48. https://doi.org/10.1080/14241277.2020.1731513

McQuail, D. (2010). *McQuail's mass communication theory*. Sage.

Michailidis, K. (2019). An investigation into the motivations of offline eSports consumption [Master Thesis, Lincoln International Business School] https://www.researchgate.net/publication/337544411_An_investigation_into_the_motivations_of_offline_eSports_consumption

Neus F. (2020) Differences and Similarities in Motivation for Offline and Online eSports Event Consumption. In: *Event Marketing in the Context of Higher Education Marketing and Digital Environments*. Handel und Internationales Marketing Retailing and International Marketing. Springer Gabler, Wiesbaden. https://doi.org/10.1007/978-3-658-29262-1_6

Neus, F., Nimmermann, F., Wagner, K., & Schramm-Klein, H. (2019). Differences and Similarities in Motivation for Offline and Online eSports Event Consumption. *HICSS*. Doi: 10.24251/HICSS.2019.296

Oliver, P. (2010). *The student's guide to research ethics*. McGraw-Hill Education.

Orleans, M. & Laney, M. (2000). Children's Computer Use in the Home. *Social Science Computer Review. 18*(1), 56–72. https://doi.org/10.1177/089443930001800104

Parelius, R. (2019). *The Return of the LAN*. Steel Series. https://steelseries.com/blog/return-of-the-lan-89

Pons, F., M. Mourali, & S. Nyeck, (2006). "Consumer Orientation Toward Sporting Events", *Journal of Service Research*, 8(3), 276–287. https://doi.org/10.1177/1094670505283931

Przybylski, A. K., Rigby, C. S., & Ryan, R. M. (2010). A motivational model of video game engagement. *Review of general psychology*, 14(2), 154-166. https://doi.org/10.1037/a0019440

Pöyhtäri, A. (2016). *Social gaming in online games*. [Master Thesis, University of Oulu]. http://jultika.oulu.fi/files/nbnfioulu-201605221858.pdf

Qian, T. Y., Wang, J. J., Zhang, J. J., & Lu, L. Z. (2020). It is in the game: dimensions of esports online spectator motivation and development of a scale. *European sport management quarterly*, 20(4), 458-479. https://doi.org/10.1080/16184742.2019.1630464

Rubin, A. M. (2002). The uses-and-gratifications perspective of media effects. In J. Bryant & D. Zillmann (Eds.), *Media Effects: Advances in Theory and Research* (pp. 525–548). Lawrence Erlbaum Associates Publishers.

Ruggiero, T. E. (2000). Uses and gratifications theory in the 21st century. *Mass communication & society*, 3(1), 3-37. https://doi.org/10.1207/S15327825MCS0301_02

Ryan, R., & Deci, E. (2000). Intrinsic and extrinsic motivations: Classic definitions and new directions. Contemporary Educational Psychology, 25(1), 54–67. https://doi.org/10.1006/ceps.1999.1020

Scholz, T. M. (2019). eSports is Business. In *eSports is Business: Management in the World of Competitive Gaming*. Springer International Publishing. https://doi.org/10.1007/978-3-030-11199-1

Scholz, T.M. (2012). New broadcasting ways in IPTV–The case of the Starcraft broadcasting scene. In: *World Media Economics & Management Conference*.

Scheibe, K., K.J. Fietkiewicz, and W.G. Stock, "Information Behavior on Social Live Streaming Services", *Journal of Information Science Theory and Practice*, 4(2), 2016, pp. 6–20. https://doi.org/10.1633/JISTaP.2016.4.2.1

Seo, Y. (2013). Electronic sports: A new marketing landscape of the experience economy. *Journal of Marketing Management*, 29(13-14), 1542-1560. https://doi.org/10.1080/0267257X.2013.822906

Seo, Y. (2016). Professionalized consumption and identity transformations in the field of eSports. *Journal of Business Research*, 69(1), 264–272. https://doi.org/10.1016/j.jbusres.2015.07.039

Seo, W. J., & Green, B. C. (2008). "Development of the motivation scale for sport online consumption". *Journal of Sport Management*, 22(1), 82-109. https://doi.org/10.1123/jsm.22.1.82

Sepehr, S., & Head, M. (2018). Understanding the role of competition in video gameplay satisfaction. *Information & Management*, 55(4), 407-421. https://doi.org/10.1016/j.im.2017.09.007

Severin, W. J., & Tankard, J. W. (1997). *Communication theories: Origins, methods, and uses in the mass media*. Longman.

Sherry, J. L. (2001). The effects of violent video games on aggression: A meta-analysis. *Human Communication Research*, 27(3), 409-431. https://doi.org/10.1111/j.1468-2958.2001.tb00787.x

Sherry, J. L., Lucas, K., Greenberg, B. S., & Lachlan, K. (2006). Video game uses and gratifications as predictors of use and game preference. *Playing Video Games: Motives, Responses, and Consequences*, 24(1), 213-224.

Sjöblom, M., & Hamari, J. (2017). Why do people watch others play video games? An empirical study on the motivations of Twitch users. *Computers in Human Behavior*, 75, 985-996. https://doi.org/10.1016/j.chb.2016.10.019

Sjöblom, M., Macey, J., & Hamari, J. (2019). Digital athletics in analogue stadiums: Comparing gratifications for engagement between live attendance and online esports spectating. *Internet Research*, 30(3), 713–735. https://doi.org/10.1108/INTR-07-2018-0304

Stafford, T. F., Stafford, M. R., & Schkade, L. L. (2004). Determining uses and gratifications for the Internet. *Decision Sciences*, 35(2), 259–288. doi:10.1111/deci.2004.35

Sun, T., Zhong, B., & Zhang, J. (2006). Uses and gratifications of Chinese online gamers. *China Media Research*, 2(2), 58-63.

Sundar, S. S., & Limperos, A. M. (2013). Uses and grats 2.0: New gratifications for new media. *Journal of Broadcasting & Electronic Media*, 57(4), 504-525. https://doi.org/10.1080/08838151.2013.845827

Saunders, M., Lewis, P., & Thornhill, A. (2016). *Research methods for business students* (Seventh ed.). Pearson Education.

Tang, T., Cooper, R., & Kucek, J. (2021). Gendered Esports: Predicting Why Men and Women Play and Watch Esports Games. *Journal of Broadcasting & Electronic Media*, 65(3), 336-356. https://doi.org/10.1080/08838151.2021.1958815

Tang, T., Kucek, J., & Toepfer, S. (2020). Active within structures: Predictors of esports gameplay and spectatorship. *Communication & Sport*, 1–21. https://doi.org/10.1177/2167479520942740

Tang, W. (2018). Understanding esports from the perspective of team dynamics. *The Sport Journal*, 21, 1-14.

Taylor, T. (2006). *Play between worlds*. MIT Press.

Taylor, T., & Witkowski, E. (2010). This is how we play it: What a mega-lan can teach us about games. Paper presented at the Proceedings of the Fifth International Conference on the Foundations of Digital Games, Monterey California. https://doi.org/10.1145/1822348.1822374

Teng, C. I., & Chen, W. W. (2014). Team participation and online gamer loyalty. *Electronic Commerce Research and Applications*, 13(1), 24-31. https://doi.org/10.1016/j.elerap.2013.08.001

Trail, G. T., & James, J. D. (2001). The motivation scale for sport consumption: Assessment of the scale's psychometric properties. *Journal of Sport Behavior*, 24(1). https://psycnet.apa.org/record/2001-14557-008

Trepte, S., Reinecke, L., & Juechems, K. (2012). The social side of gaming: How playing online computer games creates online and offline social support. *Computers in Human Behavior*, 28(3), 832-839. https://doi.org/10.1016/j.chb.2011.12.003

Tuting, K. (2020). *5 esports facts that will blow your mind.* One Esports. https://www.oneesports.gg/gaming/5-esports-facts-that-will-blow-your-mind/

Wang, Q., Yang, Y., Li, Z., Liu, N., & Zhang, X. (2020). Research on the influence of balance patch on players' character preference. *Internet Research.* https://doi.org/10.1108/INTR-04-2019-0148

Wang, X., Abdelhamid, M., & Sanders, G. L. (2021). Exploring the effects of psychological ownership, gaming motivations, and primary/secondary control on online game addiction. *Decision Support Systems*, 144, 113512. https://doi.org/10.1016/j.dss.2021.113512

Wann, D.L., Grieve, F.G., Zapalac, R.K. & Pease, D.G. (2008). Motivational profiles of sport fans of different sports. *Sport Marketing Quarterly*, 17(1), 6-19. https://hdl.handle.net/20.500.11875/2973

Weiss, T. (2011). Fulfilling the Needs of eSports Consumers: A Uses and Gratifications Perspective. *Bled eConference*, 30, 572-580. http://aisel.aisnet.org/bled2011/30

Whiting, A., & Williams, D. (2013). Why people use social media: a uses and gratifications approach. *Qualitative Market Research: An International Journal.* DOI 10.1108/QMR-06-2013-0041

Williams, D., Yee, N., & Caplan, S. E. (2008). Who plays, how much, and why? Debunking the stereotypical gamer profile. *Journal of Computer-Mediated Communication*, 13(4), 993-1018. https://doi.org/10.1111/j.1083-6101.2008.00428.x

Xiao, M. (2020). Factors influencing esports viewership: An approach based on the theory of reasoned action. *Communication and Sport*, 8(1), 92–122. https://doi.org/10.1177/2167479518819482

Yee, N. (2006). Motivations for play in online games. *CyberPsychology & Behavior*, 9(6), 772-775. http://doi.org/10.1089/cpb.2006.9.772

Yee, N., Ducheneaut, N., & Nelson, L. (2012). Online gaming motivations scale: development and validation. *In Proceedings of the SIGCHI conference on human factors in computing systems.* 2803-2806. https://doi.org/10.1145/2207676.2208681

Yu, E., Jung, C., Kim, H., & Jung, J. (2018). Impact of viewer engagement on gift-giving in live video streaming. *Telematics and Informatics*, 35(5), 1450-1460. https://doi.org/10.1016/j.tele.2018.03.014

Traditional Sports Organizations' Expansion to eSports

By Eric Gargallo Serrano

The eSports industry has experienced exponential growth in recent years which has raised the awareness of many organizations about the industry. This fast-paced growth created interest for these organizations to enter eSports. The eSports industry generated a 947.1M revenue in 2020, it grew to 1.08B in 2021 and is forecasted to grow to 1.6B by 2024 (Newzoo, 2021). These numbers imply the dimensions of eSports, reaching a remarkable market size and attracting the interest of a big part of society. However, the industry processes, governance, and stakeholders have not adapted to this increase. In other words, eSports has not been professionalized enough to handle the humongous growth of the industry. The lack of knowledge and professionalization might hinder the future of the eSports scene. This thesis will explore the industry and provide recommendations on how the industry could evolve to better adapt to general consumer and market trends. Moreover, how traditional sports organizations bring value, maturity, and business expertise into the eSports industry will be presented. The concept of traditional sport organization will be explained in chapter 1.5. but, in short, refers to the conventional and long-established sports which require physical effort and are broadly accepted by everyone.

The first eSports organizations emerged around the 1970s but, according to Scholz (2019), the beginning of the ongoing exponential growth started around the 2000s with a cultural and technological development that enabled the monetization of videogames. Therefore, many of the current organizations were born around that time. Afterwards, with the release of new videogames titles such as League of Legends in 2009 or Starcraft II in 2010 and the founding of Twitch in 2011, catalysed the industry creating a momentum that is still present nowadays. Different stakeholders realized the potential and started creating tournaments and ways to monetize eSports.

Currently, eSports are of high relevance to their audience and the top players are real celebrities. According to Scholz (2019, p. 142), the League of Legends World Championship's finals between the European team Fnatic and the Chinese team Invictus Gaming in 2018 gathered an audience of more than 200 million online viewers.

Therefore, eSports are presenting new opportunities for different brands to reach very specific and unique audiences. Principally the Gen Z, with sponsorships, advertising, and partnerships (Sparham, 2021).

Problem Area

The outlined developments and potential of eSports in terms of fanbase, audience, and repercussion has been shown in the previous chapter. Yet, the eSports industry has not been able to catch up and adapt its processes proportionally to its growth and this might handicap the further growth of the industry. Personally, I have followed the development of the industry closely for the last ten years since I started playing videogames and noticed the competitive side of eSports. Also, as a person that has been involved and enjoying sports all his life, playing, coaching, and scouting in basketball; seeing how eSports were implementing in many of the sports areas and many sports organizations started to show interest in it, further raised my interest. Thus, with this long-term understanding of both industries, being passionate about sports and an eSports enthusiast, more specifically on League of Legends, I got interested in why these sports organizations were entering and how they were doing it from a strategic point of view. Also, I noticed and constantly read certain trends about eSports organizations and the issues that need to be addressed, and that is what the purpose of this thesis is, so eSports can keep growing sustainably.

The eSports organizations need to develop their business models and look for additional revenue streams since currently there is a high dependency on the sponsors, which is not sufficient for the sustainable success of their businesses. Scholz (2019, p. 136) argues that any organization has found a way to monetize fans and that the audience's monetization is low compared to traditional sports. Hence, this thesis tries to find the reasons for this issue and provide potential solutions for the organizations to be able to efficiently monetize the audience in a sustainable manner.

In addition, there is a lack of overall academical material about eSports, so the thesis aims to fill this need and raise awareness about the industry and its possibilities, while further research is incentivized by the creation of this thesis, as well as the development of the eSports. Therefore, the thesis will explore the industry and provide an understanding of what needs to change and how traditional sports organizations bring value, maturity, and expertise from a business point of view.

Purpose of the study

The thesis purpose is to provide an understanding for sports organizations to succeed in their expansion and identify the outcome of eSports in the following years. Therefore, this research plans to give insights about why the expansion into eSports by non-endemic organizations, which are not born within eSport, can be considered an interesting growth opportunity for sports organizations. Furthermore, the advantages and disadvantages of the different relevant expansion methods are explored in this thesis. In addition, the thesis wants to provide a good overview about the structure of the eSports industry and understand what the forthcoming years of eSports might look like, as well as filling an academic literature gap. This will be done through the insights of the eight interviews

conducted with relevant people from sports organizations in eSports and providing a market overview and information about the business side of eSports. Moreover, I aim to research the methods traditional sports organizations use to expand their businesses, specifically their horizontal growth to a different market: eSports. Therefore, the research questions that will be used for the thesis will be the following:

- RQ1: Why do traditional sports expand to eSports?
- RQ2: How do traditional sports expand to eSports?
- RQ3: What does the future of eSports look like?

By answering these research questions this paper aims to acquire a complete understanding of how and why traditional sports organizations enter the eSports market. Moreover, it aims to understand how the future of eSports might be, its issues, and what needs to be improved for the further success of the industry.

Research Method

This study conducts qualitative research on the eSports topic and how traditional sports organizations are implementing their growth strategies to enter eSports. For the data collection, interviews are the main chosen method. Eight interviews, as shown in Table 2, with relevant people from sports organizations present in eSports have been done. These interviews provided insights and helped to understand why and how traditional sports organizations entered eSports. With the data being collected, the different strategies taken by different organizations are compared, aiming for conclusions to be drawn.

The data analysis starts with coding the interview by thematic areas to provide a better visualization of the data. Afterwards, the relevant data from each thematic area is gathered in tables so the comparison is easier to do, and patterns can be identified more efficiently. Besides that, some online information is used to complement this data and to provide a better understanding of the eSports industry. The research method, philosophy, and quality of the thesis are further developed in chapter 3.

Limitations

ESports is a broad industry comprehending many videogames which can be divided into different genres. Scholz (2019, p. 8) explains that eSports is an umbrella term for any competitive videogame. Many different genres can be identified, which might contain different games. Examples of these genres are Battle Royale, with games like Fortnite or PUBG, sport simulation games, with titles like FIFA, PES, or NBA2k; MOBAs, with games like DoTA2 or League of Legends, or the first-person shooters, with games like CS:GO or Call of Duty. Each of these genres could be compared to the different modalities of the traditional sports and that is why Scholz (2019) argues that the term "eSports" could be compared to the term "sports".

In addition, the thesis wants to provide a good overview about the structure of the eSports industry and understand how the forthcoming years of eSports might look like

Therefore, to narrow down the research, only one region, genre, and videogame will be researched. This thesis will study the expansion methods of the traditional sports organizations into eSports but centered on League of Legends and in the European market.

The choice for this thesis in genre and game is to focus on the MOBA game League of Legends since it is arguably the biggest eSport in terms of viewership, with 1.5 billion live hours watched on Twitch during 2020. Furthermore, it has the most structured tournament system which makes it more similar to a traditional sport. Moreover, it is found that League of Legends is the game title with more sports organizations already involved (excluding sports simulation games like NBA2K, FIFA, or PES).

In addition, every region or country comprehends different governances and authorities behind the tournaments. Therefore, a single region will be selected for this thesis: Europe. The reason for this decision is convenience. Reaching and talking to European organizations is a challenge so it is to be assumed that contacting Asian or American organizations would be more challenging due to language, time zones, or socio-cultural constraints.

Definitions

ESports might comprehend certain concepts that are new for some. Hence, this chapter will provide definitions for the key concepts of this thesis and tables with the most relevant acronyms.

Traditional Sports

The definition of what can be considered a sport varies from source to source. For example, for the International Olympic Committee (IOC), a sport will be governed by an International Federation (IF) and afterwards accepted by the IOC Session (Olympics, 2021). By dictionary, the interpretations might differ, wherein some it is defined as "an athletic activity requiring skill or physical prowess and often of a competitive nature, as racing, baseball, tennis, golf, bowling, wrestling, boxing, hunting, fishing, etc." (Dictionary.com, 2022) in other dictionaries is defined as "Sports are games such as football and basketball and other competitive leisure activities which need physical effort and skill" (Collins, 2022). It must be noted that in the first definition, physical effort is not essential whilst in the second one, it is. In addition, some activities such as chess are accepted by the IOC as a sport. To avoid confusion, traditional sport (or just sport) in this thesis will be used to define the activities that require physical effort and are commonly accepted by society such as basketball, football, athletics, or swimming.

ESports

ESports are also difficult to define and one of the main discussions in the last years is whether they would be a sport or not. Often, eSports are considered equivalent to professional gaming, but it is perhaps argued to be too broad a definition. Wagner (2006, p.3) defines eSports as "an area of sport activities in which people develop and train mental or physical abilities in the use of information and communication technologies". However, this definition does not provide an understanding of what can be included in eSports. Scholz (2019) argues that eSports is an umbrella term for any game that can be used in competitive gaming in a similar way that the term sport would group all its different competitive disciplines. Yet, competitive gaming remains broad, you can compete with other people in barely any game in multiple ways. So, for this thesis, the term eSport will be defined as the competitive activities in established competitions of videogames, such as Counter-Strike, Dota2, League of Legends, FIFA, or Rocket League.

Theoretical Framework

This chapter will describe the theoretical framework for the thesis. The chapter aims to provide relevant knowledge and information about the topics that will be discussed throughout the thesis, creating a basis for the research. The material presented in this section will be used to answer the research questions. The literature will consist of different academic papers but, as mentioned in the previous chapter, due to the mentioned lack of academic resources the book *"ESports Is Business: Management in the World of Competitive Gaming"* has high relevance for this thesis' theoretical framework.

ESports background

ESports and gaming have been part of society since around the 1970s (Young Hoon, Nauright and Suveatwatanakul, 2020) however, in recent years the industry has grown exponentially, which has attracted interest from many individuals and external organizations (Scholz, 2019).

Describing eSports is not an easy task and is still being discussed.

For instance, there is still discussion about the correct terminology, whether it should be *Esports, eSports, or esports*. In this research, the term eSports will be used since according to Scholz (2019) is the term that appears most in academic research. In addition, it is important to understand that eSports acts as an umbrella term that groups many actors and consists of any videogame that can be played competitively (Scholz, 2019, p.3). ESports' term acts similarly to the term sport, but instead of grouping different sports practices, eSports gathers different game titles. These game titles can be categorized into different types of genres of videogames, for example, sports simulations, multiplayer online battle arenas (MOBAs), battle royals, or shooters.

The potential of eSports is already being argued, and even though the measuring tools are being criticized for their inaccuracy (Hetsroni and Tukachinsky, 2006, p. 150), they are still valuable to see the growth and impact it has on their audience. According to Young Hoon et al. (2020), the *League of Legends* (LoL) 2017 World Championship was watched by over 80 million people, which could be compared to the 111.3 million that the Super Bowl captured that same year. Moreover, Young Hoon et al. (2020) mention that the industry generated 1 billion dollars of revenue in 2019 and that the numbers are expected to keep growing. The accumulation of these factors attracts the attention of non-endemic sponsors and organizations to join the industry. An example of that is Amazon's acquisition of *Twitch*, in 2014 for 970 million dollars (Scholz et al., 2019, p. 3) beating other interested companies such as Google. Twitch is a relevant stakeholder in the gaming and eSports industry, it is a live-streaming platform that allows its streamers to broadcast their gameplays while interacting with their audiences in real-time (Burroughs and Rama, 2015, p. 3), as well as tournament organizers to broadcast their tournaments and events (Scholz, 2019, p. 32). Twitch's success and main competitive advantage comes from the fact that anyone can stream which has enabled streaming to quickly grow (Scholz, 2019, p. 32). Twitch became a stabilizing factor for eSports and a steady source of revenue for different stakeholders, such the streamers, organizations, and sponsors. Moreover, Twitch has established itself as the fourth most visited website in the US and it is used by many organizers as their first option to broadcast their tournaments (Burroughs and Rama, 2015, p. 2). Burroughs and Rama (2015) explain that streaming plays a big part in the gaming culture and Twitch and their streamers have a big role in it, which keeps growing, offering a new experience that is preferred over other platforms such as YouTube and has attracted attention from traditional sports media organizations, such as the Entertainment Sports Programming Network (ESPN). Another non-endemic actor that joined the industry was the sports organization Beşiktaş J.K., which became the first sports organization that entered eSports and has been followed by many more (Scholz, 2019, p. 6).

However, joining such a growing industry and the expectation of solid returns are not the only drivers to join the eSports industry, Scholz (2019) acknowledges 5 reasons for people and companies to join eSports.

Firstly, reaching a digital and international audience: Due to the product being videogames, it becomes evident that the industry is highly digital and with big technological inputs. In addition, the globalization of the Internet enabled this industry to reach an international audience, enabling people from different countries to play together and watch tournaments. This industry is born digital and global, and it is trying to turn analogue and local, which makes it an interesting case since it is completely opposite to many of the other industries' tendency to become global and more digital.

Secondly, the eSports industry has a noticeably younger audience in comparison to other traditional sports. This is of high relevance since traditional sports have been struggling to reach this type of audience and their viewership is going down (Scholz, 2019, pp. 3-4).

As an example, Scholz (2019, p. 4) discusses that football has an average viewer age of 39

years old and the NFL of 50 years old, and these numbers have been increasing with time. Therefore, traditional sports are struggling to reach younger audiences. However, the eSports audience shows to be aged from 18 to 34 years old (Nielsen 2017). This struggle to reach the young audience of the organizations, especially sports ones, creates an interest for them to invest in eSports due to the fast amortization that it has.

Thirdly, joining the industry in the emerging state of growth that eSports is currently in involves low market entry barriers, as well as exit barriers (Scholz, 2019, p. 4). This implies that it is currently easy to join, as well as to leave if things are not going well. However, McKinsey & Company (2020) argues that even though it is not always to be expected, there is a reputational risk that needs to be considered. In addition, the authors note that eSports has an overall positive reputation but there is a need to be aware that some brands might be concerned that a negative reputation might arise due to how skeptical some people are of the industry, which is increased on realistic-looking violent titles.

Fourthly, the eSports industry, which differs from traditional sports by being industry driven. Nonetheless, Scholz (2019, p. 5) clarifies that even though sports are not industry driven, European football or American football are, with federations like FIFA that follow the market rules. Moreover, the main difference is that every eSports title is based on a videogame, therefore, every videogame is designed, curated, and managed by the videogame developer. In consequence, every videogame developer has the power to change the rules, create new content, and theoretically, even shut down the videogame.

Finally, eSports in its current form is around 20 years old and has been a relatively isolated industry and even branded as a nerd phenomenon in some cases (Scholz, 2019, p. 5), so in a way, ignored by many. This gave the eSports industry time to grow on its own, creating its own rules and principles, and without a governance structure and outside pressure. ESports' self-regulatory dynamic allowed the industry to be innovative and selectively imitate beneficial structures from other sectors (Schulz, 2019, p. 6). This enabled eSports to grow on its own without anybody imposing structures or rules in the industry.

ESports stakeholders

ESports is an industry that involves many different stakeholders due to its size and recent growth. All of them contribute to the value chain by creating relevant value and integrating the audience for many eSports products (Scholz, 2019, p. 43). Moreover, due to the exponential growth that the industry experienced many new stakeholders joined the market in recent years. Scholz (2019, p. 43) argues that stakeholders are highly intertwined and interconnected, making all of them relevant and dependent on each other.

This vast pool of stakeholders requires categorization according to their role within the eSports network. Scholz (2019) proposed a division between primary stakeholders and secondary stakeholders, which will be shown later in this chapter. Primary stakeholders, according to Darnall, Henriques, and Sadorsky (2010, p. 1074) would be the stakeholders with a direct economic stake in the industry with a direct part of the value chain and will interact with internal actors. On the other hand, secondary stakeholders are not directly involved with the market economical transactions and usually are societal stakeholders and environmental regulators (Darnall et al., 2010, p. 1075).

An overview of the stakeholder environment can be seen in *Fig. 1.1*. It can be seen how the different stakeholders interact with the critical stakeholder, the audience. It is seen that game developers, professional teams,

tournament organizers, and professional players have essential roles in the industry and are the ones closer to the audience. Then, other stakeholders act as a support for those to influence the industry indirectly. Each one of these stakeholders has specific needs, expectations, interests, and politics. (Scholz, 2019, p. 45)

Scholz (2019) argues that the core of all stakeholders is the audience, therefore, all of them aim to monetize it. The stakeholders' dynamics are distinctly linked to each other and all of them require their active interconnection for the further development of the industry.

Primary Stakeholders

Game Developer

The game developer is arguably the most crucial stakeholder since it creates the videogame that eSport is built upon and controls most of the aspects around it. The game developer owns the intellectual property so creating a product from it requires technical and legal permission from them (Scholz, 2019, p. 49).

The eSport titles are constantly updated in many cases with new patches and content, which directly impacts the other stakeholders and creates a constantly evolving competition that the organizers, teams, and players need to adapt to which, according to Scholz (2019, p. 50), is done to increase the lifespan of the game. In addition, different strategies can be taken by the game developer, depending on the level of involvement that they want to partake in, examples of these can be seen in Figure 1.

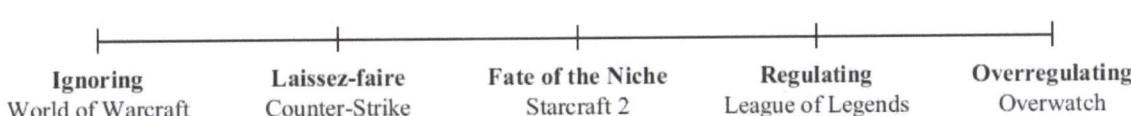

Figure 1. Game developer strategies (Scholz, 2019)

Tournament organizer

Tournament organizers are key to the development of the eSports scheme since they are the ones managing the competition. Tournament organizers cooperate with the game developers and that cooperation depends on the level of involvement of the game developer and the strategy that they decide to take. They have a vital role in the eSports ecosystem and act as a connector between many other stakeholders, such as the audience with the game developers, as well as with the players, teams, communities, or sponsors. Hence, tournament organizers have a big role in improving the interconnection of the different stakeholders (Scholz, 2019).

This stakeholder has been a driving force for eSports and crucial to the creation of the current vibrant eSports scene, mainly due to the game developer's negligence towards the eSports title (Scholz, 2019, pp. 58-59). Tournaments are not necessarily linked to a single game title and can include various eSports. Due to that, ventures and arenas are filled with large amounts of audiences and the online public for the events is also extensive (Scholz, 2019, p. 59). Thanks to that, tournament organizers achieve enormous international audiences.

These ventures are benefiting from the fact that many of these tournaments happen in an onsite manner. Many of these venues are starting to emphasize their efforts on attracting eSports, as an example, the Madison Square Garden in New York, the Staples Center in Los Angeles, and the Wembley Arena in London have hosted eSports events (*see more in Appendix 1)*. These are examples of how traditional sports arenas are willing to enter eSports to attract higher audiences and are adapting to the environment and market needs (Jenny et al., 2018). In addition, many new venues are being created with the specific purpose of hosting events, such as the Yongsan eSports Stadium in Seoul with a capacity of 1000 seats or the Esports Arena in Santa Ana with the same capacity *(see more in Appendix 2).*

Professional teams

ESports teams have a big role in the eSports scheme since they enable other stakeholders to succeed. Scholz (2019, pp. 62-63) argues that teams are necessary for the creation of a sustainable environment at the highest level. In addition, through the professional teams, players have a place to showcase their skills, sponsorships have a display where they can advertise themselves, and tournaments have the means to create their competitions.

The game developer is arguably the most crucial stakeholder since it creates the videogame that the eSport is built upon and controls most of the aspects around it.

These teams have increased their professionalism massively (Scholz, 2019, p. 63) with a similar structure to the traditional sports teams. They provide salaries to their players, premiums, health insurance and, sometimes, pension funds. Professional teams try to have the best players, coaches, trainers, possibilities to psychologists, physiotherapists, and other enablers in order to help achieve the best possible results (Scholz, 2019, p. 63). In addition, the teams monetize their players through merchandise, sponsorships, streaming, or other possibilities.

Professional players

Professional players are probably the most important stakeholder in the eSports industry, however, there is a big pool of amateur players willing to become professional players, which enables professional teams to have a wide market to choose (Scholz, 2019, p. 67). Nonetheless, it is important to be aware that, as a player, building your own career can become more challenging than in traditional sports.

These players get a salary, premiums, insurance, and other compensations from their teams; however, they assume a high risk. This risk comes from two factors: firstly, their need to specialize in a certain videogame, which happens in a similar way to traditional sports where players specialize in a specific sport (Scholz, 2019, p. 67). Players invest many hours to master their videogame and that is a risk by itself. The second risk is the lifecycle of an eSports career, which is notably shorter than in traditional sports (Scholz, 2019, p. 67). In addition, when these two risks are combined, the overall risk of pursuing an eSports career becomes greater.

The short longevity of an eSports career as a player makes the player aim to earn as much money as possible during their short professional period, being in many cases highly opportunistic. On the other hand, professional teams are aware of that, and due to the wide market of players, teams also become opportunistic agents. Thus, creating a very competitive industry and environment where only a few players, who would be the stars, have the negotiating power to get good deals. (Scholz, 2019, pp. 67-68)

Providers and communities

Following Porter's (1985) value chain, we can classify game developers, tournament organizers, professional teams, and professional players as primary activities. Yet, there is a need for certain support activities to create a product for the audience and ensure the success of the industry (Scholz, 2019, p 70). The audience is key to the monetization of the industry; hence, the support activities are key to reaching a broader audience. Scholz (2019, p. 70) defines these support activities as the infrastructure providers, service providers, hardware providers, and community enablers.

Firstly, streaming platforms are a key supporting activity within the infrastructure providers since it enables the audience to follow the matches and tournaments. Twitch can be named as the main provider, and for a long time was the only one, but nowadays there are many others, such as Azubu, Facebook, YouTube, or other smaller platforms. Hence, this competition is beneficial for the industry, since the ongoing competition between the platforms ends in a better viewing experience for the audience (Scholz, 2019, p. 71). Cur-

rently, the game developers are also interacting with the platforms to further incentivize the viewership of the matches and keep the audience hooked. Scholz (2019) exemplifies this by saying that Overwatch or League of Legends provides drops for the viewers while they watch the matches, earning skins and other in-game content. Moreover, physical infrastructures such as the venues where tournaments happen, the training facilities or gaming houses, or eSports cafés are also relevant support activities (Scholz, 2019, p. 71). In addition to the previously presented venues, Jenny et al. (2018, p. 12) discuss that some cities are opting to build their own venues to be primarily used for eSport purposes which acts as an example of public organizations responding to the environment. Therefore, Scholz (2019, p. 71), argues that this development creates a comprehensive infrastructure for any eSports-related topics.

Secondly, the service providers act as enrichers for the eSports environment. One of these service providers is the journalistic coverage of eSports, with platforms like Dot Esports or ESPN Esports which create an environment that is comparable to traditional sports journalism (Scholz, 2019, p. 71). These journalistic services cover insight information, transfer rumors, investigative reports; but, in addition, other services are comparable to the traditional sports ones, such as the Esports Observer that provides business information, consulting agencies focusing on market research, or game analytics organizations (Scholz, 2019, p. 71). Furthermore, law firms and representation agencies are also increasing in terms of presence in the eSports industry. The last group of services that support the eSports industry could be defined as the betting companies. In eSports, these go beyond cash bets and fantasy leagues, the betting expands to bet and speculate on skins and other virtual items, accelerating the growth of the industry by providing additional value for the audiences (Scholz, 2019, p. 71).

Thirdly, hardware providers are as important as in traditional sports. Whilst in traditional sports we have companies like Nike providing the best equipment, in eSports companies like SteelSeries, HyperX, Razer, Intel, or

Logitech, provide mice, keyboards and other specialized hardware (Scholz, 2019, p. 72). The hardware companies also invest in the teams and players with sponsorships and developing their products to provide better equipment and better tools for the players to perform better, as well as for the audience to buy them.

Lastly, the community providers help the different and international audiences to unite and nurture their interactions. Scholz (2019, p. 73) cites that the community enablers go beyond the stakeholders in bringing people together and are self-organized. The communities have a strong presence on social media and sometimes organize events such as viewing parties, which are important to keep the audiences hooked.

Secondary Stakeholders

Governing bodies

Something that has been mainly criticized about eSports is the lack of governance within the industry (e.g., Hollist 2016; Chao 2017; Holden et al. 2017a, b). This is due to the unstructured and hectic evolution that eSports had, added to the isolation without any external parties interfering with its growth, which makes it a comprehensive critic (Scholz, 2019, pp. 109-112). However, there are certain entities in eSports that try to create governance. For instance, traditional sports federations like the Olympic Committee are trying to include eSports as one of their sections and demanding the industry to create certain rules and regulations according to the Olympic movement (Carrabine, 2019). In addition, Carrabine (2019, p. 5) explains that the strongest federation candidate to achieve the International Olympic Committee recognition is the

International eSports Federation (IeSF), which was established in 2008 in South Korea. With that purpose, the IeSF became an official signatory of the World Anti-Doping Agency (WADA) and created an Athletes Commission to protect their players' welfare and interests. Furthermore, IeSF applied to the Global Association of International Sports Federation (GAISF) membership and

is working on achieving the criteria (Carrabine, 2019, p. 5). Hence, there is an intention from the industry to create certain regulations and efficient governance. Yet, eSports is an umbrella term for all the different videogames, which is sometimes not understood by all the stakeholders, and the process takes time and might not even fit in the traditional sports structure (Scholz, 2019, pp. 74-75). That is why Scholz (2019, p. 75) further explains that eSports are governable by one authority, with organizations such as the IeSF, but they sometimes like legitimacy. Scholz (2019, pp. 74-77) claims that the term "governance" is understood differently by everyone, and it is essential to consider the term in more depth since the different embodiments are making it difficult to find the right governance solution for such a unique industry as the eSports.

Sports organizations

Traditional sports organization link in eSports is notable and many are the discussions about it (e.g., Franke, 2015; Hutchins 2008; Jenny et al. 2017). The real tendency in recent years is that more sports organizations are investing heavily in eSports. According to Scholz (2019, p. 78), the tendency comes from three different angles.

Firstly, many traditional sports organizations are struggling to gain international audiences and cannot compete anymore with powerhouses such the Real Madrid, FC Barcelona, or Bayern Munich. In addition, there are not that many fields remaining with potential for a global market, Scholz (2019, p. 78) mentions that the current star markets are the FIFA World Cup, the English Premier League, and the NBA, therefore, the potential and relevance of the eSports increases.

Secondly, Scholz (2019, p. 78) explains that the sports audience is going grey. This means that the age of traditional sports spectators is increasing year after year. For instance, the NFL had an average of 46 years in 2006 and in 2016 grew to 50, or the NBA which moved from 40 in 2006 to 42 in 2016; even football is already around the 40s (Scholz, 2019, p. 78). That is where eSports is key, it enables the reach to a younger and international audience while remaining a market with the potential to keep growing and is a way for sports organizations to diversify their businesses.

Scholz (2019, pp. 78-79) suggests that over 200 sports organizations are involved in eSports. This number grew exponentially from 2015 when less than 10 sports had a presence in eSports. Scholz (2019, pp. 78-79) explains that not all the teams take the same approach, he divides them into diverse types of action. Firstly, when individual players are part of the digital version of the business, this describes the approach taken by many European football teams where they collaborate with FIFA or PES players, and these wear their team equipment. This is an easy and efficient way for a football team to bind fresh players to the professional team and potentially lead to new fans (Scholz, 2019, p. 79).

Secondly, the creation of eSports teams for a variety of games which involves commitment from the sports organization to specific games which are not directly related to the business (Scholz, 2019, p. 79). Schmidt and Holzmayer (2018, cited in Scholz 2019) show the example of the FC Schalke 04, which has a League of Legends team with the purpose of enlarging their fans, attracting an international audience, and introducing eSports to their football fans. FC Schalke 04 had a considerable success in 2018 almost qualifying for the LoL World Championship, which would have been important for their international success since playing in the world championship enables the brand to be recognized on a larger scale.

Thirdly, the creation of eSports teams for a variety of games in a different country is seldom done but aims to use the current brand of the organization to make it more accessible (Scholz, 2019, p. 79). An example of this was the Olympique Lyon partnering with a Chinese eSports team as their internationalization strategy to collect a fanbase in China.

Fourthly, creating joint ventures with existing eSports teams and creating a new brand. which is useful since it utilizes the existing experience and capabilities of an eSports organization (Scholz, 2019, p.80). An example

of this could be the Paris Saint-Germain FC and the LGD Gaming team which partnered in Dota2 finishing second in The International, the most important Dota2 tournament. Scholz (2019, p. 80) explains that this is an easy and natural way for a sports organization to grow into eSports since it does not require them to have their own structure.

Fifthly, the creation of own leagues creates a digital structure for the traditional sports. For example, the NBA 2K League has a strong commitment of the NBA, or the E-Divisie, a pioneer in the football eSports leagues, involved Dutch football clubs, and was aimed to increase their fans and to generate added content (Scholz, 2019, p. 80).

Lastly, buying a franchise team's existing spot has been increasingly popular since tournaments like the League of Legends and Overwatch started to implement a franchise system in 2018. For instance, in League of Legends, the slots were around 10 million dollars in the North American scene (Scholz, 2019, p. 80). This implied the locking-in of the franchises in the league which could lead to long-term planning and profitability for the sports organizations and is like the sports structures that are commonly used in the United States. Examples of these are the Kraft Group, which owns the New England Patriots, acquired the Boston Uprising in Overwatch, or the Houston Rockets investing in Clutch Gaming in League of Legends.

Challenges are there, though. Seeking an eSports journey requires effort and knowledge and choosing the best way to expand to eSports as a traditional sports organization relies upon many factors and is not easy. But eSports is an alternative answer to the ageing of sports audiences are appealing to sports organizations since it allows them to reach an international, young, and digital audience (Scholz, 2019, p. 81).

Sponsors

Sponsorships are a driving force in eSports. Scholz (2019, pp. 81-82) explains that around a third of the eSports' economy could be attributed to sponsorship activities. Indeed, the data verification is not there, and the numbers in eSports should be taken carefully. However, even though the numbers regarding sponsorships differ slightly, their relevance can be noted. Moreover, Scholz (2019, pp. 82) adds that eSports business models have been on sponsorships and advertisements for a long time since it has been the most doable way to monetize their activities. Sponsorships are highly relevant for organizational growth, are a powerful component of communication strategy, and contribute to a strategic advantage (Dolphin, 2003), which might explain the dominance of these in the business models of the eSports organizations.

At the beginning of the eSports run, endemic sponsors were the ones that were prone to invest in eSports due to their eSports knowledge, examples of these were Nvidia, Logitech, or Intel (Scholz, 2019, p. 82). That was a time when it was hard for eSports organizations to share returns on investments and other metrics, so was hard to attract non-endemic investors. However, in the most recent years non-endemic sponsors are increasingly joining and have broadened their involvement in eSports, examples of these would be Deloitte sponsoring the ESL Dutch Championship, Mercedes-Benz to ESL and LoL World Championship, or Mastercard as a LoL World Championship partner (Scholz, 2019, p. 82). Similarly, as with sports organizations, these sponsorship companies aim to reach a unique, young, and international audience through eSports. However, Crompton (1993) raises awareness of the importance of selecting correct and ethical sponsors in sports due to their power and influence on the audience decision-making. This gets amplified in eSports due to the young age of the public and there is a need for eSports organizations to consider this when making a deal with a sponsor.

For sponsors, it is not only enough with paying some money and having their logo somewhere, but Scholz (2019, p. 83) also points out that there is the need of being authentic, speaking the language, feeling the eSports' passion, and giving up control in order to succeed. Due to the unique eSports audience, real involvement and creating authentic partnerships with the primary stakeholders are needed to seek new branding opportunities and innovative ways of interacting with the audience.

Sponsorship activities are relevant for other reasons than investment and play an important role in the strategy of organizations (Demir & Söderman, 2015). These further strategies are grouped in animation, which involves the alignment and activation activities in terms of communications and engagement of consumers; and in relational, which discusses the relationships, influence, and power levels between the sponsor and the sponsored party. Understanding the importance of sponsors and the implications that a certain sponsor might have for the organization is crucial for the success of the deal and to achieve corporate objectives (Dolphin, 2003) and it is relevant to find a good fit between both organizations.

General public

The general public is understood as the broader public that interacts with eSports, larger than the audience itself. This secondary stakeholder is relevant because it affects the perception of the industry. Scholz (2019, p. 83) argues that the general population has had the perception that eSports are bad for people, making people aggressive, leading to shootings. Also, he mentions that there is the perception about videogames being addictive which makes people lose control of their life. Thus, these arguments and perceptions by the general public act and have been acting as a handicap for the evolution of the eSports industry and the profitability of the business. Therefore, it is important to tackle the issue and aim to reduce the risk, making the general public more pleasant with videogames and the eSports industry.

Furthermore, the general public also influences eSports from other angles. For instance, in terms of gender representation. Women, despite being half of the gaming population, have low representation in professional eSports. Scholz (2019, p. 84) introduces that there is an ongoing discourse about the reasons and that, for example, the AnyKey organization is currently fighting to diminish the stereotypes in the industry.

Also, reaching a point of actual gender diversity could be greatly beneficial for not only the general perception of the industry, but also for improving the performance of the teams through achieving mixed-gender teams which are currently non-existent (Apesteguia, Ghazala, and Nagore, 2012). On the other hand, cultural diversity is also beneficial for the industry, teams, and organizations but this is something that is currently well utilized in eSports, where teams gather diverse cultures and language is not a barrier.

Investors, entrepreneurs, media, and shareholders

Lastly, various stakeholders also have an impact on the eSports industry but do not seek a direct influence or to change the industry, just taking a part in the eSports profitable market. Investors, entrepreneurs, and shareholders are the ones that aim to earn money through eSports. On the other hand, media is included in this section since despite trying to change the industry in the beginning, they learnt that they need to adapt to the eSports scene and adopt a more passive role (Scholz, 2019, p. 42).

Investors have been flooding money into the eSports industry, Scholz (2019) cites that in just the first half of 2018 over 700 million dollars were infused into the industry in disclosed investments. Certainly, the investors will require a return on their investment, and this is something that is argued by some to be over valuated and rumored to be the new bubble. In addition, there is a risk of not achieving the returns that everyone is expecting, leading to dangerous endeavors with the purpose of forcing the success of the industry (Scholz, 2019)

Secondly, media is gaining importance in eSports. Due to the lack of monetization opportunities, some organizations are trying to emphasize content creation as a source of income, hiring streamers and putting efforts into their social media content. Therefore, media companies are playing a crucial role in eSports to digitalize the industry (Scholz & Stein, 2017).

Lastly, shareholders request an increase in their shares and a growth in revenues. However, Scholz (2019) argues that eSports is a long-term investment but that they apply pressure for a shorter-term shareholder value, which he demonstrates with the case of Tencent owning Riot Games. In this case, Tencent was crucial for the transition to a franchise model leagues in League of Legends, like the systems in the NBA.

Characteristics of eSports stakeholders

Some characteristics are fundamental to understanding stakeholders. These are primarily found in the primary stakeholders, but not exclusively. Most of the stakeholders evolved from within, and when a non-endemic organization joined eSports and tried to enforce its rules, they failed (Scholz, 2019, p. 47). Thus, eSports organizations grew on their own without much interference.

Hence, the stakeholders developed certain common components. Scholz (2019, p.47) argues that the eSports industry is in a lock-in stage in terms of cultural similarities that might make outsiders difficult to enter, since eSports also evolved globally. The six characteristics that Scholz and Stein (2017) distinguish are explained followingly.

Firstly, there is a high ambition in the industry. The stakeholders want to be the best in what they do. As an example, the eSports organizations want to be the best in their videogame and deliver the best experience to their fans. This, according to Scholz and Stein (2017), increases the innovation of the industry and has been one of the main reasons for its improvement. Secondly, the globality of the eSports activities makes the audience able to take part both onsite and online, filling stadiums like Madison Square Garden whilst entertaining thousands of fans on the online broadcast (Scholz and Stein, 2017). Thirdly, the constant development of the industry. ESports stakeholders are not content with mediocracy and regularly strive to excel, for instance, Scholz and Stein (2017) explain that players and organizations are constantly reinventing themselves until they succeed. Fourthly, due to the evolution of eSports, the resources have been allocated in a bottom-up fashion, with everyone contributing in a decentralized manner for the collective benefit (Scholz and Stein, 2017). Fifthly, the overenthusiasm of the endemic stakeholders is one of the key characteristics (Scholz and Stein, 2017). Gray (1978) talks that over-enthusiasm, together with being over-energetic, and over-dynamic are key characteristics for innovative stakeholders which is very linked with the characteristics and nature of the eSports industry. Lastly, the digitalization as a logical characteristic of eSports is mentioned by Scholz and Stein (2017) when they explain the importance of the Internet, the technology, the channels of eSports, and how stakeholders such as the teams, tournaments organizers, and media are tightly linked to these.

> *eSports is continuously evolving, but a common thing among all the stakeholders is the intention to monetize the audience, acting as a driver for the business models of the organizations within the eSports industry.*

These characteristics make the industry and its stakeholders unique. This is due to the history and how isolated has eSports been from other industries. Therefore, for new stakeholders aiming to enter eSports, such as the sports organizations, it is important to be aware, understanding, and adapting to these.

ESports business models

Scholz (2019, p. 118) shows that due to the stakeholders' interactions, eSports can be considered as an interwoven network where all the stakeholders require each other to succeed. The industry has evolved independently and very differently from other industries, which led to an industry driven by innovations and technology, but also by the interaction of people capitalizing on the technologies to their maximum.

It is true that eSports is continuously evolving, but a common thing among all the stakeholders is the intention to monetize the audience, acting as a driver for the business models of the organizations within the eSports industry. Scholz (2019, p. 118-119) explains the focus of these business models on value integration with an emphasis on cooperation rather than a threat. It appears logical for all the stakeholders that the threat of new entries, buyer and supplier power, risk of substitution, or competitive rivalry exist, but the need for cooperation is more important for the success of the industry and, therefore, of all the stakeholders. Hence, it occurs to be cooperation and competition in the industry, bringing up the term coopetition. This concept highlights that the network needs to cooperate in certain areas to thrive while competing in others (Brandenburger & Nalebuff, 1996) to increase profitability throughout the system.

Furthermore, it is important to be aware that the role of a certain stakeholder might influence the overall business model network. For instance, Scholz (2019, p. 120) explains that the game developer in Overwatch is notoriously dominant while in Counter-Strike it is not dominant. These differences in such an important stakeholder as the game developer make the different stakeholders of every videogame need to interact differently. That is why the different interconnections require efficient usage of dynamic capabilities, which are important for eSports organizations to rapidly adapt to the changing environment (Teece, 2010).

Coopetition, Co-Destiny, and Convergence

Scholz (2019, pp. 120-124) proposes coopetition, co-destiny, and convergence as common rules in all the eSports business models. These will be explained following and their impact on the industry.

Coopetition

Coopetition, as previously mentioned, is one of the driving forces in the eSports industry due to the need of collaborating while competing, and many stakeholders follow the rules of coopetition aiming to ensure the success of themselves as well as the success of the industry. Mutual recognition of interdependence is a precondition for coopetition and, especially in eSports, it becomes evident that a game developer may require tournament organizers but depends on professional teams and professional players.

Walley (2007, p. 11) talks about coopetition as "a situation where competitors simultaneously cooperate and compete with each other". In addition, Scholz (2019, p. 121) argues that coopetition is essential for the eSports industry and has helped to create new and innovative ideas. Some eSports stakeholders compete very aggressively when reaching the audience, but they do so while cooperating to encourage growth. All the organizations learn and share knowledge with each other, creating a better and more profitable market.

Co-Destiny

The eSports industry has shown a particular behaviour with a specific shared vision or co-destiny (Scholz, 2019, p. 122). A shared vision in an industry is relevant for the enablement of the co-destiny process (Davidow and Malone, 1992) which happens in eSports with several stakeholders sharing a long-term goal and strategy, aiming for eSports to grow. Scholz (2019, p. 121) suggests that despite eSports not having a governing body, associations, federations, or big enough institutions to create a shared vision, eSports is strongly driven by co-destiny. This happens because the people involved in eSports really love eSports, and they want to see it grow. The co-destiny driver is increased with long-term stakeholders, but also this tendency is starting to be seen in younger stakeholders.

However, Scholz (2019, p. 121) says that trust between eSports organizations is crucial to ensure co-destiny. This was enhanced at the beginning of the eSports industry when everything was even more hectic and less structured, with fewer rules and not as many business experts as nowadays. Hence, eSports relies upon a network based on trustworthiness and a certain informal code of conduct (Scholz, 2019, p. 121)

Convergence

Due to the fundamental rules of coopetition and co-destiny, it can be seen in the eSports industry that there is also a certain tendency towards convergence (Scholz, 2019, p. 123). Beckert (2010) explains that organizations tend to become more and more similar over time, which is enhanced in eSports due to the relationships between stakeholders. In addition, DiMaggio and Powell (1983) stated that this convergence is increased within the context of newer institutions and organizations. Scholz (2019, p. 123) adds that eSports is facing a tendency towards sigma-convergence which occurs when the dispersion of certain variables between different countries tends to decrease over time (Young, Higgins & Levy, 2008). The sigma-convergence is relevant when we align it with the coopetition and co-destiny because when stakeholders share these makes them become more similar with time. Then, the importance of new stakeholders is notable due to the potential of bringing innovative ideas, changes, and challenges to the industry that might disrupt the industry (Scholz, 2019, p. 123).

Sports organization expansion to eSports

Sports organizations are already an important stakeholder in the eSports industry due to the many ways that these are involved. Entering eSports requires certain knowledge and adapting to the specific ways of doing of the industry and the needs of its audience.

Understanding the strategic expansion methods and the advantages and disadvantages of those is important. Johnson, Whittington, and Scholes (2011) explain that the main methods to pursue strategic growth are acquisitions, alliances, and organic development. These are methods relevant for eSports and there are examples of those in eSports. Figure

2 provides a good understanding of the positives and negatives of each method from different perspectives. It is good to acknowledge that there is no better or worse method, and it depends on the capabilities, needs, and context of the growth.

	Buy	Ally	DIY
High urgency	Fast	Fast	Slow
High uncertainty	Failures potentially saleable	Share losses and retain buy option	Failures likely unsaleable
Soft capabilities important	Culture and valuation problems	Culture and control problems	Cultural consistency
Highly modular capabilities	Problem of buying whole company	Ally just with relevant partner unit	Develop in new venture unit

Figure 2. Buy, ally, or DIY (Johnson et al., 2011)

However, when talking about how the sports organizations have been expanding into eSports the more concurrent methods are organic growth and alliances, therefore, these two will be explained further in this section.

Organic development as a growth strategy

Organic development is, according to Figure 2, the slower way to grow. This is because it requires the process of learning and understanding and relying on the own organizational resources. However, Lockett et al. (2011) mention that a way to accelerate this growth is by bringing in and training new managers, which then increases the cost of the strategy. Johnson et al. (2011, p. 328) define organic development as the strategy of building on and developing an organization's own capabilities. Moreover, they describe four main advantages of organic growth.

Firstly, it is the expertise gained by the organization. Even if it takes a certain time to adapt and learn, the direct involvement in a new market or technology enhances the organizational knowledge. Secondly, the investment and expenses of the organization are distributed over time which compared with acquisitions requires a larger expenditure in the beginning. In addition, an extra of flexibility is added, allowing the organization to reverse or adjust the strategy if needed. Thirdly, developing a company by itself does not require any other organization to be available to acquire or ally with, so there is the advantage of not depending on the availability and not having to wait for the perfect match. Lastly, it brings independence to the organization since there is no compromise with any other organization.

Moreover, Johnson et al. (2011) separate organic development between radical and continuous development. Radical organic development, also understood as corporate entrepreneurship, is defined as a radical change in the organization's business that is principally driven by its own capabilities (Johnson et al., 2011, p. 328). However, relying too much on organic growth might create problems in terms of path dependence and might hinder the possibilities of learning outside the areas where the organization has prior knowledge (Lockett et al., 2011).

Alliances as a growth strategy

Alliances play an important role in eSports, Wheelen & Hunger (2011, p.125) define them as "an agreement between firms to do business together in ways that go beyond normal company-to-company dealings but fall short of a merger or a full partnership". Many organizations opt to share resources and activities to pursue a strategy (Johnson et al., 2011, p. 338). For some sports organizations, this has been the best option due to the possibility of knowing the unique ways of doing things of the eSports industry and its stakeholders. Johnson et al. (2011) discuss that a core thing about alliances, differing them from mergers, is that in alliances there are minor or no ownership changes at all. Establishing an alliance has benefits in comparison with organic growth, such as being a faster method or involving less risk, since the organization can share the losses, as seen in Figure 2. In addition, Elmuti & Kathawala (2001) highlight that alliances are used to diffuse recent technologies rapidly, to enter a new market, and to learn quickly from the outstanding organizations in a certain industry, which really fits the needs of certain sports organizations. However, one of the main drawbacks of alliances is the potential cultural and control issues, which might handicap the success of the alliance, therefore, a considerable amount of effort must be put in by all the involved parties. It is necessary for both organizations to outline the expectations, roles, requirements, and benefits so a favorable outcome of the alliance can be expected (Elmuti & Kathawala, 2001).

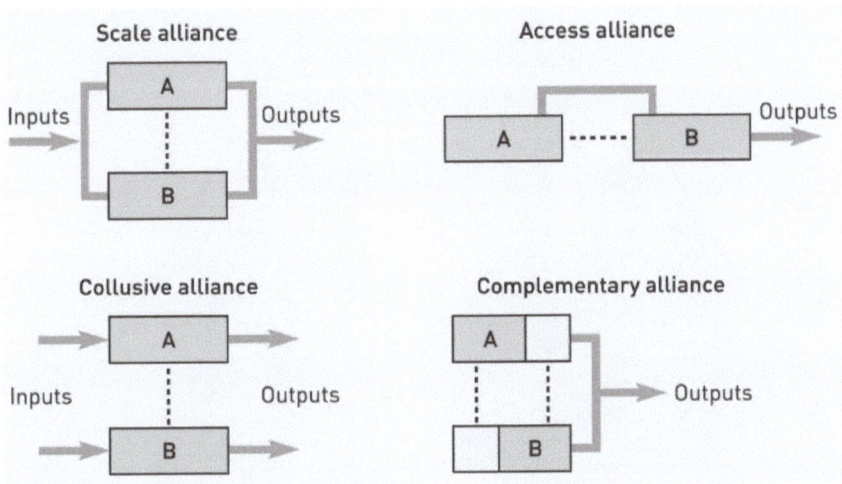

Figure 3. Types of alliances (Johnson et al., 2011)

Alliances can happen in different ways. First, in regards to the type of ownership, Johnson et al. (2011, p. 340) explain that some alliances involved the creation of new entities with shared equity. In that case, the most common form is through a joint venture, where two organizations remain independent but set up a new organization owned by the parents. On the other hand, alliances can happen with any commitment in terms of equity. Johnson et al. (2011) define franchising as the most common way of nonequity or contractual alliances.

Secondly, the types of alliances can be differentiated in regards to the motives and how the resources and activities are shared. Figure 3 shows four different alliances. First, scale alliances where the two organizations with similar capabilities combine in order to achieve advantages that otherwise they would not. In addition, through scale alliances risk is shared between both entities which allows these to not have to commit so many resources and not threaten the existence of the whole organization. Secondly, access alliances are commonly done when the organizations require accessing another organization's knowledge or resources in order to develop their activities. Thirdly, complementary alliances, which are similar to access alliances, allow organizations to combine resources in order to overcome each other difficulties, limitations, weaknesses, or boost their strengths. Lastly, collusive alliances happen when organizations secretly and illegally collude to increase their market power. By doing that they achieve competitive advantages in the forms of higher prices or lower costs. (Johnson et al., 2011, pp. 340-342)

Alliances are usually seen as positive for strategical purposes. It could be argued that the positive aspects get enhanced in an industry where there is high dependence and need for cooperation between the different stakeholders. Yet, proceeding with a strategical alliance comes with some risks, the main ones being trust issues, operational differences, lack of coordination, lack of clear goals and objectives, and clash or incompatibility of cultures (Elmuti & Kathawala, 2001) which need to be taken in consideration when establishing the initial strategical plan.

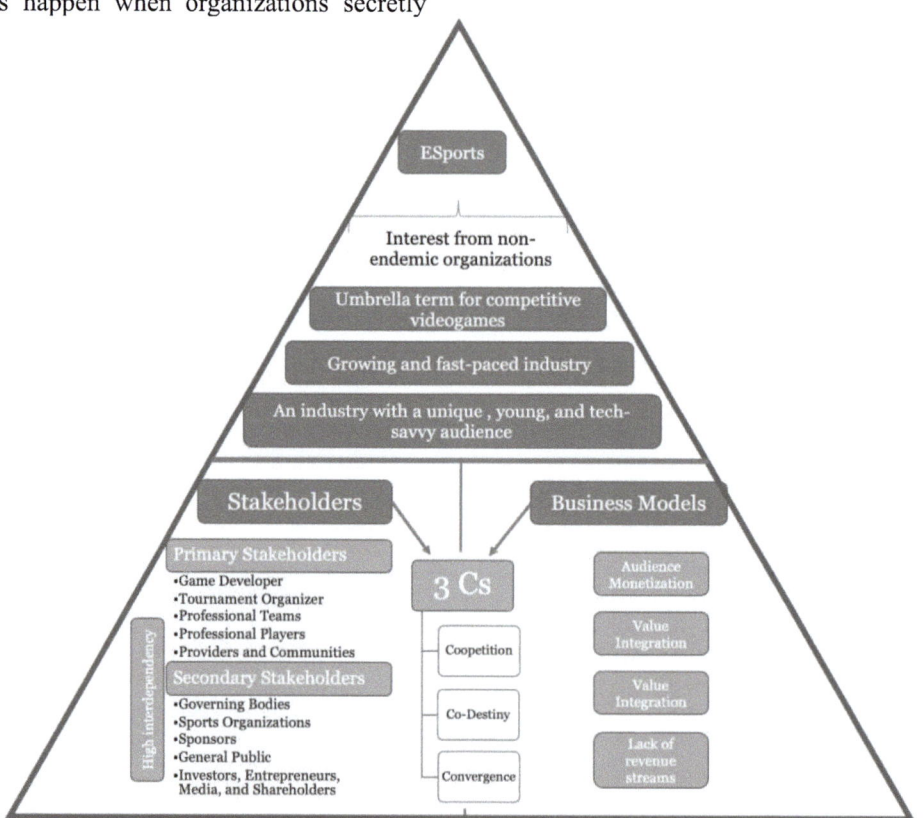

Figure 4. Theoretical framework pyramid

Methods

This section depicts the methodology used in the research. Here, the thought process and the reasons of why a certain method has been chosen over alternative ones will be explained. The chapter consists of the research philosophy, where the beliefs about the reality and how it influences this research are shown; the research strategy, where the approach taken in the study is explained; the data collection process, where the sampling and the eight interviews design shown in Table 2 are described; and lastly, how the quality of the research is ensured.

Research Philosophy

Before knowing the approach that a researcher will have to the study, it is important to know about how the researcher sees the world, the beliefs, and attitudes towards it. Saunders, Lewis, and Thornhill (2016, p. 124) describe research philosophy as the beliefs and assumptions about the development of knowledge. It explores concepts like ontology, meaning the beliefs about the nature of reality; epistemology, referring to the theory of knowledge, or in other words: how do we know what we know? Lastly, axiology, which is explained by Lincoln & Guba (2005, pp. 197-198) as the way that the values influence the research, like with the choice of problem, the choice of the theoretical framework or the choice of presenting the findings.

There are different philosophies, and different authors make different distinctions. There is not a universal way of categorizing them. This research adopts an interpretivist approach. Hudson & Ozanne (1988, p. 513) explain that interpretivist researchers are characterized by a continually evolved research design and they try to explain different realities that cannot be known beforehand because these are time and context-specific. Moreover, it is understood that realities change, contexts evolve, and the researchers come to the study with different preunderstandings (Hudson & Ozanne, 1988, p. 513). However, despite the prior knowledge, interpretivists are open to new information and knowledge that is acquired during the research. In this philosophy, an evolving design is utilized and there is the belief in human capabilities to adapt to different contexts and scenarios.

These factors are consistent with the philosophy of this research. I, as a researcher, had prior knowledge of the subject and eSports environment, however, I have been open to listening to others' realities and perceptions on the subject and integrating the findings into the research. Moreover, the current reality of eSports might change with time, new ways of entering the industry might appear, as well as the best or most successful expansion approaches might vary. I believe it is important to be aware of the time and context sensitivity in a novel and evolving industry as eSports is.

Research Strategy

This thesis is based on qualitative research. Patton (2014, p. 107) explains that qualitative data consists of quotations, observations, excerpts from documents, and entries from social media. Thus, the data that is aimed to be collected is non-numerical data that can be collected through interviews, surveys, or observations, among other data-collection methods. Denzin & Lincoln (2008, p. 3) define qualitative research as a set of interpretative practices that make the world visible, turning the world into a series of representations studied in its natural settings helping to make sense of it and interpreting the world in the way that people bring it. When studying why the traditional sports organizations wanted to expand to eSports and how they have done it, the qualitative approach must be the preferred option because it enables the researcher to find out their experiences, hear their stories and examples, and understand how and why they perceived the situation (Patton, 2014, p. 67).

The purpose of using a qualitative inquiry lies in being able to describe what is happening while understanding the logic of it. Sanders et al. (2017, P. 177) explains that the research strategy shows how the researcher answers the research question, therefore, in this subsection the process is be explained.

The research is be constructed in an abductive manner. Denzin (1978b) defines abduction as a combination of inductive and deductive thinking. In addition, he explains it as "working from consequence back to cause or antecedent" (p. 109) where the observer records a particular event and works back in time to reconstruct the causes and consequences in question. The choosing of this approach is due to the nature of eSports. There is not much theory nor knowledge on the subject, hence, learning while doing and being able to learn from the data and redo and adapt the theory is needed when studying such a topic.

Data Collection

In order to succeed with a research, data is needed. Bryman & Bell (2015) explain that the most common data collection methods are observation, interviews, focus groups, and other documents. For this research, there are two different sources of data. Firstly, through the eight interviews that are conducted, which are displayed in Table 2. The sampling strategy and a thorough logic about them is explained in the following subsections. This data enables me to understand the reasons and logic behind the traditional sports organization's expansion process, as well as deepen the knowledge about the industry, its stakeholders, business models, and issues. Furthermore, it enables me to hear about specific stories and examples, which are highly important in qualitative analysis (Patton, 2014). Secondly, public online material is collected to support the interview's findings. Due to the lack of academic resources, this additional material is relevant to provide an accurate overview of the industry. These sources were found thanks to the previous research with endemic people from the industry as well as the acquired knowledge of following the industry for many years. Examples of these sources are Leaguepedia as a database or the journal DotEsports for analysis, news, and eSports coverage.

With this, I aim to provide an analysis of the market and research if esports is a profitable market to enter for traditional sports organizations. These two different approaches are needed in order to answer the three different research questions that were previously stated in chapter 1.2.

Sampling Strategy

Patton (2014, p. 448) sampling strategies can be described as the different choices that a researcher does in aiming to obtain the information and data needed to progress with the research. Aiming to achieve a homogeneous sampling and fulfil the requirements of this thesis research, purposeful sampling is used (Patton, 2014, p. 428). Purposeful sampling is when the sampling is specifically created for the study purposes with the objective to provide the best sample for the research. The choice of using purposeful sampling in the research is clear because it enables to achieve consistent data that will enrichen the qualitative study.

> *Before knowing the approach that a researcher will have to the study, it is important to know about how the researcher sees the world, the beliefs, and attitudes towards it.*

Moreover, critical case sampling will be used as a sampling strategy. Within the League of Legends European environment, the sports organizations that already have a presence in eSports were contacted and acted as relevant cases providing the most knowledge for future cases of other sports organizations aiming to expand to eSports (Patton, 2014, p. 460). This strategy was chosen because the experience and knowledge that is extracted from these chosen cases can permit logical generalization to other similar cases, hence, providing value and being similar to other sports organizations aiming to expand to eSports (Patton, 2014, p. 404). Moreover, the snowball or chain sampling technique is utilized. After studying the market and discovering certain personalities, they provided guidance on who could be useful for the purpose of the research, therefore, accumulating valuable and important informants (Patton, 2014, p. 451). To achieve this, in addition to my own knowledge, I reached out to a few people from the eSports scene and set up some calls to talk with them. Examples of these are former pro-player DanDan or the current head of scouting of Real Betis, MrOrxata. These calls were very valuable, I was able to create a list of the organizations to reach and some contact persons and I got a better understanding of the eSports market.

After having the names and organizations to contact, I started reaching out to them mainly on Twitter and by email. The response time for these first messages was slower than anticipated which was a small issue. In addition, on some occasions, I was redirected to other people within the same organization and the process had to start all over again, but it was useful to find the correct person to talk to.

The final number of interviewees was eight, which are shown in Table 2. Even though I reached out to all or most of the European eSports organizations, it was impossible to interview more, most often due to the lack of response. It was considered interviewing other people from eSports, like professional players, but it was decided not to, again, because just very few replied and would not provide significant data. Even though this number is seen enough by some for this type of research, it can be seen as non-sufficient by others. But, due to the faced constraints that have been previously mentioned and the limitations of the research, there was no other choice. However, it has provided valuable and significant results and the quality of the data is good. There has been variety and the interviews happened to be long enough to cover all the topics and go in deep on them.

Table 2. Interviewees list

Interviewee	Organization
R1	FC Barcelona
R2	Schalke04
R3	Team Orange Gaming (Ulm)
R4	Cream Real Betis
R5	Anorthosis Famagusta
R6	FC Nantes
R7	Penta 1860
R8	PSV Eindhoven

Interviews

Interviews will be used to understand the cases of these companies. Patton (2014) explains that through the explanation of the interviewees' experiences, opinions, and attitudes it is possible to obtain insights and information that are valuable for the purpose of this research. A realistic approach will be of interest for the interviews since Silverman (2005, pp. 154-157) mentions that is the preferred way to understand the experiences of the interviewees in certain events, facts, or actions. This approach is chosen because it will provide the best understanding of the

reasons for the expansion into eSports, the opinions of the interviewees, and why they entered the market the way they did. Moreover, the interviews will be conducted individually due to the possibility of studying every case deeper and perhaps personalizing the questions or asking follow-up questions if needed (Patton, 2014, p. 45). Lastly, the interviews were prepared in a semi-structured manner. Therefore, an interview guide is produced (found in *Annex 1.3.*) but when this one appears to be insufficient, follow-up questions will be asked *in situ*. Moreover, thanks to this semi-structured approach the interviewee will be able to freely speak, enabling him or her to create valuable stories and, as Patton (2014) says, having an informal conversation.

When creating the interview guide, the first step was to come up with themes. These themes made it easier to formulate the questions and helped to have an organized interview. The interview had six different themes: eSports market, business model, strategy, culture, audience/stakeholders, and others. The eSport market theme aimed to understand the eSports market overall and the interviewee's organization's presence in it. Therefore, questions like "Which principles regulate eSports" or "Would you explain about your organization's presence in eSports" are asked. Secondly, the business model questions aim to understand the organization's plans to be profitable and how they are changing with time, that is why questions like "How does an eSports organization differ from the traditional sports" are asked. Thirdly, the strategy theme aims to deep into the expansion itself, why and how was the process of diving into eSports. Questions from these themes are "Why did your organization decide to grow to eSports?" and the followup question, if needed, "Which factors were key for the decision". The culture theme aimed to understand how the organization ensure that the employees have the same goal and work efficiently towards it, and questions like "How does your organization integrate different cultures in order to achieve the goals". Fourthly, the audience/stakeholders theme aims to understand the relationships of the organization with their stakeholders, with a specific focus on the audience due to its importance, with questions like "How is the unique audience of eSports reached". Lastly, a theme of others was included to different but relevant questions like "what is the role of technology and digitalization in eSports". But also, before ending, an open question for the interviewee to add anything else if it is needed is proposed.

The interviews are slightly adapted to the interviewees. That is because the organization or position of each of the interviewees varies from one to another. There are eSport organizations that are analysed that partner with a sports organization, whilst others are a department from a sports team. Moreover, managers and players are interviewed and in order to learn the most about their experiences and perceptions, different questions are needed.

Due to the current pandemic of Covid-19 that is happening, the interviews take place primarily in Microsoft Teams in an online method, unless objection from the interviewee. Another reason for this is that the interviewees are all around Europe and an online interview creates an easy way to set the interviews. However, Bryman & Bell (2011, p. 660) show that face-to-face interviews are better than online ones because enables the interviewer to maintain rapport with the interviewees, that is why is specifically asked to the interviewees to have their camera on during the interview, which also enables to observe their reactions and non-verbal communication. Most of the interviews are being held in English. However, there is a need for awareness that English is not the mother tongue of almost any, if not any, of the interviewees and that might influence their answers. Two of the interviews were held in the mother tongue of the interviewees (one in Spanish and one in Catalan) for their convenience and to ensure the quality of the data, the material that will be used from these interviews is translated for this thesis.

Finally, the interviews are transcribed and recorded. The transcriptions are done in a verbatim manner, transcribing what is actually said, the repertoire of false starts, incomplete sentences, with a detailed description of the non-verbal behaviour, including scratching, fidgeting, coughs, and so on (Bryman & Bell, 2015, p. 537). In addition, for the interviews that were conducted in the native language of the interviewee (Spanish or

Catalan), the interview fragments and citations that are used for the thesis are translated. Patton (2014, p. 767) cites that transcriptions are important to afterwards analyse the data and verbatim transcriptions are also important because not everyone talks the same way.

Furthermore, regarding the privacy of the data and the ethics, which follows the GDPR guidelines, and it is stored in the Hanken School of Economics cloud service, being deleted after 12 months of the thesis submission; anonymity is granted to all the interviewees. This is communicated to them since the first approach. In addition, prior to the interview, a consent form is signed or verbally agreed upon in the interview's recording where the usage of the data is explained. Lastly, before starting the interview or while recording there was a verbal agreement of the interview's recording, communication regarding their power to decide if something needs to be excluded and that if they do not want to answer a question, they can skip it.

After analysing the interviews and their data, citations are used in the empirical chapter sections. But each of the interviewees is contacted in order to have their acceptance to that. In that last email, it is reminded that the interviews are anonymous, but the organization's name will be used, unless objection.

Data Analysis

Analysing the data is crucial for research since it is where results might appear and the researcher gets to draw conclusions and interpretations from them, achieving new knowledge (Patton, 2014). Moreover, he adds that the purpose and the own judgement of the criteria defines the analysis and must be created anew each time.

Spiggle (1994) talks about the importance of actually understanding the data and not falling into the mistake of merely describing it. In addition, he proposes to reduce the data as much as possible, simplifying it and identifying the most interesting and relevant data. Then, a researcher should organize it in order to display it efficiently, which will enable the researcher to conclude easier. Lastly, Spiggle (1994) recommends forming frameworks, revealing the data in terms of importance, and making it easier to interpret it and understand the theoretical and practical implications. This thesis analyses the interview's transcriptions through a thematic analysis which is the qualitative analysis most used by researchers (Bryman & Bell, 2015) and the steps will be explained followingly.

Step 1: Coding and preliminary categorization

After transcribing the interviews, it is important to spot the concepts that better describe the experiences and insights of the interviewees. Spiggle (1994, p. 493) defines the categorization process as the technique of classifying and labelling the units of data. In order to proceed with the categorization is necessary to identify the chunks of data and name them and, for this purpose, coding was used. The coding provides an understanding of the data through visualization and helps with the analysis. done by was used for the coding. In order to simplify the data some themes were established, each one with a different colour. In addition, notes and a summary of the highlighted part were written next to it. This method provided a simpler and more visual data that was easier to analyse afterwards. Initially, the transcripts were reviewed, and the most relevant data was highlighted. In addition to the highlighting, notes were added to every data bulk which provided extra information for afterwards making the labelling and thematic analysis easier.

Step 2: Establishing the themes

For a better visualization, understanding of the data, and to ease the rest of the analysis certain main themes were set up. The process of establishing these core categories was through observation, a preliminary understanding of the data, and the help of the interview guide's structure and initial themes. Therefore, the final themes were: "Why – Reason", "How-Method", "Evolution – Future", "Drivers", "Stakeholders", "Governance", "Business Models", "Culture", and "Other". These themes were present in more or less capacity in each of the transcripts and that is why, after identifying the chunks of data, they were established.

The interviewee's answers for each of the themes in the tables were grouped. An example of how this was done in practice, for the *Why* theme where I organized all the organization's reasons for entering eSports, can be seen in Table 2. These tables were helpful to organize, structure, and visualize the data, hence, to draw tendencies and conclusions for each one of the themes.

Step 3: Grouping the data by theme

After identifying the themes, it is useful to group and bring the data units together for the better afterwards analysis. To start, the previously highlighted transcripts were reviewed again with the purpose of colouring with different colours the relevant data according to the established themes. With this, a higher level of visualization is achieved and allows a better identification of the crucial data for the research (Spiggle, 1994). With the colouring done, the next step for grouping the data is copying the sets of data per category or theme of all the interviews in a separate document. With that, nine different documents were created with all the data structured in an organizational order, allowing the next steps of the analysis and the identification of the most relevant information per theme and per organization.

Step 4: Creating tables

With the data already organized in the documents, the next step was to create tables per theme which would allow comparing the data, in order to answer the research questions and to fill the purpose of the research. As can be seen in Table 3, the previous data that was in the documents was simplified and summarized providing a more pleasant analysis. This simplification is important according to Spiggle (1994) who explains that reducing the data is key for the understanding of it and for the success of the qualitative analysis. There were nine total tables created, one per each theme, and the content of the tables depended on the answers of the interviewees. These tables are essential since they display the data clearly and efficiently, which allows a better analysis.

Table 3. Data analysis "Why - Reason"

Organization	Reason 1	Reason 2
Barça	Connect with young audiences, which cannot be reached with traditional sports – traditional sports audiences are getting older.	
Nantes	Football fans are getting older – need to grow a new fanbase (young audience) – feed both audiences.	Used by Nantes as a marketing practice
PSV	Increase fans and followers. Football struggles to fill the gap and connect with young fans (12-25).	eSports as a competitor for sports. Entertainment revolution.
Schalke	Fill a complementary but young audience for sports	
TOG	New market with a new audience (but with a different language)	Chance to rejuvenate the sports organization. Opportunity to develop the know-how to be professional for eSports org. And for sports orgs in terms of digitalization
TSV PENTA	Big market that enables to reach a new audience easily	

Anorthosis	Reaching a new and more international.	Help the club with digitalization and spread the values of the club and issues about Cyprus.
Betis	Gets to an audience that otherwise cannot be reached. A young audience. Because the sports audience is stuck.	The audience needs to be reached in a very specific form and channels.

Step 5: Comparing and pattern identification

Lastly, with the data sorted, organized, and simplified the interpretation of the tables starts. In order to analyze the table and extract the insights and findings for the research, the comparison method was used. In order to display the process that was utilized, Table 3 will be taken as an example. So, all eight organizations' reasons for entering eSports are contrasted and certain patterns are tried to be found. In this case, it was clear that the reason was to reach an audience that traditional sports organizations are struggling to attract. In addition, as some organizations had extra reasons this is taken into consideration as well.

Quality of the research

Having a well-done and relevant analysis is important, however, doing so with quality is key for the success of a research. Quality, according to Wallendorf & Belk (1989) can be defined as the reliability, validity, and trustworthiness of a study. Assessing the quality must be something done in every study and constant throughout the research. To measure and ensure that the research is done with quality, is important to know how to assess it and what to do to guarantee the trustworthiness, reliability, and validity of the study. There are different assess the quality, according to the view of the researcher. Lincoln & Guba (1986), propose to assess the quality of qualitative research differently that the proposed internal and external validity plus internal and external reliability standards that are used in quantitative research. This is, according to Bryman & Bell (2011), because there are no absolute truths about the social world and there are more than one, and possibly several, accounts of social reality.

Therefore, to assess the trustworthiness and the authenticity of research, Lincoln & Guba (1986, pp. 76-77) suggest credibility as an analogue of internal validity, transferability as an analogue to external validity, dependability as an analogue to reliability, and confirmability as an analogue to objectivity.

Firstly, credibility is explained by Wallendorf & Belk (1989) as the adequation and reliability of the representations of the constructions of the study and the provision of sufficient representations of how the study is constructed. To ensure credibility Lincoln & Guba (1986, p. 77) propose a prolonged engagement, a persistent observation, a triangulation and cross-checking of data, peer debriefing, negative case analysis, and/or member checks. In this thesis, an example of the credibility and cross-checking and persistent observation would be how during the interviews is that follow-up questions and confirmation of what was said in the interviews with online data were done.

Secondly, transferability according to Wallendorf & Belk (1989) is when the working hypotheses can be employed in other contexts. Lincoln & Guba (1986, p. 77) propose to use thick descriptive data so that others that want to use the totality or part of the findings elsewhere can do so. The detective work that was done prior to the interview and the meetings that were set to help understand and support the data collection criteria providing descriptive data which was helpful to secure the transferability of this thesis.

In addition, the research methods explain all the steps comprehensively and a detailed background is provided.

With a publisher like Riot, they are the owner

of the competition. And that's a big difference.

Thirdly, dependability is defined by Wallendorf & Belk (1989) as to whether the results would be the same if another person would have done the study. And the last criterion, confirmability, is referred to by Wallendorf & Belk as the neutrality of the data and the ease of tracking the process and construct of the researcher. For both of these criteria, Lincoln & Guba (1986, pp. 77-78) propose the need for external competent auditing to examine the process results. In this thesis, all the processes are thoroughly explained, from the data collection to the findings which allows a good understanding of what is being done.

Empirical Results

In this chapter, the empirical findings of the research are shown. The findings are from the interviews conducted with eSports managers and other relevant persons from sports organizations that have a presence in the European League of Legends, but also from research on publicly available content such as consultancy reports or from journalist sites.

The eSports industry

The eSports industry and a market overview will be presented in this chapter. ESports is a concept that joints diverse videogames, so in the same way that the term sports groups in-corporate different disciplines such as football, basketball, or water polo, eSports group different videogames with different competitions. Figure 5 provides a visual representation of how it is structured, with examples of different videogames. Each of these videogames comprehend different competitions with different competitive formats, different organizations, and different stakeholders involved. But the main difference between eSports and sports industries is the role of the Game Developer in eSports.

"…and the thing is that the difference is that actually, the publisher is mainly the owner of the eSport itself. So, game developer is the owner of the game where in football is, of course, regulated by FIFA or UEFA, in a sense. […] With a publisher like Riot, they are the owner of the competition. And that's a big difference. […] Also, in terms of rules and regulations… so, the publisher, make it Riot, they are creating the rules for the competition of League of Legends. So those publishers are very important in terms of rules and regulation"

Interview with R8 - PSV

In traditional sports, no one owns the IP of the game, in football for example. However, in eSports, the publisher or game developer owns the rights to their videogame. For example, in League of Legends, Riot is the game developer, whilst in FIFA, EA Sports is the organization with the videogame rights. Then, the role of the game developer varies from videogame to videogame, as Scholz (2019) clarifies some publishers get more involved than others.

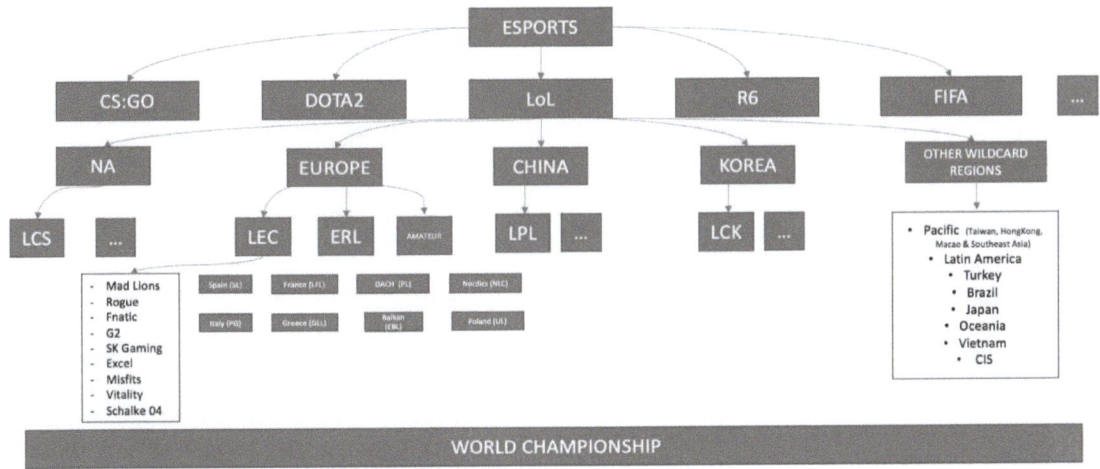

Figure 4. ESports overview

However, one of the main differences between the eSports and the sports industry is that in eSports there are issues with the governance and regulatory bodies in eSports, which are developed during this chapter. The eSports' governance has not developed as far as the rest of the industry and that might hinder the future of the scene. In League of Legends, this gets accentuated when looking at the European Regional Leagues (ERLs) and the amateur scope where the game developer does not have as much involvement as in the main league, the LEC.

"And they [Riot] actually govern the high-level eSports at least. So, there's still a grey area, which I think is a problem. The governance of high-level eSports for League of Legends is decent, Riot is overlooking the contracts, and actually is taking care of professional contracts being held, which is one of the biggest and most important governance functions that you need in order to have a professional sports system because otherwise, players could use us whatever they want, and they would just leave any day for the next highest bidder. But actually, Riot prevents that because they govern the entire player market at the high level. Now the thing is that at some level, Riot stops doing that. And that's the issue. So, if you're too small, and if you're not playing at that level yet, players can just leave you, they can just or they can ignore any contract"

Interview with R3 - TOG

In addition, this governance structure creates issues for the eSports organizations' revenue streams and their business models. One of the main sources of income for traditional sports organizations is the media rights, however, due to the game developer power and eSports governance, this is not possible and that hinders the industry development.

[Translated from Spanish] "In eSports, there is a monopoly of the publisher, which is a monopoly that I sincerely believe must be broken and will be broken because in Europe there cannot be one, an actor with as much power as the publisher today with the excuse that it has the rights of the game. [...] Currently, the publisher is the one who totally sets all the rules of what can be done and what cannot be done. Here in the value chain of several actors, the publisher, on the one hand, and the league organizers, on the other, to whom the publisher gives a license. For example, here in Spain, in the Superliga, it is MediaPro to whom Riot gives the license to operate. [...] That's why a few years ago what we set up is the ACE basically to be able to correctly negotiate the joint interests of the clubs or this will be impossible to sustain because in the end we have to start with some league rights like it occurs in sports which is the main source of income for football clubs, for example, and here we don't have it, it is not the main source of income for the esports clubs. But this will end up happening just as I tell you that the sector is maturing, the forces in this value chain will compensate and the regulation will also make the publisher stop exercising the force that it has today and it will be highly relevant in the competitive eSports industry, but not with the monopoly that it has now I am convinced that this will happen"

Interview with R4 - Betis

Moreover, this creates a high dependency on the sponsors as a revenue stream for these organizations. Many of these organizations rely greatly on sponsorships to sustain their business.

"the sponsors… it is the main source of income and therefore the most important stakeholder for a club"

Interview with R4 - Betis

"To give you an example of the sources of income, the great dependence on the eSports industry, and whose fault makes that the vast majority of teams are in deficit, is that there is a great dependence on sponsors, this means that according to the latest data I consulted, 90% of the sources of income of the organizations. Which means that there is a very clear lack of sources of income. Or of diversification, in this case. And this denotes a lack of maturity in the sector, in which we believe that new monetization formulas should be sought"

Interview with R1 – FC Barcelona

Associations like the ACE, which has been mentioned above, are key to develop and to build a sustainable industry where all the interconnected stakeholders rely on each other for the success of the industry. All the parties need to be protected and develop ways to self-sustain. But more involvement also from governmental regulatory bodies and law is needed. Some organizations have highlighted the need for a change in the law system where eSports players can have similar contracts to the athletes. This lack of recognition in the law is obstructing many deals and brings difficulties for many stakeholders.

"[Translated from Catalan] I have encountered a lot of problems at the contractual level, to regulate the situations of my players. In Spain, as you know there is no specific regulation for eSports, for professional eSports players. This means that I have to hire

my players with an employment contract with a category that does not belong to them […] I may have potential issues if I need this player who is from a specific region, outside the EU or Schengen area, and so on, to be in Barcelona"

Interview with R1 – FC Barcelona

"because of the lack of bargaining power for teams, because it's right, the contracts are not protected"

Interview with R3 – Schalke04

In order to monetize the audience, the eSports organizations decided to look for other ways. Monetization of the audience is key to develop the business models and the revenue streams of the organizations, and one alternative that has been used is content creation. And organizations need to understand the importance of content creation and its importance for the fans and the audience, and ultimately monetize it.

> *The sponsors… it is the main source of income and therefore the most important stakeholder for a club.*

"For us, content is the core. Okay? It's the show's core business. In the end, entertainment is what people want to see. The future in this regard, and the for the other clubs, must be clearly focused on creating content. Your bet has to go here, because in the end all these assets … you are selling the commitment and engagement in the end and you have this commitment in the social media, you have it in the streaming, and you can monetize it at this moment but also you can pack it and sell it to sponsors"

Interview with R1 – FC Barcelona

But many organizations also highlighted that the players have too much power compared to traditional sports where the eSports players play a big role in the strategic decisions and roster and project management. More specifically and where it differs more from traditional sports is that, in some eSports, the organization itself does not own the spot in the league but the player does, which puts the eSport organization in a tough position.

"For example, there is a big difference between Superliga, in which Barça owns the place, or Rocket League, in which the player owns the place, all right. This means that surely in Rocket League I have to be much more careful with the players, in terms of relationship and more than in Superliga, although we are obviously careful in both cases. But in Rocket League, one player is taken and the rest falls very heavily on the players. [...] And this is something that in medium / long term projects are very complicated in eSports."

Interview with R1 – FC Barcelona

Then, establishing healthy power relations between all these stakeholders is very important for the maturity and professionalization of the industry. This is an ongoing process but still needs time.

Traditional Sports in eSports

Various European sports organizations have decided to join the growing market of eSports, and the number is increasing year after year. The biggest representative of traditional sports in eSports has been Schalke04 which competed in the top League of Legends European league, the LEC. However, currently, there are no sports organizations in the LEC, or in any of the major LoL competitions; but there is a presence in the so-called wildcard regions, such as in the Turkish league with Fenerbahçe, Galatasaray, or Beşiktaş, PSG Talon in the PCS, or Flamengo in the Brazilian competition

(CBLOL). Therefore, when I interviewed the organizations, I focused on the European Regional Leagues (ERLs), where many sports organizations are competing that are more accessible. Examples of these organizations are FC Barcelona or Real Betis in Superliga (Spain), FC Schalke04 or Penta 1860 in Prime League (DACH). Also, since the eSports scene is constantly evolving, some organizations' presence in the scene has changed. For example, Real Betis is no

longer in the Superliga (Spain), but in the 2nd division, PSV is not currently competing in LoL, or as mentioned, Schalke sold its LEC spot and now only competes in the Prime League.

Moreover, it is worth introducing that sports are finding other ways to be involved in eSports. For instance, many sports professionals have developed their own organizations in eSports, mainly in Spain. Examples of these are Gerard Piqué's co-owning KOI with the Spanish streamer, Ibai Llanos which competes in the Superliga, Casemiro's team Case Esports and David De Gea's team Rebels Gaming, both competing in the 2nd Spanish Division, among another eSports. In addition, another way that sports organizations are being involved in eSports is seen in LEC's organization Misfits, which has been involved in a partnership with the NBA Franchise Miami Heat since 2018 and recently since 2020 also with the Orlando Magic (DotEsports, 2020).

Why do traditional sports organizations expand to eSports?

But why do these organizations have an interest in joining an industry like eSports? This is an important question. Understanding the reasons underlying the strategic decision of expanding into another industry is of relevance to first, further understanding the advantage and profitability of the niche sector of the eSports for their organization and, secondly, having access to the very unique audience and stakeholders of it.

The conduction of the interviews provided valuable insights to answer one of the core research questions of this thesis. It can be noticed after conducting all the interviews that one of the reasons has been homogenous for all the sports organizations: the audience. ESports audience was argued to be unique and niche by all the interviewees.

"… it's a huge difference for any sports organization to reach that target group, instead of a professional sports organization such as Ratiopharm Ulm. I think that Ratiopharm Ulm reaches […] like the youngest, the youngest children of them. I think that being an eSports organization makes it a lot easier to interact with his audience because the eSports audience is very interested in what they like, their interests, being gaming and eSports. And they are hardly interested in other sports. So, I think an Esports organization has it a lot easier to reach that demographic, especially since there's a difference between young sports fans and young eSports fans, they can be the same, but they're not"

Interview with R3 – TOG

"eSports has a pretty young target audience like if you compare it to traditional sports where like, I don't know, in football, I would say that the average is probably 30, 30 or more, you know, and in eSports, it was proven to be much lower, like, I don't know, beginning of the 20s, right"

Interview with R2 – Schalke04

And, moreover, many of these same organizations brought up that the importance of joining eSports is because traditional sports, such as football, is struggling to reach this young audience and that this is due to the fact that traditional sports audience is ageing.

"But mainly because football fans are getting older, I would say, and they try to like to broaden their diligence by reaching young, younger people. And yeah, basically trying to grow a new fan base, I would say, that could translate from eSports to sports or the other way around"

Interview with R6 – Nantes

So, connecting with these fans and filling the age gap that traditional sports find hard to reach is increasing in importance for these organizations. Moreover, is not only just to reach a young audience, but because this unique audience has acquisitive power and specific demographic characteristics that are important from a business perspective to reach.

"[Translated from Catalan] …the reason we get into it, and it is to connect with audiences that are very young, that are different, or partially different from those that can consume traditional sport. It does not mean that it is one thing or another, in some cases it is, and in other cases they consume both. But it is true that there is a high incidence or a high percentage in which, I could not tell you the exact number, but there is a percentage of people who we can no longer catch with football, with 90 minutes of a game or we can't catch them with basketball, or we no longer catch them with handball. We need to create a new product for this new audience, which is also an audience that brands, in general, globally, are very interested in, why? Because it is very young, very young, and because part of that young audience that we could mark is mostly between the ages of 18 and 35, they tend to have a high purchasing power. Therefore, the potential for monetization is huge, compared to audiences you can target, 10 and 15 years. Therefore, the purchasing power is completely different. They've noticed that and they have seen that the traditional product, the traditional sport, yes, it still has a huge impact, it's huge. It's getting older, it's also a reality, and we need, or needed, a much more targeted product for this new audience."

Interview with R1 – FC Barcelona

But that is not the only reason, some organizations also highlighted the importance of rejuvenating sports organizations and how eSports help to do so. Digitalization and technology are core for eSports due to its nature and having a presence in those, helps traditional sports organizations to adopt some of the practices, and learn from eSports in that area.

"…one of one of the biggest reasons the target group is just very different […], a lot of people who are directly in, invested in esports are usually quite tech-savvy, at least that's, that's like I said, my experience with it. So, they are very, very keen on all things digital. Then there's, there's, if you will, new methods that are being that they actually come from, they come from eSports. Like, today, we as a basketball team, we are using live streaming, right. And live streaming is actually something that comes from the eSports part and not from the sports area. So, you get in touch with a new target group"

Interview with R3 - TOG

This is of high relevance because of the times we live in, where many things are digital and where the importance of digital content, having your brand online, and connecting with the young fans through different channels is growing in importance. Some of the organizations also highlighted the entertainment revolution aspect. Sports and eSports share the property that in the end, for the audience, is a source of entertainment. Hence, being keen on how entertainment is evolving and adapting to it is seen as essential for the future of sports organizations

eSports are global, and the organization reaches a larger audience more easily and might attract fans from different parts of the world.

"...from **PSV Eindhoven**, we created our vision 2030. One of the macro developments we identified is the entertainment revolution. So, what we see is, driven by the newest technology, the new generation is being raised in a digital world. So gaming is just part of their life, as is, having everything on demand. Think about watching a video on Netflix, or YouTube, or Spotify, or whatever. So, we need to understand what their interests are, how they are raised, and what they expect from brands and sports organizations like us for example. We live in an experience economy driven by those technologies. This is why we can better acknowledge the esports and gaming market and see how we can play a role within like we do with our FIFA22 activities for example to keep the connection with the new generation and stay relevant to them."

Interview with R8 – PSV

In addition, the eSports audience is an international one. Even if the sports organization is based in a certain country or city, eSports are global, and the organization reaches a larger audience more easily and might attract fans from different parts of the world.

"...the factor surprised them (the board) was that we had fans from Omonia and Apoel,

which, if I can put it in perspective is like a fan of Real Madrid, they would come to Camp Nou to buy the shirt of Barcelona eSports. So, this is the level of... as soon as they saw that an Apoel fan came to football stadium during one of the events that we have to take pictures with the players and buy a jersey, they saw... they said they were shocked to say these things doesn't happen. And I said: no! These things happen. Because people who are into eSports, who are into League of Legends or Hearthstone, or Rocket League, or the of the gaming community, let's say they don't care about the football team. They don't care. So, we built the brand around it, they see them the value that we bring, you will bring in new fans"

Interview with R5 - Anorthosis

Furthermore, some organizations used eSports as a channel to revendicate certain local issues due to its international reach. By reaching a broader audience, they can raise awareness about the events happening in their cities or countries and take advantage of the visibility and technology of the eSports audience.

"So, by the time we had to also announce our roster, it was the last day that we had to announce.

And I didn't want to do this. I was feeling very, very, bad you know [with the political situation in Varosha], I couldn't do it, and I had to do big discussion with the organized fans, and you know, the team and all of that, and they tell me: 'No, you have to do it. You have to bring awareness, do your video announcement, but bring awareness', you know, and I finished the video with big letters saying, 'freedom to Famagusta', you know, and it was being shared in Greece and Cyprus, and people are seeing it. So, there was that, well, why freedom to Famagusta? Why are they saying this? Again, so this is something that we are taking advantage of technology, and the viewability and the visibility that we have as an esports team to raise awareness of what's happening outside of Cyprus"

Interview with R5 - Anorthosis

All organizations have specific reasons, due to their specific context. But in general, it was a constant reason for the need of attracting the niche and global audience of eSports, and it is important to be able to adapt to the channels and manners of the eSports audience.

How do traditional sports organizations enter eSports?

It is not only important to the reason of entry, but also, understanding how these organizations enter eSports, the expansion methods, and the advantages of these, are as important to understand. When researching how the organizations entered eSports, it is evident that all of them had a different journey, with different methods, and experiences. However, two tendencies can be defined. On the one hand, some of the sports organizations clearly created the eSports organization from within. On the other hand, other sports organizations had to partner with endemic eSports organizations.

Furthermore, it was a uniform answer about having to adapt to the audience. Since it is a unique audience, you cannot treat it as another sports audience. Organizations had to make an effort to understand what is driving the audience, the channels, and their interests.

"eSports fans and the traditional football fans are different audiences. So, the way to approach these fans should be different. But managing eSports and traditional sports from a management perspective can be done in a similar way. But being a football club, you need to understand that the gaming or eSports audiences are different from your traditional sports. So, copy-pasting your communication will fail"

Interview with R8 - PSV

And if you adapt correctly to the audience, you will get the results. Most of the organizations have had a short experience in eSports, but the ones that have been longer managed to succeed and fill the age gap for their organizations

"And this is the reason why they enter eSports and I think it makes total sense from a business perspective also. And I think these four years in the EULCS/LEC showed that we were really able to, yeah, build a fan base and attract people that otherwise would not necessarily be interested in Schalke04"

Interview with R2 – Schalke04

Passion is key in eSports, and that influences how the beginning of the eSports journey raises within an organization. Many of the organizations started with the passion of someone in the organization that built a case and took responsibility for it. This passion is important, first, because it brings certain knowledge about the eSports scene and, secondly, brings commitment and drive to the project.

"When I joined the club three years ago, […] I was able to convince the CEO back then, to see it the same way as me. And I told him the entire idea of, you know, like having a new target group, join, on what the club is, like, get to know the brand, but because this is what it's all about, getting to know getting in touch with the brand"

Interview with R3 - TOG

As introduced before, some organizations learnt by themselves through their journey. Starting from the bottom and learning day by day. These organizations want their brand to be recognized in eSports and have the capabilities and resources to learn about the industry and the know-how. This approach is slower and requires time or external aid.

[Translated from Catalan] "…since May 2019 I have been leading together with other people, and people from the digital department, and with an eSports agency that supports us, the whole of eSports of Futbol Club Barcelona"

Interview with R1 – FC Barcelona

[Translated from Catalan] "The model and the culture are totally different. This is a reason and I think it is the most important. So, we don't need another club or another brand to get into the Superliga"

Interview with R1 – FC Barcelona

On the other hand, other organizations wanted to establish their brand in eSports at a quicker pace and at lower risk. For that, they establish a collaboration deal with an endemic eSports club or another endemic organization.

"They had the opportunity to join the French second division, which was a new competition at the time. But they had no idea on how to build a team that just basically didn't know anything about the game. They only had the big name and Riot Games wanted them to be in the second division. So, they basically made a partnership deal with a school which is called Gaming Campus that has both players, young players trying to get into eSports, professionally, and also a business school, which I was a part of that aims to train eSports managers overall"

Interview with R6 - Nantes

When the interviewed organizations discussed which eSports videogame they chose and their strategy regarding that, most of them answered similarly. It was consistent that these sports organizations entered first through a sports simulation videogame and then they made the jump to higher-rated videogames, such as League of Legends. All the organizations agreed that being part of League of Legends was a clear choice. LoL is one of the eSports with more visibility and a very dedicated audience. Therefore, with these organizations having teams competing in the different European leagues they have been able to have access to interact with this audience. In addition, it is important to consider that other very relevant videogames with high audience numbers, such as CS:GO or Valorant, are not eligible for some of the organizations due to the type of game. Shooters, which is a videogame genre that is characterized by the usage of weapons to defeat the enemies, are treated as violent for a part of the society and are considered as a higher risk for some organizations, whilst it also might break with certain core values of the organizations.

[Translated from Catalan] "…the most interesting part of eSports that was, in the end, to go for the tier 1, to the tier 1 eSports that as you know are League of Legends, it could be a Counter-Strike, it could be an eh … a Dota2, but considering what we had it on the table, and considering that we are Barça, we can't get into shooters so League of Legends was the obvious choice"

Interview with R1 – FC Barcelona

These first steps are important for two reasons, and it is a natural and logical way to understand the industry. First, because it enables the sports organization to have a first taste of the eSports scene and learn about its audience, ways of doing, and stakeholders of the industry.

"The easiest way to enter eSports for a football club is to enter something football-related right? So, FIFA and Pro Evolution Soccer obviously, I mean, and Schalke was present or still is present in both I think it is it is the easiest way to combine you know the love for football and the love for video games is to have a video game about football and to be active there Right. So, it was the first step into eSports but then we pushed it further right we pushed it into other games that you know with League of Legends that don't really or like are not linked to football it is simply put a video game, but it has no like no link, I would say to the core business of Schalke04. And so, they are present there they are present obviously or they were present until now in the LEC and they are present in the Prime League which is the National League basically for Germany. And in the future. They will keep the team in the PrimeLeague so they see Although they had to sell the sport in LEC, they see the value of having a team in PrimeLeague, they also see the potential has, you know, for the Schalke, and they will stay in PrimeLeague can continue to compete, you know, for, for the title in PrimeLeague Can I think it's really to see that although they sold to sports, they keep the commitment to League of Legends"

Interview with R2 – Schalke04

And, secondly, because this entrance through a sports simulation videogame acts as a pedagogical tool to help understand the people within the organization and the current fans about eSports and its potential.

"[Translated from Catalan] ... the quintessential tier 1 is League of Legends. This reasoning, which is very simple, or the transition we have made, from pro evolution soccer to League of Legends, is something that only with outside staff would surely not have been possible. You may have been stampeded and left at Hearthstone because in the end, this internal pedagogy is only done internally. An outside agency does not have the opportunity to meet with Barça's general manager or Barça's digital boss. It's something that must be done from the inside, and it's fundamental, and that's why I think we'll have a long way to go and probably why others have stayed the course.

Interview with R1 – FC Barcelona

But the pedagogy is not only needed for the organization itself. Making non-endemic organizations, sponsors, and other stakeholders understand about eSports, its potential and to eliminate the stereotypes about it has taken time. Some organizations expressed the difference when dealing with these external stakeholders and how making them understand that it is an opportunity for them has been a process and a long effort.

[Translated from Spanish] "Brands… basically there has been a very big process and there still is, but the last four years, since I started now that four years ago, you talk to a brand and they had no idea what esports are so there has been an evangelization or a job of pedagogy, the brands of this enormous sector and four years ago when I talked to them about what it had set up, people was very surprised and said: oh, and you pay the players to play video games? And many other things that when we explained before what we were doing, well, they said like, he's crazy"

Interview with R4 - Betis

Reciprocal benefits of eSports

The entrance of sports organizations to eSports has numerous benefits, both for the sports organization itself and the eSports organizations that they might have allied with. In addition, these benefits might also extend to the whole eSports scene. Therefore, this section will present the findings regarding these benefits.

For the sports, the main benefit is the reason why they join the industry which is the access to the niche audience that eSports has. But as was mentioned previously, there are additional benefits that the eSports organizations bring to traditional sports such as access and understanding of new digital channels, the possibility of dealing with new brands and stakeholders and the whole knowledge and ways of doing about this very unique sector, and freshness and change on the manner of communicating.

Making understand the non-endemic organizations, sponsors, and other stakeholders about eSports, its potential and to eliminate the stereotypes about it has taken time.

"We can help them to understand eSports to get reach into another group of people they wouldn't reach with old media and their current ways of approaching. Furthermore, we have contacts in endemic and new eSports contexts, that could be sponsors interesting for them as well, that could be… players that could influence them, because they live near that, or they have a story to tell. This could also be the way to present yourself in a new media because this is the biggest strength of eSports. And what they are experts on, especially orgs like G2, that they fully understood how new media works completely to the last point whereas a second-division German football club like Munich TSV, like they have no clue of that. So, they can ask us, and we can tell them this and this, and this is how it works. And this is how it interacts. And these are KPIs you need to look at and all of that stuff"

Interview with R7 - PENTA

However, there is also an interest for eSport organizations to collaborate with sports organizations since it is an opportunity to learn about a mature industry and its processes. In the end, the essence of the business is the same where teams compete, deal with players, and prepare them and organizations have relationships with the stakeholders. The organizations are part of transfer markets, player contracts and negotiations, as well as how to prepare, train, and provide support to their players, which is something that sports has a lot of experience on.

[Translated from Spanish] "eSports in the end, beyond the debate of whether it is a sport or not, the business itself is the same and the sport knows very well what it is to sign players and sell players, contact people, prepare a team sportingly... that is, the business is exactly the same, looking for sponsorships, there is an audience. So, the business of eSports is in the end really similar and it's something that sports know, right? So, we have something that they didn't have, and they have things that we don't have, basically because of the maturity we're talking about"

Interview with R4 – Betis

In addition, an important aspect that eSports get from sports is the backup and trustworthiness that is achieved by being aligned with a more known and mature organization. Mostly when dealing with non-endemic stakeholders, having the support of the sports organization has been of benefit to achieving sponsorship deals and other cooperation bringing reliability to the eSports brand.

[Translated from Spanish] "…we had associated ourselves very badly with brands, for example, in sponsorships. And Real Betis, well, today it has a consolidated brand, when we did this, what I told you was a bit outdated was that I had to do a lot of pedagogical work [...] that is, if I had the idea that, well, If a sponsor wants to enter the esports sector and doesn't trust it because he doesn't know, well, in the end, the Real Betis brand gives him a solidity that it's proven and that no one is going to tease him, you know? So, it makes a lot of sense to us. What is most important is also an important infrastructure, an important fanbase, removing things that we did not

have, and we gave them all the knowledge of the sector that no soccer team today very few have"

Interview with R4 – Betis

Having a connection to traditional sports leadership provided value in terms of better business understanding and culture, focusing on the long term and acting as a brake to the fast-paced and impatient business of eSports.

"They always were patient, you know, and I feel like some of the players we had, for example, needed time to develop, which I know some other teams would not give them that much time. And I think it was really important that from the beginning, they said to us: "Hey, guys, stop being impatient". I think in eSports, people, in general, are really impatient. And I think it paid out in the end. And it was something that came straight from the club, from the football club, to be patient to be human"

Interview with R2 – Schalke04

Some of the eSports organizations highlighted how they acquired the values of the sports organization and how it shaped the ways of doing in the eSports organizations for its success.

"Basically, the core value that we took over, I would say from the football team. It was really important to us to stay humble to be, you know, to be funny, but humble and to implement the roots of the football club as well, you know, and this was basically what we did. And I think it worked out pretty well in the in yet"

Interview with R2 – Schalke04

Another reason of interest for eSports is that many sports organizations provide the infrastructure, facilities, and technology for the players to be able to do their activities. Also, they provide the possibility for the staff to learn and exchange knowledge from very experienced professionals from the sports organization and access and support from the different departments of the sports organization.

[Translated from Catalan] ... They will come with their clothes that we bring them; they also have a training centre provided by us with all the necessary technology so that they can carry out their activities. [...] What more, for example, already in the coaching staff. We have very good, wellqualified in-house professionals, the people who have come with Xavi [Hernández, current Head Coach of Barça's first team], and other people who are also part of the club's executive structure. Well, for example, what I've already talked about with our League of Legends coaches is that, as they're interested in sports and health sciences, I've given them a number of talks with coaches from other FCB professional teams. As a result, there is a very interesting exchange of knowledge that allows these coaching staff, who may be spending a year or two at Barça, to grow as professionals thanks also to the experience we have in the field of traditional sport. And we're one of the only sports clubs out there that can do this. They don't have these qualified professionals and I think that, as I told you at the beginning, the part of eSports and traditional sports is very close, therefore this wisdom, knowledge, experience that we have in this field, transferring to eSports is also literally, take the coaching staff you have for League of Legends and bring them closer to the coaching staff of the other sections.

Interview with R1 – FC Barcelona

Yet, eSports is a far more immature and young industry than traditional sports, which raises the concern of many of the organizations concerning the sustainability of the business. However, there is room for development and professionalization and learning from core aspects of traditional sports is relevant for the progress of eSports. One of the issues that was brought up by most of the interviewed organizations is the power of the game developer, which holds the IPRs of the videogame. In the League of Legends case, it is Riot Games that owns the IPR and therefore the one in charge of the competitions and acting as the main regulator.

"Then another regulators Riot games, who have a complete monopoly on how they want to do it. So, if they want to ban a team, they just ban it, there's no way to save it. Something like that can't happen in football, without a reason. But you don't have like this institutional infrastructure that saves you from

doing that. So theoretically, we could do what Blizzard, for example, has done that with banning a player for saying Free Hong Kong"

Interview with R7 - PENTA

Moreover, there is currently no presence of eSports regulation in European law or in the law system of the countries.

"there's no word about eSports. under German law, for example. So, every team is basically company. And for example, if you want to get like someone out of Europe to play for you, you need to do the classical import, like import worker way, which is really, really unsustainable for Esports completely, because you have those rules of minimum two years of this, and that which does not fit the needs of eSports at all"

Interview with R7 - PENTA

However, things are developing, slowly but they are. In some countries, there is a will to start regulating eSports. These regulations need a lot of work and regulators perhaps do not fully understand the eSports industry and its stakeholders, but it is a starting point.

"So recently in Greece, the Ministry of Sports sent us the draft planning of the rules or regulations they wanted to implement to, let's say, put inside the legislation eSports" [...] "My main concern is the one I raised is that they classified eSports only the sims [simulation eSports]. So, everything that could be tied to physical sport, they tied it to eSports. And they neglected FPS games, mobile games, there was no mention of League of Legends, CS, Valorant... And that was my first comment when I told them: guys, it's a nice step forward, I feel that we are doing a nice step forward, but also, we are doing 10 steps backwards"

Interview with R5 - Anorthosis

An important thing that has been already mentioned and discussed by other organizations is the need of establishing eSports players as athletes. With that, the organizations would get a relief in terms of contracts which are currently a headache for many of them.

"So, the eSports players of a team to be recognized as athletes. And in that way, how can a club, esports team can be an organization or a club or a company. So, then you will have to give contracts, you have to employ people, you know, because so far, it's like fully a grey area, on how you employ eSports players or content creators, all of that. So, I think that doing good steps, the countries in general, in Cyprus, we still have no, any indication of what they're going to do, if they're going to do it. People don't seem to still understand or grasp the idea behind eSports on and how big of a market it is, and how big of an impact this industry has. In Greece, they are going in a good direction"

Interview with R5 - Anorthosis

But these first steps are important, again, for the need of making the non-endemic people understand what eSports are, for the pedagogical process that was previously discussed.

Conclusion

This last chapter will conclude the thesis, presenting the findings and learnings from this work and answering the research questions. The thesis had the purpose, firstly, of providing awareness and knowledge about eSports. This is accomplished in this thesis in a multitude of ways, providing a thorough review of previous research, showcasing the potential and journey of the eSports, and providing an overview of the eSports scene. Secondly, the thesis aimed to research about sports organizations' implication in eSports, how has been the growth and expansion of the existing sports organizations to eSports, and why these organizations wanted to expand to the industry. This goal has also been achieved thanks to the interview guide that was prepared for conducted interviews and the results and answers to the research questions are presented below.

Answering the research questions

1) Why do traditional sports organizations expand to eSports?

The first research question wanted to understand the logic and reasons that traditional sports organizations had to expand to a different and unique industry such as the eSports one. The answers to these questions were mainly found in the interviews. The interviewees' main answer regarding why they entered eSports was unanimous: to reach a unique audience that traditional sports organizations are struggling to reach. It was argued that traditional sports are struggling to reach the young target and that their audience is ageing. This is a very important audience, because of its specific demographics, its acquisitive power, and its passion.

In addition, Scholz (2019) argues that the importance of the audience is not only for the organizations, but it is also the key stakeholder for the industry and due to the dynamics of the industry and its stakeholder relations and characteristics makes it perhaps the most relevant one, such as the coopetition, co-destiny, and convergence. That is why most of the other stakeholders enter the industry, with the purpose of monetizing the audience.

However, reaching this unique audience is not the only reason why traditional sports organizations are expanding into eSports. The industry is profitable and that is an attraction in itself. According to Newzoo (2021), the industry generated 947.1M revenue in 2020 and is projected the generate around 1618M in 2024. These numbers are per se very appealing for outsiders, but most importantly, the potential 71% growth between these years is humongous.

Lastly, some sports organizations added that the eSports industry was a chance for them to renovate and modernize their processes. ESports endemic stakeholders are born digital and global (Scholz, 2019), and it is an opportunity for the sports organizations to learn about the new channels and ways of communicating where eSports organizations excel. ESports organizations have certain ease and understanding of how to use social media platforms and acquiring this knowledge is important to bring these processes, which are being so useful and novel for eSports, to their industry. Nonetheless, it is important to acknowledge the target audience. Adapting to the channels is important and sports organizations must not fall into the mistake of using the same communication strategy in all of the channels. Every channel has its specific audience and ways of doing and it is important to be aware of it.

2) How do traditional sports expand to eSports?

When studying the expansion methods that the sports organizations have been using, two tendencies can be defined. On the one hand, certain organizations choose to organically expand to eSports. Johnson et al. (2011) find that culture is a key aspect for the organization. The most significant example of this would be FC Barcelona, which emphasized in the interviews the importance for the organization to control everything that happens and correctly communicate the values of Barça. In addition, this method provides more flexibility, both in terms of the investment and expenses, which are distributed over time, and in terms of strategy and approach, which can be adjusted or reversed when needed (Johnson et al., 2011). The sports organizations have to learn about what eSports are, the unique audience and its ways of doing, the channels, or the stakeholders, which involves a learning journey that some other organizations might not want to go through due to the time and other resources that are associated with it. In addition, there is a pedagogical labour that is important to make understand, not only the rest of the organization but also the fans, about the potential and relevance of entering eSports. However, going through the journey brings the advantage that the acquired knowledge about eSports is internalized by the organization and makes them not rely on anyone else (Locket et al. 2011).

On the other hand, some organizations do not have the time and resources to expand organically to eSports, and it was found that the preferred alternative is to create an alliance with an endemic eSports organization, which usually was an eSports club. When organizations choose this method, Johnson et al. (2011) argue that the reason is that it involves less risk, and it is a faster method to enter the industry. However, an alliance involves a higher initial expense, less control, and reliance on the other party. Many eSports organizations claimed alliances to be beneficial because it enables them to also acquire knowledge, professionalize their processes, and use the infrastructure that traditional sports organizations provide them. Even though sports and eSports industries are different, some organizations mentioned that allying with a sports organizations provided them knowledge about market transfers, contracts, game preparations, or trainings. Scholz (2019) argued that eSports is still a young and unprofessional industry and that is why for some eSports organizations partnering with experienced organizations like the sports ones gives them a lot of value.

> *Moreover, some interviewees argued that the national legislation needs to catch up and integrate eSports' needs within the law.*

ESports, as argued by Scholz (2019) is an umbrella term for different videogames, therefore it is important for eSports organizations to further research on the expansion process and knowledge of which videogames to enter. Many organizations started with sports simulation games, such as FIFA or NBA2k, because it is a natural way to enter the eSports industry and even start the pedagogical process that has been mentioned. Then, the interviewees agreed that it is important to enter the tier 1 videogames since are the ones with more audience and it was unanimous to choose League of Legends as the most relevant one.

3) What does the future of eSports look like?

This paper projects that the industry is to keep growing and the revenues are projected to be on the rise. According to Escharts (2021), the League of Legends Worlds Finals had a peak concurrent viewership of over 4M on the online broadcast. In addition, the entrance of non-endemic stakeholders is professionalizing the industry and making the people that do not know much about eSports to start to normalize it, which both of these things are very beneficial for eSports. However, through the literature review and the empirical research, some issues were found that obstruct and hinder the future of eSports. These matters need to be addressed for the sustainable development of the industry and for its stakeholders' wellbeing.

Firstly, both literature and interviews show that there are issues with the business models of the eSports organizations. As Scholz (2019) argues, organizations struggle to monetize the audience and the reason for that is the immense power of the game developer, which in LoL's case is Riot Games. This huge role of the publisher repercusses in a limitation on the revenue streams that the organizations can look for. Currently, the main, and perhaps only for many, source of income for these organizations is through sponsorships. This is not sufficient nor sustainable for the needs of the organizations. That is why some organizations are starting to look for other opportunities such as content creation or ticketing, which are further discussed in the following section. As mentioned by the interviewees, one of the main differences in the business models between sports organizations and eSports organizations is that the sports organizations have media rights as one of the main revenue streams. This does not happen in eSports because of the structure of the industry, how eSports are broadcasted, and the monopoly of the game developer.

Secondly, as presented before the power of the developer or publisher can be a constraint for the development of the eSports industry. The game developers have full control of the tournaments and leagues, and they are the main regulators of how these are executed and, hence, are very influential for the organizations and the industry overall (Scholz, 2019). In the previous paragraph, it was explained how eSports organizations are affected by the immense power of the publishers in this industry. However, this paper finds that some eSports organizations in certain countries are starting to take actions to solve

this, like grouping into syndicates and defending their rights and interests, like the ACE in Spain. Yet, more involvement from local authorities and global regulators is needed, and organizations such as what FIFA is in football are needed in eSports. Scholz (2019, p. 142) adds that the issue gets enhanced when you notice that a single organization, Tencent, owns Riot Games, has a majority in Supercell, and a 40% in Fortnite, along with minority stakes in Activision Blizzard. That means that a single private organization has so much power in the competitive scene of eSports. Having to regulate a private entity might be tricky but, perhaps, having certain legal guidelines on how they can operate in certain regions, or establishing agreements with the clubs for the tv rights could be potential solutions.

Lastly, an issue that was raised by certain organizations is the level of regulation within the eSports industry, which was introduced in the previous paragraph. There is a need to stop the monopoly that organizations such as Riot have over the League of Legends scene, or broader, the big power that Tencent has over the eSports industry, and that can only come with major legislation. Moreover, some interviewees argued that the national legislation needs to catch up and integrate eSports' needs within the law. One of the main issues that was explained is the need of including eSports players in the same contractual category as traditional sports athletes. Otherwise, the eSports organizations need to offer regular contracts when they make a transfer, with the limitations that it has, or are discouraged to acquire players from certain regions.

In conclusion, the future of eSports might look bright at first sight but there are certain aspects that need to be addressed in order to secure the potential of the industry. Audiences and viewership are growing, sponsors and non-endemic stakeholders are seeing the capabilities of eSports, and new and more professional organizations are entering the scene, which brings fresh ideas and professionalization, but anything of that will matter if the industry does not solve the fundamentals, provide a clear regulatory terrain for organizations to develop, allow healthy power relationships so the organizations within the industry can create sustainable business models, and in the end, integrate eSports within society rather than considering it as a solitary phenomenon.

Managerial Implications

The previous chapter has already provided a good understanding of what this research's implications are for the decision-makers in traditional sports organizations which want to expand into eSports. To further elaborate, this sub-chapter will present the practical actions that the organizations can consider in order to succeed in this strategic decision.

Firstly, it is necessary to understand the industry, its audience, and its stakeholders. ESports is a unique industry with unique actors involved and it is crucial for any sports organization that wants to enter eSports to perform market research before joining, no matter which entry method is chosen. Moreover, it might be important to look for the support of a specialized eSports agency since it could help with branding, media, or content strategies. It has been shown that even if eSports' audience is extensive, their ways of behaving are different from the traditional sports audiences and there is a need for adaptation to their needs and channels. Learning about effective social media communications, the difference between the different social medias, learning about the importance of content creation and certain niche channels such as Twitch is essential for the accomplishment of the growth strategy.

Secondly, it is important to be aware of the own organization's capabilities and resources, such as time, prior knowledge, and financial assets. This highly influences the entry method to eSports whether is organically or by an alliance with an endemic organization. An aspect that is decisive in the expansion process is the values, culture, and heritage of the sports organization. Preserving this when proceeding with an alliance might be complicated and that is why certain organizations opt to follow an organic growth when they can acquire the specific eSports' knowledge in a longer period of time whilst assuming a higher risk.

Lastly, it is relevant for the sports organizations that enter eSports to be aware of the governance and regulatory issues of the industry, which ends up in inefficient business models due to the lack of revenue streams. These organizations might play a big role in the professionalization and sustainable development of the industry, and it is imperative that they use their size and experience to cease the dominance of the publishers. Their experience in negotiation, the establishment of federations, or seeking new revenue streams. There is room for improvement of the current business models such as opening new eSports venues which bring ticketing as a potential additional income, and here traditional sports organizations have experience. Jenny et al. (2018) talked about how existing venues and arenas are looking to eSports as an opportunity for their activities and new venues were being opened before the Covid-19 pandemic. This would need a restructuring of the competitive system, but it is something that some interviewees are hoping for in order to connect more with regional fans, which, as Scholz (2019) argues, helps the objective of eSports to be more local and analogue.

Suggestions for future research

This thesis has provided an overview of the eSports industry, its structure, and its potential. In addition, it has provided guidelines for sensemaking on the strategical decision of sports organizations expanding to eSports. However, eSports is a novel topic which offers many opportunities for further research. Hence, this sub-chapter will contribute to incentivising the study of the field with the following recommendations.

Firstly, this study has been done when many of the organizations have recently entered. Therefore, I would suggest following up on the journey of the sports organizations, seeing how they progress with time, and drawing conclusions about it. Looking at which method is being more beneficial for the sports organizations in terms of expansion in a couple of years and further analysing the pros and cons of each method might be highly relevant for strategical research. Furthermore, keeping an eye on how the channels, communications, and audiences evolve might be significant. The entrance of new organizations might shift or include new demographics into the current eSports audience.

Secondly, it would be interesting to research in-depth how to solve the issues that were previously mentioned. In this thesis, it has been argued that the power of the publisher should be diminished, but with that, there would be a lot of work to do to establish a sustainable industry. As an example, it would be relevant to explore possibilities for the development of the business models and the improvement of the revenue streams. As discussed in this research, how to implement media rights is one of the main sources of income for many sports organizations. But another source could be ticketing. It has been argued by Jenny et al. (2018) that venue owners are being more and more interested in eSports, perhaps there could be a day when the eSports league games could be streamed in arenas. This would be aligned with the tendency of eSports to become more local (Scholz, 2019) and the need to satisfy regional and national audiences, as was explained in the interviews. It has been shown that certain organizations are having huge success on certain events such Ibai and Piqué's team presentation of KOI filling the Palau Sant Jordi's venue in Barcelona and their showmatch against the French powerhouse

Karmine Corp in December 2021 with more than 15,000 onsite fans and around 360,000 (Tejedor, 2021). How ticketing can become an option for eSports is a research opportunity but, as argued, more research on the opportunities would be interesting to see in the future.

Lastly, a study on how to implement a sustainable and effective regulatory framework for eSports is relevant in order to support the organizations in a correct manner and reduce their struggles. Regulation and law are out of the area of expertise and relevance for this research, but they are still highly relevant to be researched in the future.

However, I think it is important a potential outcome of the entrance of traditional sports organizations and other non-endemic eSports organizations might be that endemic eSports organizations might be forced to disappear since they might not have enough resources, power, and knowledge to compete with sports organizations that have been in the competitive business for many decades. Because in the end, despite the discussion if eSports should be sports or not, the business is the same.

References

Apesteguia, J., Ghazala A., and Iriberri N., (2012). The Impact of Gender Composition on Team Performance and Decision Making: Evidence from the Field. Management Science 58 (1): 78–93.

Brandenburger, A.M., and B.J. Nalebuff. (1996). *Co-opetition.* New York: Doubleday.

Beckert, J. (2010). Institutional Isomorphism Revisited: Convergence and Divergence in Institutional Change. Sociological Theory 28 (2): 150–166.

Burroughs, B., & Rama, P. (2015). The eSports Trojan Horse: Twitch and Streaming Futures. *Journal For Virtual Worlds Research*, 8(2). doi:10.4101/jvwr.v8i2.7176

Carrabine, Z. (2019). Paris 2024 GLHF: Esports' Quest for Olympic Inclusion. *Sports Law. J., 26*, 229.

Collins. (2022). Collins Dictionary | Sport Definition. [online] Available at: <https://www.collinsdictionary.com/dictionary/english/sport> [Accessed 27 March 2022].

Crompton, J. L. (1993). Sponsorship of sport by tobacco and alcohol companies: a review of the issues. *Journal of Sport and Social Issues*, 17(3), 148-167.

Demir, R., & Söderman, S. (2015). Strategic sponsoring in professional sport: a review and conceptualization. *European Sport Management Quarterly*, 15(3), 271-300.

Denzin, N. K. (1978). *The research act: A theoretical introduction to sociological methods* (2nd ed.). New York, NY: McGraw-Hill.

Denzin, N. K., & Lincoln, Y. S. (2008). Introduction: The discipline and practice of qualitative research. In N. K. Denzin & Y. S. Lincoln (Eds.), *Strategies of qualitative inquiry* (pp. 1–43). Sage Publications, Inc.

Dictionary.com. (2022). Definition of sport | Dictionary.com. [online] Available at: <https://www.dictionary.com/browse/sport> [Accessed 27 March 2022].

DiMaggio, P. J., and Powell, W. W. (1983). The Iron Cage Revisited: Institutional Isomorphism and Collective Rationality in Organizational Fields. *American Socio-logical Review* 48 (2): 147–160.

Dolphin, R. R. (2003). Sponsorship: perspectives on its strategic role. *Corporate Communications: An International Journal.* Vol. 8 No. 3, pp. 173-186. https://doi.org/10.1108/13563280310487630

Elmuti, D., & Kathawala, Y. (2001). An overview of strategic alliances. *Management decision.* Vol. 39 No. 3, pp. 205-217.

Escharts. (2022). *LEC Spring 2022 / Statistics.* [online]. Esports Charts. Available at: https://escharts.com/tournaments/lol/lec-spring-2022. [Accessed 17 April 2022]

Franke, T. (2015). The Perception of eSports— Mainstream Culture, Real Sport and Marketisation. In *eSports Yearbook* 2013/14, ed. Julia Hiltscher and Tobias M. Scholz, 111–144. Norderstedt, Germany: Books on Demand.

Gray, H. L. (1978). The Entrepreneurial Innovator. *Management Education and Development*, 9(2), 85–92. doi:10.1177/135050767800900202

Hetsroni, A., and Tukachinsky, R. H. (2006). Television World Estimates, Real World Estimates, and Television Viewing: A New Scheme for Cultivation. *Journal of Communication.* 56 (1): 133–156.

Hudson, L. A., & Ozanne, J. L. (1988). Alternative Ways of Seeking Knowledge in Consumer Research. *Journal of Consumer Research*, 14(4), 508. doi:10.1086/209132

Hutchins, B. (2008). Signs of Meta-Change in Second Modernity: The Growth of ESport and the World Cyber Games. *New Media & Society* 10 (6): 851–869.

Jenny, S. E., Keiper, M. C., Taylor, B. J., Williams, D. P., Gawrysiak, J., Manning, R. D., & Tutka, P. M. (2018). eSports venues: A new sport business opportunity. *Journal of Applied Sport Management, 10*(1), 8.

Jenny, S. E., Manning, D. R., Keiper, M. C., and Olrich, T. W. (2017). Virtual(ly) Athletes: Where eSports Fit Within the Definition of 'Sport'. *Quest* 69 (1): 1–18.

Johnson, G., Whittington, R. & Scholes, K. (2011). *Exploring strategy.* 9th Edition. Harlow, Essex: Pearson Education Limited.

Saunders, M., Lewis, P., & Thornhill, A. (2009). Research methods for business students. *Pearson education.*

Schmidt, S. L., & Holzmayer, F. (2018). A framework for diversification decisions in professional football. *Routledge handbook of football business and management*, 3-19.

Scholz, Tobias M., & Barlow. (2019). *ESports is Business: Management in the World of Competitive Gaming.* Springer International Publishing. ProQuest Ebook Central, http://ebookcentral.proquest.com/lib/hankenhttp://ebookcentral.proquest.com/lib/hanken-ebooks/detail.action?docID=5717907ebooks/detail.action?docID=5717907. Created from hanken-ebooks on 202109-21 11:04:49.

Scholz, T. M., and Stein., V. (2017). Going Beyond Ambidexterity in the Media Industry: eSports as Pioneer of Ultradexterity. *International Journal of Gaming and Computer-Mediated Simulations* 9 (2): 47–62.

Silverman, D., (2006). Interpreting qualitative data. 3rd ed. *Sage publications*, London.

Sparham, I. (2021). *The gaming industry shows no signs of slowing down* [Blog].
Available at:
https://pwc.blogs.com/pwcresearch/2021/07/gaming_industry.html [Accessed 12 September 2021]

Spiggle, S. (1994) Analysis and interpretation of qualitative data in consumer research. *Journal of Consumer Research*, 21 (3), 491-503.

Teece, D. J. (2010). Business Models, Business Strategy and Innovation. *Long Range Planning* 43 (2): 172–194.

Tejedor, O. (202). *Resumen de la presentación del equipo de eSports de Ibai Llanos y Piqué |*

KOI es el nombre elegido [online]. Lo + Gaming – Marca. Available at: https://www.marca.com/videojuegos/lo-mas-gam-ing/2021/12/15/61ba2973268e3eb16e8b45 70.html [Accessed 17 April 2022]

McKinsey & Company, (2020). *ESports as a sponsorship asset.* [online] McKinsey & Company, pp.1-22. Available at: https://www.mckinsey.com/~/media/McKin-sey/Business%20Functions/Mark eting%20and%20Sales/Our%20In-sights/E%20sports%20and%20the%20next % 20frontier%20of%20brand%20sponsor-ships/esports_whitepaper_03_06_202 0_vfinal.pdf [Accessed 29 August 2021].

Michael, C. (2020). Misfits Gaming Group signs partnership deal with the Miami Heat and Orlando Magic. [online] Dot Esports. Avail-able at: <https://dotesports.com/business/news/misfits-gaming-group-signspartnership-deal-with-the-miami-heat-and-orlando-magic> [Ac-cessed 21 January 2022].

Newzoo. (2021). Global Esports & Live Stream-ing Market Report (pp. 1-43). Newzoo. Nielsen. 2017. The Esports Playbook. Max-imizing Your Investment Through Under-standing the Fans. Cincinnati, OH: Nielsen.

Lincoln, Y. S., & Guba, E. G. (1986). But is it rig-orous? Trustworthiness and authenticity in naturalistic evaluation. *New directions for program evaluation*, *1986*(30), 73-84.

Lockett, A., Wiklund, J., Davidsson, P., & Girma, S. (2011). Organic and acquisitive growth: Re-examining, testing and extending Pen-rose's growth theory. *Journal of manage-ment studies*, 48(1), 48-74.

Olympics. (2021). Sports, programme and results. [online] Available at: <https://olympics.com/ioc/faq/sports-pro-gramme-and-results> [Accessed 27 March 2022].

Patton, M.Q. (2014). *Qualitative research & Evaluation Methods.* 4th ed. Thousand Oaks: Sage Publication

Porter, M. E. (1985). *Competitive Advantage: Creating and Sustaining Superior Perfor-mance.* New York: Simon and Schuster.

Reuters. (2018). Olympics. E-Sports Could Be Sports Activity. Accessed 7 November 2021. https://www.reuters.com/article/us-olym-pics-summit/

Wagner, M. G. (2006). On the Scientific Rele-vance of eSport. In Proceedings of the 2006 International Conference on Internet Com-puting and Conference on Computer Game Development: 437–440

Wallendorf, M., & Belk, R. W. (1989). Assessing trustworthiness in naturalistic consumer re-search. *ACR special volumes*.

Walley, K. (2007). Coopetition: An Introduction to the Subject and an Agenda for Research. *International Studies of Management & Organization* 37 (2): 11–31.

Wheelen, T. L., & Hunger, D. L. (2011). *Strategic Management and Business Policy: Toward a Global Sustainability*, 13th ed., Prentice Hall., New York, NY.

Young, A. T., Higgins, M. J., & Levy, D. (2008). Sigma convergence versus beta conver-gence: Evidence from US county-level data. *Journal of Money, Credit and Banking*, 40(5), 1083-1093.

The Electric Brain: New Intelligent Agents in eSports

By Ziqi Wang

Game playing has always been a topic of Artificial Intelligence (AI) research. Modern video games turned out to be a good examination of intelligence. Most games have a fixed set of rules, where problem-solving techniques can be developed and evaluated before being applied to more complex real-world problems (Schaeffer, 2001). Some games offer multiple advantages to AI research (Vinyals et al., 2017):

1. They have clear objective measures of success.
2. Computer games typically output rich streams of observational data.
3. They are externally defined to be difficult and interesting for a human to play. This ensures that the challenge itself is not tuned by the researcher to make the problem easier for the algorithms being developed.
4. Games are designed to be run anywhere with the same interface and game dynamics, making it easy to share a challenge precisely with other researchers.
5. In some cases a pool of avid human players exists, making it possible to benchmark against highly skilled individuals.
6. Since games are simulations, they can be controlled precisely, and run at scale.

eSports are competitions using some video games where skills are heavily weighted. So, they serve as a good multi-agent adversarial testing platform in AI research. Apart from the video games themselves, eSports now have become a type of commercial activity involving professional players, sponsors, organizers, commentators, audiences etc. This paper intends to give a summary of the principle of eSports AI and the effect to the community as well as the possibilities in the future. Therefore, there are 3 research questions to be answered later:

1. Do the methods of creating those AI players have a certain level of generality that allows the procedure to be reused, or makes the agents (AI players) adaptive?
2. From players' perspective, what impact does the invention of such AI players have, to the gaming community?
3. How possible is the cooperation between the AI and human players?

AI Technologies

Before video games

The history of AI game playing is even longer than eSports. Back in 1950, there were people developing computer program to play chess (Shannon, 1950), including Alan Turing (A. M. Turing, 1953). In 1997, IBM's Deep Blue made history as it became the first machine to beat a reigning world chess champion. Deep Blue is designed as a massively parallel system for carrying out chess game tree searches. It is equipped with some chess chips: specially customized hardware unlike general purpose CPU, GPU (Campbell, Hoane, & hsiung Hsu, 2002). Deep Blue could calculate the basic moves it could make in response to its opponent, exploring up to 100 million possible chess positions per second (Goodrich, 2021). The result was intriguing: Deep Blue defeated Garry Kasparov by a score of 3.5-2.5, but a rematch was demanded, expressing unsatisfaction. The rematch was rejected by IBM and Deep Blue was soon retired (McCorduck & Cfe, 2004).

The research did not end here as Go is a much more complex board game with immense possible states which was not conquered at that time. However, most programs fall short of human performance. They did not even achieve a beginner-intermediate level. A common misconception from the chess research is that brute force techniques, utilizing good search and evaluation algorithms, is sufficient to solve any problem once it has been formally specified (Burmeister & Wiles, 1995). Unfortunately, in the history before 2000, the biggest advances in computer game playing had come because of work done on the alpha-beta search algorithm (Schaeffer, 2001), just like Deep Blue.

For a period, Go was considered too difficult for machines. But the overall performance of computers did not stop growing. This enabled more and more machine learning application to be implemented (Jordan & Mitchell, 2015). In 2015, under spotlight, Korean professional Go player Lee Sedol had several broadcasted matches against the new Go playing AI, named AlphaGo created by the research group DeepMind. He had confidence of winning the series without losing a single game, but eventually he lost the series 1-4.

For a period, Go was considered too difficult for machines. But the overall performance of computers did not stop growing.

What made AlphaGo so powerful was a subtype of machine learning technology called Deep Learning. Deep Learning used to be named Connectionism back in 1980s-1990s (Goodfellow, Bengio, Courville, & Bengio, 2016). Terrence Deacon even suggested in his book that connectionism is the defining characteristic of humans (Deacon, 1998) because the model in deep learning, artificial neural network (ANN), is inspired by neuroscience (Marblestone, Wayne, & Kording, 2016). In deep learning, artificial neural networks do not rely on hard-coded knowledge, but extract patterns from raw data (Goodfellow et al., 2016). In an examination process, an algorithm called backpropagation compares the output by the neural network with

the expected result and indicate how the network's neuros should change its internal parameters that are used to compute from the input to the output. The process was made possible due to the advent of fast graphics processing units (GPU) that enabled high speed computation (LeCun, Bengio, & Hinton, 2015).

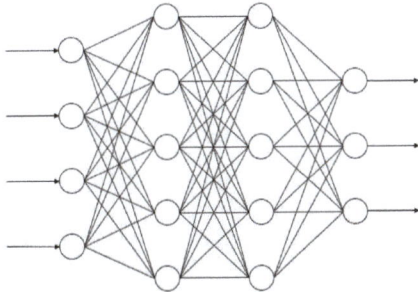

Figure 1: Example of a small neural network.

Every circle represents a neuro, which provides calculated output (a number) from left layer's results and their weights. So, the connections represented by the lines between them carry the weights, also known as network's parameters. Users feed leftest input and get rightest output through several matrix multiplications.

Apart from deep learning, AlphaGo also uses other methods and was upgraded several times. The early version, AlphaGo Fan, has separate policy network and value network. Policy networks select moves and value networks evaluate board positions. They are combined with Monte Carlo tree search. Moreover, the deep neural networks are trained by both human expert games, and reinforcement learning from games of self-play. In later version named AlphaGo Zero, there is no human data anymore. It abandoned two networks design and only uses one. The new AlphaGo Zero achieved superhuman performance, winning 100-0 against previously published champion-defeating AlphaGo (Silver et al., 2016, 2017).

Video Game AI

Unlike the research being conducted by scientists in the recent years, AI has been developed and used by the game developers for a long time. Those agents are put in the games mostly because the vacant role of player needs to be filled to make the game enjoyable. A lot of games marked as eSports nowadays have built-in agents. In the book *Artificial Intelligence for Games*, Ian and John divided AI in games into 3 categories (Millington & Funge, 2018):

1. Hacks (ad hoc solutions and neat effects)

2. Heuristics (rules of thumb that only work in most, but not all cases)

3. Algorithms (the "proper" stuff)

The method of hacks only wants the character to look right, as there used to be some debate around whether the machines think or not (A. M. Turing, 1951). For this question, Turing invented the famous Turing Test, a.k.a the Imitation Game (A. Turing, 1950). However, in conclusion, Turing Test is subjective because it only observes the result, not how the machine works. It is more a psychological approach that correlates behaviourism. Quake II has the "gesture" command where characters and players can flip their enemy off so they feel emotional, but it has nothing to do with the gameplay (Millington & Funge, 2018). Hack goes wrong if the behaviour is triggered beyond the rule. Street Fighter II agents fight back in a cheating way that could not be copied by human players (Desk, 2019). Research into the source byte code reveals that the moves of agents are simply executed as instruction, skipping the game rule (Sf2platinum, 2017).

Heuristics are general principles that do not guarantee working all the time, often related to goal-oriented behaviours. In eSports, majority of agents belong to this type. Plus, agents may be expected to play "normally and intelligently" like human.

Algorithms are the once-and-for-all solution, but most of them are designed for smaller tasks such as movement, pathfinding, decision making (Millington & Funge, 2018). Scripted input for speedrun games could be considered as a type of algorithm, when the script is proved optimized (Ramblings, 2021). For mainstream multiplayer eSports, there is no such silver bullet agent.

The Quake III Arena Bot is a well-designed, well-documented agent example from the last century competitive classic. The detailed description mentioned some attributes the agents should have, such as being indistinguishable from human player concerning movement, fighting, communication. The designer also required the agents to be computational resource efficient, modifiable and customizable (Van Waveren, 2001). The list of requirements is comprehensive, but some elements are redundant in serious eSports's view, where some linguistic hacks are not needed.

Since the developers know how to play their games, they could simply adopt traditional top-down approach AI to build their agents. The intelligence is built by applying existing knowledge (top) to specific tasks (down). For example, having both the area descriptions and reachabilities in 3D environment, routes between areas can be calculated with Dijkstra's algorithm (Van Waveren, 2001). The developers could teach and code so the agents behave reasonably given the situation. However, when the game is extremely complicated, such as eSports, it becomes very difficult to handcraft a good agent. Particularly, Blizzard's RTS game StarCraft, had attracted a large amout of AI research around 2010, due to its immense depth in gameplay and competitive challenge (Ontan˜´on et al., 2013).

As the wave of deep learning started around 2006 (Goodfellow et al., 2016), some people began using games as deep learning testbed. Especially, following the introduction of the Arcade Learning Environment (ALE), a platform providing an interface to emulated Atari 2600 game environments (Bellemare, Naddaf, Veness, & Bowling, 2013), there came some good results demonstrating that neural networks works well with these simple video games (Hausknecht, Lehman, Miikkulainen, & Stone, 2014; Mnih et al., 2013). Artificial neural networks were used for StarCraft unit control early in 2011, 2012 (Robertson & Watson, 2014). At this stage, deep learning was still used only "partially" in eSports.

The years of 2018 and 2019 were mind changing. Within 6 months, in StarCraft II and Dota 2, the most difficult eSports, show matches were played together with the professional players where the agents, AlphaStar and OpenAI Five performed in exceptionally great, humanlike ways.

AlphaStar is DeepMind's StarCraft II playing agent. The training process is enabled by SC2LE, a toolset released by DeepMind and Blizzard consisting of an application programming interface (API) called StarCraft II client, a dataset of anonymized game replays, a python component of API called PySC2, a series of simple reinforcement learning mini-games and a joint paper that outlines the environment and reports initial agents' baseline results on the mini-games (Vinyals et al., 2017).

StarCraft II has a very rich action and observation space for human players. The game outputs the 3D world, economical information, command cards, etc. to the monitor for human. In PySC2, the RGB pixels are only available for the screen and the minimap, plus, the screen is rendered from a top-down orthogonal camera, as opposed to a perspective camera that a human would get. Unit sizes do not change as any unit moves. Moreover, the PySC2 exposes feature layers from the RGB pixels of minimap and screen, which represent decomposed, structured information. The feature layer contains features such as height map, visibility, unit's owner, and for screen exclusively, units' hit points, energy, unit _density. The screen resolution is much lower than human's physical monitor, which could be like 64^2. Normally human sees several pixels as one unit on monitor, but agents could see inaccurate number of units on one pixel in PySC2. For most of the nonspatial data, PySC2 delivers them to the agent as tensors. This information mainly mirrors the information shown in the human UI interface such as mineral and vespene stock, supply, control groups, selected units' status (Vinyals et al., 2017).

The SC2 action space is very big. In addition to selection on screen, all possible moves which could be issued by human to units are shown in the command card. Many of them take a point in either screen or minimap. Instead of flattening the action space into a single dimension, PySC2 created function actions that are rich enough to give composability, without the complexity of an arbitrary hierarchy. The full set of valid types and functions are hardcoded in ValidActions in pysc2.lib.actions, and then each observation specifies which of the available function is valid this frame. For example, high frequency command

"Attack" is partially defined as 12/ Attack _ screen, which accepts a screen point as a parameter (Vinyals et al., 2017).

AlphaStar is trained by a hybrid of supervised learning and reinforcement learning. Agent parameters were initialized by supervised learning using a public human replay dataset.

AlphaStar's behavior is generated by a deep neural network of complex architecture that receives all observation from the start of the game as inputs and selects actions as outputs. The agent architecture consists of general-purpose neural network component that handle StarCraft's raw complexity. Observations are processed using a self-attention mechanism (Vaswani et al., 2017). Scatter connections are included to integrate spatial and non-spatial information. To deal with fog of war, a deep long short-term memory (LSTM) (Hochreiter & Schmidhuber, 1997) system is at the core of the network, allowing the agent to remember some information. An auto-regressive policy and recurrent pointer network (Vinyals, Fortunato, & Jaitly, 2015) are utilized to manage the combinatorial action space (Vinyals, Babuschkin, Czarnecki, et al., 2019).

AlphaStar is trained by a hybrid of supervised learning and reinforcement learning.

Agent parameters were initialized by supervised learning using a public human replay dataset. The network was trained to predict actions given all the observations and summary of strategies. This procedure created a diverse set of agents adopting human play styles (Vinyals, Babuschkin, Czarnecki, et al., 2019).

Then the agents enter the reinforcement learning stage, aiming at maximizing the win rate. It is conducted in a continuous league, a system similar to the StarCraft ladder. The league functions as a match-making manager, so the agents could play against others. The agent's policy is updated from experience generated by a previous policy, which is also known as off-policy learning. At some stages of training, some agents are added to the league, by branching from the existing ones, while some others are frozen. This keeps diversity of strategies in the league. After training using Google's v3 TPUs for 14 days, each agent has experienced up to 200 years of SC2 play, and the final agent is discovered from the most effective mixture of strategies, that could run on a single desktop GPU. Finally, AlphaStar was rated at Grandmaster level for all three races and above 99.8% of officially ranked human players (Vinyals, Babuschkin, Czarnecki, et al., 2019).

OpenAI Five is OpenAI's bots playing the competitive 5 vs 5 game Dota 2. OpenAI Five agent sees the game state with Valve's Bot API, which is the programming interface provided by the game's developer. One agent at each step observes around 16000 inputs from the game state. The observation is mostly real numbers plus some integer categorical data.

This makes up a long array. The agent's observation is more semantic than human's observation on screen. Visual processing is not a research focus here, and all observations are done instantly, whereas a human needs to click into various menus or units to get these data. The main feature of OpenAI Five's observation is "unit centrality". The observable properties about the unit are dependent on the unit type. For example, allied hero units have the most observations such as buyback status, while creeps have much less. There are only 189 units observations, so if there are less visible units, the rest are padded with zeros. If more, only the closest units to allied heroes are observed, similar to how human player pays more attention to the units around. Heroes are always registered. When enemy heroes are in fog of war, the last-seen data are used (OpenAI et al., 2019).

Without the peripherals, the action space presented to the agents is divided into two parts. One part is represented as "primary action", which is controlled by the deep neural network. The other part of actions is scripted, which is defined by a rules-based system to handle the decisions. Primary actions are most of the actions in a game, which are mostly combinations of high-level command (attack, use a certain spell, or activate a certain item) and a target. A primary action is joined by a set of parameters, which are delay, unit selection and offset. At the start of OpenAI Five, the scripted actions were more than how there remained at the end. The scripted logic takes in charge of the actions which are less frequent during a game. The remaining scripted actions are 1. Ability builds, 2. Item Purchasing, 3. Item Swap, 4. Courier Control (OpenAI et al., 2019).

Dota 2 is famous for its immense dynamics. Over 100 heroes and items make super big possibility of this game. For OpenAI Five, it does not handle all the situations because it would cost tremendous amount of effort to support everything in the full game. Matches with OpenAI Five are played under a set of restrictions, such as no Roshan, no summons/illusions. Before facing world champion team OG, the AI system eventually included 17 heroes, as Lich was removed from the pool because his abilities were changed significantly in version 7.20 (OpenAI et al., 2019).

The core of OpenAI Five program is a recurrent neural network acting as a policy function from the history of observations to a probability distribution over actions. The neural network consisted of 4096-unit long short-term memory. The game passes the current observation to the network as input and the network samples an action from the output distribution at each timestep. Though the goal is to win the game, the single winning reward would be very inefficient in training. Therefore, OpenAI Five uses a reward function which included additional signals such as characters dying or collecting resources. Most of the time, they do not conflict with the final goal and represent advantage in the game. The policy is trained using Proximal Policy Optimization, a new class of reinforcement learning algorithm by OpenAI (Schulman, Wolski, Dhariwal, Radford, & Klimov, 2017). The optimization algorithm uses Generalized Advantage Estimation to stabilize and accelerate training (Schulman, Moritz, Levine, Jordan, & Abbeel, 2015). There are 4 types of machines running the self-play environment. Forward Pass GPUs hold the recurrent neural network and open its port for receiving game observation and producing action output. Rollout workers run multiple Dota 2 games on CPUs. Optimizers run gradient updates based on the game results received from rollout workers. Controller works as a storage, receiving the updated parameters from the optimizers and providing new parameters to the Forward Pass GPUs. OpenAI Five is trained without any human gameplay data and most of the games in training were played against the latest set of parameters (OpenAI et al., 2019).

Interestingly, none of AlphaStar and OpenAI Five used the native graphical interface for observation. Both research teams clearly wanted to avoid graphical issues and run the games at higher-speed simulation. This differs from some Atari agents, as well as a Quake III agent by DeepMind where they use direct graphics or down sampled graphics (Hausknecht et al., 2014; Jaderberg et al., 2019). OpenAI Five even proved the robustness that the agent could respond to a missing piece of visual effect that is related to an areal damage, by walking out of it (OpenAI, 2018). The way of action is affected by the observation: OpenAI Five's unit-centralized observation caused the action to be some unit-centralized. AlphaStar's camera-based observation made the action still similar to clicking, but PySC2 provided prior knowledge of abilities. Both approaches have certain level of semantic conversion and demonstrated to be fair and successful. Coincidentally, both AlphaStar and OpenAI Five contain LSTM units at the core of their deep neural networks. Neural network seems to be the only choice for managing the mapping from the input to the output in high skilled eSports. AlphaStar has an exclusive bootstrap period when agents are trained by replays. Even though it could not make them masters in StarCraft, it helped the agents start playing the game. OpenAI Five, has a reward system which gives clearer objectives than that of AlphaStar. This makes it easier to induce a behaviour that is occasional but important, as there are plenty of different things to do in Dota 2. The concept "self-play" is not fully loyal to its literal meaning that one agent plays against itself. In fact, the so called "self-play" involves multiple agents playing in a matchmaking league. Not all agents eventually become the best one and many of them developed a playstyle that is not optimized. The playstyle can be considered as the ability that arises from the pursuit of the goal of winning, thus maximising the reward drives that behaviour (Silver, Singh, Precup, & Sutton, 2021). But at the same time, the league of "self-play" has become a selective process, hinting that learning does not start with a tabula rasa, a blank state, but with a set of representational commitments (Roitblat, 2021), which in eSports agents, is the initial random parameters in the neural networks. The social environment of the AlphaStar league reserved some victories for the agents of massive Void Ray playstyle, but these agents just fail to become among the best, while league system keeps feeding the reward that does not negate their playstyle (Vinyals, Babuschkin, Chung, et al., 2019).

There are several scenarios to examine the generality. The first scenario is the agent handling patches. Firstly, just like how Lich was removed from the hero pool in OpenAI Five due to the new patch, patches could decrease the performance of agents dramatically. Pure numerical change (e.g., skill damage, hit points) does not change the interface, so the agent could still invoke the function to issue that action. However, it could be confusing to agents. If none of the neural network parameter is changed, in the same game state with unchanged settings, the agent would have the same behaviour. Secondly, if the patches introduce a redesign like a new ability, then mostly the new ability comes with a new id or new effect. Even though, from PySC2 random agent it could be seen that illegal order does not crash the game, but there could be severe performance decline of the agent. Thirdly, it does not seem possible that the agent could accept community-created games in the arcade mode of these games, without researchers' heavy rework on the agent. However, cross game support existed on a simpler level. One deep learning architecture could be used to play multiple Atari games (Hausknecht et al., 2014; Mnih et al., 2013). The complexity of those old games is not on the same level as today's ones. So, they are easier to adapt.

Intelligent agent created for certain kind of eSports has only limited generality that only allows it to handle minor changes to the game.

To adapt to games, neural networks need training. Deep learning technology is notorious for its high cost of computational resources. In AlphaStar, each agent was trained using 32 third-generation tensor processing units (TPUs) over 44 days. During league training almost 900 distinct players were created (Vinyals, Babuschkin, Czarnecki, et al., 2019). For OpenAI Five, it could be seen that tens of thousands of CPUs and thousands of GPUs were used in the training system. OpenAI Five is a long project that last 1 year with many times of surgeries and rerun (OpenAI et al., 2019). The cost of computational resource requires research group with financial background. The training needs to be implemented on computing service provider, such as a cloud platform. However, one agent in the end could run on a high-end consumer GPU, which only does network forwarding for the agent.

As a conclusion, intelligent agent created for certain kind of eSports has only limited generality that only allows it to handle minor

changes to the game. It can be enhanced by manual intervention to solve the interface adaptation, which is shaped by the game and could be changed by patches. For the best agents, many patterns are alike, including recurrent neural network, league matchmaking. The training of agents is beyond personal level in terms of cost and work but suitable for a research group.

Community Response

These new agent technologies are revolutionary technical breakthrough. There has never been a non-human player participating in any major eSports team, and it is still not likely that any agent would participate. The release of the showmatches attracted a lot of viewers and there are a lot of feedback and comments alongside the videos. A simple script for finding the most-liked comments is created since the comments are not sorted correctly at first.

The video (https://www.youtube .com/watch?v=l92J1UvHf6M), titled OpenAI + Dota 2 is the oldest video about OpenAI Five and attracted more than 1 million views. The most-liked comment in the video has 1.1K likes, talking about the question mark joke. Dota 2 players sometimes type question mark as a taunt, questioning the motivation of the opponents' actions. This assumes OpenAI Five is not going to support typing question mark, which lacks the emotional toxicity of bad players. Another important video is OpenAI Five (https://www.youtube.com/watch?v=eHipy j29Xw). The top comment's opinion is very clear here. It attracted 1.8K likes and reads:

"WE ARE DOOMED". The poster is a Dota 2 video maker with plenty of subscribers. Despite this negative view, OpenAI Five had not played the show match against Dota 2 champions at this moment and did not play the full game of Dota 2. It had not played the full version either eventually.

AlphaStar is exhibited to the world in the live stream DeepMind StarCraft II Demonstration (https://www.youtube.com/watch?v=cUT-MhmVh1qs) on 24 Jan 2019. Surprisingly the most liked comment came from the official account of League of Legends, the popular MOBA game. The comment has 4.3K likes saying "let's see your fancy robot try to win a 1v1 against our boy imaqtpie". This comment invites such research straightforwardly. The second high like numbers (1.6K) belong to this comment: "Props to deepmind for enduring 200 years of pure protoss vs protoss." Agent training time can be scaled so it could be impossibly long compared to human experience. Even in eSports, games are built partially for entertainment. Playing mirroring race can be thought as tedious and monotonous. The third top comment talks about "oversaturating mineral line" technique behaved by the agent, sharing understanding of the game.

Both AlphaStar and OpenAI Five were deployed to the official game during a period of time for the public. Despite there is worry mentioned above that such technology would create a disturbance to the game community due to abuse, the deployment of the agents was only temporary. The agents' neural network is not made available to the public. There are some successors after them. DI-Star is born under the supervision of a Chinese retied zerg player from the AI company SenseTime (Harstem, 2022). Even though this zerg-vs-zerg agent was shared to many for offline playing, there was no observation below complaining that AI ruins the official online matchmaking yet in the year of 2022.

Therefore, in terms of the impact to the gaming community, the main outcome of those projects is the announcements by the researchers that make people realize that such agents exist now. They did not bring big changes to the eSports. Apart from the time limited deployment, those agents did not stay in touch with players for long. Attitudes towards the agents are not unified. In conclusion, the impact to gamers is not very significant. It only left some new ways to think about the games.

Cooperation

The biggest ethical problem for any kind of AI is the question: how could the AI product be beneficial to human? These agents take victories in matches against human, which looks threatening. Some examples of AI human cooperation will be shown and discussed. In the future of Go Summit, Pair Go showed a feasible way to combine human intelligence and machine intelligence. Top Chinese players Gu Li and Lian Xiao are paired with their own AlphaGo teammate, and both human and machines make decisions on the next moves (DeepMind, 2017). Go is a turn-based board game, so there is time to examine agent's suggestion before moving. Though Go is not a kind of eSports, some eSports are slow paced or de facto ported board game.

In OpenAI Finals, a special match was hosted including human and agents on both sides. OpenAI Five is trained to play on the side with full agents, but it is general enough to participate in a team with some human players in the team (OpenAI, 2019). The bot teammates adapted themselves well in the game and performed not bad, though they did not respond to the human's ping messages, and they did few weird actions.

Deep neural network is the major contributor to the high performance in game playing. However, deep neural network has the issue of lack of transparency (Carvalho, Pereira, & Cardoso, 2019). It is impossible to extract knowledge from the networks' parameters to a descriptive form in any natural language. This makes game agents not only uninterpretable but also uncontrollable. Agents take actions fully autonomously towards their reward, planning the moves according to the observable game state. Therefore, to have in-game cooperation with the agent player, instead of focusing on the agent's behaviour output, a better way is to have a cooperative environment like team.

Despite the agents not being the best teammates, they can help in other ways. After training, game agents can respond to most kinds of game situations with some human-like actions. Rule-based scripted agents may have flaws or weaknesses that could be exploited by humans using anticomputer tactics. The agents from a league are more robust, thus they represent several stable skill levels by playing as polite opponents. Most agents are implemented to catch up with human intelligence in existing games. But from the training process of AlphaStar and OpenAI Five, a potential benefit is shown: The training could be used for even new game that is not published yet. Agents gradually developed different strategies by themselves. Even though they do not try all possible states computationally, they explore the game strategically, just like human compiling an opening book. The game developers used to learn this only from players when their game became online, as some developers are not best at playing skilfully. With the new agent technology, the eSports developers could know better about their game in advance, before polishing and publishing their game finally.

In general, cooperation with agents is more indirect. Lacking communication, agent's autonomy and environment settings can be obstacles of cooperation. They can be still useful to human as explorers or opponents.

Conclusion

The article studied the new eSports intelligent agents by using comparative analysis and case studies into two main agent system. The article examined technology history, the agents' design, conference show matches, feedback to the showcases and discussed cooperation opportunity. It is confirmed that the new game-playing agents acquired high performance by heavily using deep learning technology. The training process and the agents have only limited generality, meaning that it requires human guidance for adaptation to eSports and the agent handles only specific game version. Despite the agents achieved great performance in a humanlike manner, the agents did not revolutionize the game community, because they are only temporarily online. They provided a new way of thinking and opened a new field of creating bots. Agents are less cooperative teammates than human in game. However, they can act as good opponents and automatic game explorers, which help players improve and assist game developers.

References

Bellemare, M. G., Naddaf, Y., Veness, J., & Bowling, M. (2013). The arcade learning environment: An evaluation platform for general agents. *Journal of Artificial Intelligence Research, 47*, 253–279.

Burmeister, J., & Wiles, J. (1995). The challenge of go as a domain for ai research: a comparison between go and chess. In *Proceedings of third australian and new zealand conference on intelligent information systems. anziis-95* (p. 181-186). doi: 10.1109/AN-ZIIS.1995.705737

Campbell, M., Hoane, A., & hsiung Hsu, F. (2002). Deep blue. *Artificial Intelligence, 134*(1), 57-83. Retrieved from https://www.sciencedirect .com/science/article/pii/S0004370201001291 doi: https://doi.org/ 10.1016/S0004-3702(01)00129-1

Carvalho, D. V., Pereira, E. M., & Cardoso, J. S. (2019). Machine Learning Interpretability: A Survey on Methods and Metrics. *Electronics,*

8(8). Retrieved from https://www.mdpi.com/2079-9292/8/8/832 doi: 10.3390/electronics8080832

Deacon, T. W. (1998). *The symbolic species: The co-evolution of language and the brain* (No. 202). WW Norton & Company.

DeepMind. (2017). *The Future of Go Summit.* Retrieved from https://www.deep-mind.com/research/highlighted-research/ alphago/the-future-of-go-summit

Desk. (2019). *How the CPU cheated you in Street Fighter 2.* Retrieved from https://www.youtube.com/watch?v=laUAg EUunsI

Goodfellow, I., Bengio, Y., Courville, A., & Bengio, Y. (2016). *Deep learning* (Vol. 1) (No. 2). MIT press Cambridge.

Goodrich, J. (2021). How IBM's Deep Blue Beat World Champion Chess Player Garry Kasparov. *IEEE Spectrum.* Retrieved from https://spectrum.ieee.org/how-ibms-deep-blue-beat -world-champion-chess-player-garry-kasparov

Harstem. (2022). *Machine Learning AI (DI-Star) Can Beat StarCraft II Pros.*
Retrieved   from https://www.youtube.com/watch?v=fvQF-24IpXs

Hausknecht, M., Lehman, J., Miikkulainen, R., & Stone, P. (2014). A neuroevolution approach to general atari game playing. *IEEE Transactions on Computational Intelligence and AI in Games, 6*(4), 355-366. doi: 10.1109/TCIAIG.2013.2294713

Hochreiter, S., & Schmidhuber, J. (1997). Long short-term memory. *Neural Computation, 9*(8), 1735-1780. doi: 10.1162/neco.1997.9.8.1735

Jaderberg, M., Czarnecki, W. M., Dunning, I., Marris, L., Lever, G., Castan˜eda, A. G., ... Graepel, T. (2019). Human-level performance in 3d multiplayer games with population-based reinforcement learning. *Science, 364*(6443), 859-865. Retrieved from https://www.science.org/doi/abs/10.1126/ science.aau6249 doi: 10.1126/science.aau6249

Jordan, M. I., & Mitchell, T. M. (2015). Machine learning: Trends, perspectives, and prospects. *Science, 349*(6245), 255-260. Retrieved from https:// www.science.org/doi/abs/10.1126/science.aaa8415 doi: 10.1126/ science.aaa8415

LeCun, Y., Bengio, Y., & Hinton, G. (2015). Deep learning. *Nature, 521*(7553), 436–444. Retrieved from https://doi.org/10.1038/nature14539 doi: 10.1038/nature14539

Marblestone, A. H., Wayne, G., & Kording, K. P. (2016). Toward an integration of deep learning and neuroscience. *Frontiers in computational neuroscience, 10*, 94.

McCorduck, P., & Cfe, C. (2004). *Machines who think: A personal inquiry into the history and prospects of artificial intelligence.* CRC Press.

Millington, I., & Funge, J. (2018). *Artificial intelligence for games.* CRC Press.

Mnih, V., Kavukcuoglu, K., Silver, D., Graves, A., Antonoglou, I., Wierstra, D., & Riedmiller, M. (2013). *Playing atari with deep reinforcement learning.*

Ontan˜´on, S., Synnaeve, G., Uriarte, A., Richoux, F., Churchill, D., & Preuss, M. (2013). A survey of real-time strategy game ai research and competition in starcraft. *IEEE Transactions on Computational Intelligence and AI in Games, 5*(4), 293-311. doi: 10.1109/TCIAIG.2013.2286295 OpenAI, :, Berner, C., Brockman, G., Chan, B., Cheung, V., ... Zhang, S. (2019). *Dota 2 with large scale deep reinforcement learning.*

OpenAI. (2018). *OpenAI Five. Retrieved* from https://openai.com/ research/openai-five

OpenAI. (2019). *OpenAI Five Defeats Dota 2 World Champions.* Retrieved from https://openai.com/blog/openai-five-defeats-dota-2-world -champions/

Ramblings, M. (2021). *The code behind Quake's movement tricks explained (bunny-hopping, wall-running, and zig-zagging).* Retrieved from https:// www.youtube.com/watch?v=v3zT3Z5apa M

Robertson, G., & Watson, I. (2014, Dec.). A review of real-time strategy game ai. *AI Magazine, 35*(4), 75-104. Retrieved from https://ojs.aaai.org/ index.php/aimagazine/article/view/2478 doi: 10.1609/aimag.v35i4 .2478

Roitblat, H. (2021). *Building artificial intelligence: Reward is not enough.* Retrieved   from https://bdtechtalks.com/2021/07/07/ai-reward-is -not-enough-herbert-roitblat/

Schaeffer, J. (2001, Sep.). A gamut of games. *AI Magazine, 22*(3), 29. Retrieved from https://ojs.aaai.org/index.php/aimagazine/article/ view/1570 doi: 10.1609/aimag.v22i3.1570

Schulman, J., Moritz, P., Levine, S., Jordan, M., & Abbeel, P. (2015). *Highdimensional continuous control using generalized advantage estimation.* arXiv. Retrieved from https://arxiv.org/abs/1506.02438 doi: 10 .48550/ARXIV.1506.02438

Schulman, J., Wolski, F., Dhariwal, P., Radford, A., & Klimov, O. (2017). *Proximal policy optimization algorithms.* arXiv. Retrieved from https:// arxiv.org/abs/1707.06347 doi: 10.48550/ARXIV.1707.06347

Sf2platinum. (2017). *The AI Engine.* Retrieved from https://sf2platinum

.wordpress.com/2017/01/20/the-ai-engine/

Shannon, C. E. (1950). Xxii. programming a computer for playing chess. *The London, Edinburgh, and Dublin Philosophical Magazine and Journal of Science, 41*(314), 256–275.

Silver, D., Huang, A., Maddison, C. J., Guez, A., Sifre, L., van den Driessche, G., ... Hassabis, D. (2016). Mastering the game of Go with deep neural networks and tree search. *Nature, 529*(7587), 484–489. Retrieved from https://doi.org/10.1038/nature16961 doi: 10.1038/nature16961

Silver, D., Schrittwieser, J., Simonyan, K., Antonoglou, I., Huang, A., Guez, A., ... Hassabis, D. (2017). Mastering the game of Go without human knowledge. *Nature, 550*(7676), 354–359. Retrieved from https://doi.org/10.1038/nature24270 doi: 10.1038/nature24270

Silver, D., Singh, S., Precup, D., & Sutton, R. S. (2021). Reward is enough. *Artificial Intelligence, 299*, 103535. Retrieved from https://www .sciencedirect.com/science/article/pii/S0004370221000862 doi: https://doi.org/10.1016/j.artint.2021.103535

Turing, A. (1950). *Computing Machinery and Intelligence.*

Turing, A. M. (1951). Can digital computers think? *The Turing Test: Verbal Behavior as the Hallmark of Intelligence*, 111–116.

Turing, A. M. (1953). Digital computers applied to games. *Faster than thought.*

Van Waveren, J. (2001). The quake iii arena bot. *University of Technology Delft.*

Vaswani, A., Shazeer, N., Parmar, N., Uszkoreit, J., Jones, L., Gomez, A. N., ... Polosukhin, I. (2017). Attention is all you need. In I. Guyon et al. (Eds.), *Advances in neural information processing systems* (Vol. 30). Curran Associates, Inc. Retrieved from https://proceedings.neurips.cc/paper/2017/file/3f5ee243547dee91fbd053c1c4a845aa-Paper.pdf

Vinyals, O., Babuschkin, I., Chung, J., Mathieu, M., Jaderberg, M., Czarnecki, W., ... Silver, D. (2019). *AlphaStar: Mastering the Real-Time Strategy Game StarCraft II.* https://www.deepmind.com/ blog/alphastar-grandmaster-level-in-starcraft-ii-using-multi -agent-reinforcement-learning.

Vinyals, O., Babuschkin, I., Czarnecki, W. M., Mathieu, M., Dudzik, A., Chung, J., ... Silver, D. (2019). Grandmaster level in StarCraft II using multiagent reinforcement learning. *Nature, 575*(7782), 350–354. Retrieved from https://doi.org/10.1038/s41586-019-1724-z doi: 10.1038/s41586 -019-1724-z

Vinyals, O., Ewalds, T., Bartunov, S., Georgiev, P., Vezhnevets, A. S., Yeo, M., ... others (2017). Starcraft ii: A new challenge for reinforcement learning. *arXiv preprint arXiv:1708.04782.*

Vinyals, O., Fortunato, M., & Jaitly, N. (2015). Pointer networks. In C. Cortes, N. Lawrence, D. Lee, M. Sugiyama, & R. Garnett (Eds.), *Advances in neural information processing systems* (Vol. 28). Curran Associates, Inc. Retrieved from https://proceedings.neurips.cc/paper/2015/file/29921001f2f04bd3baee84a12e98098f-Paper.pdf

Balancing Acts: Copyright, Expression, and the Nintendo Paradigm in Esports Streaming

By Despoina Farmaki

Video games have not only influenced the economic landscape in Europe but have also left a lasting impact on its cultural background (Lee, 2020, p. 60). Present-day video games represent intricate works of authorship operating within a highly advanced technological framework (Lee, 2020, p. 44). The global popularity of online gaming has surged significantly. This surge is often attributed to the plethora of content created by users and the prevalence of live streaming. Among the various forms of user-generated content closely associated with video games, 'Let's Play' (LP) videos stand out. Coined by the gaming community, the term (LP) refers to pre-recorded videos that document a player's journey through a video game. These videos typically include the player's commentary and are skilfully edited to engage and entertain the online audience (Coogan, 2018; Lee, 2020, p. 60).

Two distinct types of streaming are employed for the online distribution of digital content: live streaming and on-demand streaming. Live streaming involves the simultaneous delivery of digital content to multiple users in real-time from a single source. On the other hand, on-demand streaming is utilised to provide digital content when requested by a user (Borghi, 2011). Despite the similarities in the transmission process for both types of streaming, the initiation of the transmission differs. In live streaming, data are captured from a source, processed into a digital signal, and then transmitted simultaneously to multiple users. Conversely, in on-demand streaming, data are stored on a central server, and the transmission is triggered upon a user's request (Borghi, 2011).

While streaming has become a prevalent trend in online distribution, European jurisprudence concerning the copyright implications of this technology is notably limited (Makeen 2020, p.247). A more substantial body of literature addressing video game streaming and the associated copyright law issues has primarily originated from the United States. Over the past decade, scholars have endeavoured to ascertain the relevance of the 'communication to the public' right in the context of Internet streaming and video game streaming (Borghi, 2011; Brusa, 2015; Caguioa, 2019; Larkey, 2015; Lu, 2018; Matsui, 2016). However, a significant portion of this analysis has been grounded in the doctrines of fair use and the concept of derivative works, which are specific to U.S. copyright law. Consequently, there exists a fertile ground for exploration in Europe regarding these legal aspects.

This paper delves into the realm of intellectual property litigation in the video game industry, with a specific lens on Nintendo as a case study. As video games continue to wield a profound influence on both the economic and cultural landscapes in Europe, Nintendo, a prominent player in the gaming arena, has been at the forefront of legal battles to safeguard its intellectual property. By scrutinising Nintendo's approach to intellectual property, examining notable litigation cases, and exploring the broader impact on the gaming community, this paper aims to unravel the intricacies of intellectual property disputes in the evolving landscape of video game streaming. Through this focused exploration, the author seeks to shed light on the challenges, legal precedents, and broader implications that arise when a major player, such as Nintendo, engages in intellectual property litigation within the dynamic context of video game streaming.

Copyright and Video Games

Video games, being highly interactive multimedia, comprise distinct components that result from creative ingenuity and skills. These games encompass various artistic forms, including literary, dramatic, musical, and visual elements, alongside computer programs and characters. The ongoing debate revolves around which aspect merits copyright protection: is it the entirety of the video game or its individual constituent parts? Expanding on this, the subsequent query arises: which category of protected works do these elements fall into? European case law, and particularly the case Nintendo Co Ltd v PC Box Srl (2014), and legal scholars have addressed these inquiries, asserting that video games represent complex works of authorship. In other words, an 'amalgamation of individual elements that can each individually be copyrighted if they achieve a certain level of originality and creativity' (Farmaki, 2022; Ramos, 2013).

For example, the German Urheberrechtsgesetz (UrhG) lacks specific provisions for the classification of video games, leading legal doctrine to perceive them as multimedia works. Ramos and others assert the presence of two distinct elements in video games: the computer program and the audiovisual presentation (Ramos, 2013). In Germany, the UrhG in section 2(1)(1) categorises computer programs as 'speech work' or 'literary work,' while the audio-visual presentation is primarily treated as 'film work.' French case law, including Lefranc c/ Sté SESAM (2009), recognises video games as 'works of the mind,' emphasising their complexity beyond the software dimension. In Greece, recent jurisprudence acknowledges video games as 'complex audio-visual works' due to their combination of different types of works, digital form, and interactive nature (First Instance Court of Athens (ΠΠρΑθ) case 2221/2015). British case law Techniques (Anglia) Ltd. v Critchley Components Ltd. (1997) and Norowzian v Arks Ltd. (No 2) (2000) discussed the possibility of a single work containing multiple copyright-protected elements. Notably, in Nova Productions Ltd v Mazooma Games Ltd (2006), the court rejected the protection of a video game as a dramatic work, emphasising the lack of unity for performance. However, the complexity of contemporary video games, featuring narrative structures and various components, adds layers to the classification debate.

Consisting of two major elements, namely the software and audio-visual parts, the twofold nature of video games was further discussed by the Court of Justice of the European Union. In Nintendo v PC Box (2014), the Court held that 'video games... constitute complex subject matter comprising not only a computer program but also graphic and sound elements, which... have a unique creative value... they are protected, together with the entire work, by copyright in the context of the system established by Directive 2001/29'.

Copyright Enforcement: Nintendo as a Case Study

Since its inception in the video game industry, Nintendo predominantly focused on coin-operated or arcade games. Notable releases in the 1980s included Donkey Kong, Popeye, Mario Bros., and Duck Hunt. Subsequent releases such as Super Mario Bros. (1985) and The Legend of Zelda (1986) marked Nintendo's shift from 8-bit pixel art to 2D and then 3D animated games. Since its release in March 2017, Nintendo Switch has achieved global sales surpassing 132.5 million units, becoming a formidable contender against major console rivals, Xbox and PlayStation (Statista, 2023).

While a number of companies encourage streaming of their games (e.g. Valve Video Policy, Ubisoft Video Policy, Riot Legal Jibber Jabber, Microsoft Rules, and Blizzard End-User License Agreement), Nintendo has been documented for its aggressive approach towards asserting copyright over LP videos (Hagen, 2018; Larkey, 2015; Marfo, 2019). Matsui (2016) believes that the potential benefit of permitting game streaming would outweigh the potential cost. This contrast, combined with intellectual property concerns on how the gameplay can be shared, will be contested in the coming years (Taylor, 2018, p. 245).

While Nintendo has historically grappled with the challenges posed by LP videos and the streaming community, recent developments underscore the company's proactive stance in addressing a broader spectrum of threats to its intellectual property.

Despite the potential infringement, users and gamers persist in live streaming or uploading LP videos online, and platforms continue to host such content. Matsui (2016) contends that the platforms' indifference stems from the game companies' overall reluctance to file complaints or civil actions against platforms. Notably, Nintendo stands out as an exception, having taken action against the upload of their copyrighted work by allowing it under the condition of profit-sharing from advertisements among the user, Google, and Nintendo.

Game developers and streamers have generally coexisted without significant conflicts. Online video games, like other software, are accompanied by End-User License Agreements (EULAs) that players must agree to (Kind, 2017). EULAs outline the terms of use between developers and users, typically taking the form of 'click-wrap' agreements, permitting streaming under the condition that it remains 'non-commercial' (Girasa, 2002). However, developers retain the right to prohibit streaming at their sole discretion, for any reason or none.

Nonetheless, the previously established truce showed signs of deterioration. In 2013, Nintendo took a stand against LP videos, issuing takedown notices to prominent streamers and YouTubers (Bailey, 2015). Subsequently, Nintendo introduced its partner programme, allowing the streaming of specific games with the condition that streamers share the advertising revenue (Jungar, 2016). Under this arrangement, Nintendo and YouTube divided the revenue 55/45, and Nintendo returned 60% of its 55% share to the content creator. Games outside this partnership programme faced streaming restrictions. However, in 2018, Nintendo lifted some restrictions related to how YouTube creators could monetise gameplay, introducing a new set of guidelines. Content creators on YouTube are no longer obligated to join Nintendo's partnership programme; instead, they can operate within YouTube's partner programme (Alexander, 2018).

While Nintendo has historically grappled with the challenges posed by LP videos and the streaming community, recent developments underscore the company's proactive stance in addressing a broader spectrum of threats to its intellectual property. A notable case, Nintendo vs. Sky (2019), involves Nintendo's pursuit of blocking injunctions against Internet Service Providers (ISPs). This legal action goes beyond the realm of LP videos and delves into the issue of websites advertising, distributing, offering for sale, and selling devices that allow technological protection measures on Nintendo's popular Nintendo Switch games console to be circumvented. The focus shifts from the content itself to the tools enabling unauthorised access to Nintendo's copyrighted material. This case serves as a pivotal example of Nintendo's multifaceted strategy to combat various forms of infringement, illustrating the company's dedication to protecting its intellectual property from diverse threats.

Nintendo has also been known for exhibiting minimal tolerance toward fan games, as evident in the issuance of numerous takedown notices to at least 500 fan games, exemplified by the high-profile cases of Pokemon Uranium and the Metroid 2 remake AM2R, both of which received notices in 2016 (Frank, 2016). This uncompromising approach is not confined to games alone; it encompasses copyright enforcement actions against a Metroid Fan film (Dyer, 2023), trailers for fan games (Mackey, 2020), and even an online Smash Bros tournament during the pandemic (Skrebels, 2020), where legal action was taken due to the unauthorized use of a mod enabling online gameplay.

Navigating the Intersection of Copyright and Freedom of Expression

Nintendo faces the delicate task of striking a balance between protecting its intellectual property and fostering a positive relationship with its gaming community. The issuance of takedown notices and the imposition of restrictions on certain content can be perceived as restrictive by some gamers, leading to concerns about the potential stifling of creativity within the gaming community.

The Information Society Directive 2001/29/EC governs exceptions to the communication right, aiming to strike a fair balance between right holders and users. The Directive outlines a closed list of exceptions and limitations, categorised by the European Audio-visual Observatory into three main groups: those favouring public interest, fundamental freedoms, and private use (European Audiovisual Observatory, 2017). This paper emphasises exceptions based on fundamental freedoms, specifically the exception for quotations for criticism or review (Article 5(3)(d)). Four conditions apply to such quotations, including lawfully made public availability, indication of the source, compliance with fair practice, and appropriateness for the specific purpose.

As the analysis proceeds to explore different types of LP videos, it distinguishes three categories: reviews, playthroughs with commentary, and playthroughs without commentary. Reviews, presented as video critiques with accompanying commentary, may qualify for copyright exceptions. Live streaming, considered a new dimension of game reviews, introduces challenges, particularly regarding potential spoilers and companies' preferences for experienced reviewers over player-driven reviews. The intricate landscape of exceptions and limitations, as outlined in the InfoSoc Directive, necessitates a nuanced examination of the diverse forms of LP videos within the evolving digital gaming environment.

The second category of LP videos involves playthroughs with commentary, where viewers witness the gamer playing part or the entirety of a video game while receiving commentary on the gamer's experience rather than an analysis of the game's features. A debate exists regarding whether playthroughs with commentary qualify for the exception outlined in Article 5(3)(d) of the InfoSoc Directive, which pertains to purposes such as criticism or review.

Arguments in favour of qualifying playthroughs with commentary for the exception highlight that the commentary serves a distinct purpose from the original work's story, often focusing on demonstrating game strategy without interfering with the original work (Puddington, 2015). However, stronger arguments against this qualification emerge. The extensive use of the original work, showcasing the entire game, including its plot twists and climaxes—the "heart of the game," raises concerns under Article 5(3)(d) (Carlisle, 2015).

The broader implications of these considerations extend beyond the gaming community, reaching into the broader realms of culture, democracy, and the evolving landscape of digital content creation.

The third category of LP videos comprises playthroughs with no commentary, exemplified by the "full game walkthrough" of the video game Alan Wake 2. In these videos, viewers observe the entire game being played without accompanying commentary. Postel

(2017) notes that, akin to playing the game, viewers do not actively influence on-screen actions. Since complete works are seldom permitted for criticism or review purposes, the third category of LP videos is unlikely to fall within the exception outlined in Article 5(3)(d).

Analysing video game streaming through the lens of freedom of expression requires the consideration of key factors. LP videos encompass diverse expressions, extending beyond gameplay discussions. Instances such as 'Twitch Plays Pokémon' and 'Heartstone' demonstrate innovative uses of streaming beyond traditional gameplay discussion (Frank, 2019; Stephen, 2019). However, the video game industry's varying stances on political expressions, exemplified by Blizzard's actions against a Hearthstone player supporting Hong Kong protestors, reflect a complex landscape.

Geiger and Izyumenko (2019) argue that copyright should enhance free expression rather than block access to information for fear of criticism. Legal cases, such as the one involving TotalBiscuit's negative review of Day One: Garry's Incident, highlight concerns about using copyright to stifle criticism (Ligman, 2013). The ECtHR, recognising the importance of freedom of expression in Asby Donald and others v France (2013) and Fredrik Neij and Peter Sunde Kolmisoppi (The Pirate Bay) v Sweden (2013), emphasises its role in democratic societies. Evaluating video game streaming as 'protected speech' involves determining whether LP videos are commercial or cultural, considering whether they contribute to democratic values or not. LP videos, while revenue-generating, primarily aim to entertain, making them distinct from commercial speech. The debate in the general interest criterion focuses on whether streaming contributes to democratic culture, as noted in Ceylan v Turke (1999), Von Hannover v Germany (2012) and Axel Springer AG v Germany (2012). Streaming platforms are identified as spaces for political discussion and critical work, particularly appealing to young people as fora for democratic deliberation.

Conclusion

In conclusion, the intricate landscape of intellectual property rights and freedom of expression within the realm of video game content creation, particularly in the form of LP videos, presents a multifaceted challenge for both creators and industry stakeholders. Nintendo, as a key player, faces the delicate task of balancing the protection of its intellectual property with fostering a positive relationship with the gaming community.

The examination of the InfoSoc Directive reveals a framework aimed at achieving a fair balance between right holders and users, with specific emphasis on fundamental freedoms. The delineation of exceptions, notably the exception for quotations for criticism or review (Article 5(3)(d)), forms a crucial aspect of this regulatory landscape.

As the analysis delves into different categories of LP videos, ranging from reviews to playthroughs with and without commentary, nuanced considerations arise. While reviews with commentary may qualify for copyright exceptions, debates persist regarding playthroughs with commentary and those without, each presenting distinct challenges in the context of the InfoSoc Directive.

The evolving digital gaming environment adds complexity, especially with the rise of live streaming and its intersection with freedom of expression. A number of instances showcase the innovative potential of streaming, but the industry's varied responses to political expressions underscore the complex nature of this evolving landscape. The debate over whether LP videos should be regarded as 'protected speech' necessitates a careful evaluation of their nature, purpose, and contribution to democratic values. Despite being revenue-generating, LP videos primarily aim to entertain, distinguishing them from purely commercial speech. Acknowledging streaming platforms as spaces for political discussion and critical work further underscores their potential societal value.

In the face of legal challenges and instances where copyright has been wielded to stifle criticism, it becomes imperative to strike a balance that not only protects intellectual property but also upholds freedom of expression. The broader implications of these considerations extend beyond the gaming community, reaching into the broader realms of culture, democracy, and the evolving landscape of digital content creation. As the digital era continues to unfold, a thoughtful and adaptive approach is essential to ensure the harmonious coexistence of intellectual property rights and the vibrant expressions facilitated by the diverse world of LP videos.

References

Alexander, J. (2018, November 28). *Nintendo's New Content Guidelines Make It Easier for YouTube Creators to Get Paid. The Verge.* https://www.theverge.com/2018/11/28/18117172/nintendo-youtube-monetization-partner-program-super-smash-bros-ultimate-lets-play-livestream

Asby Donald and others v France App No 36769/08 (ECtHR, 10 January 2013)

Axel Springer AG v Germany App No 39954/08 (ECtHR, 7 February 2012)

Bailey, J. (2015, April 9). *Nintendo's Copyright Blunder.* Plagiarism Today. https://www.plagiarismtoday.com/2015/04/09/nintendos-copyright-blunder/ accessed 27/03/2020.

Blizzard. *Blizzard End-User License Agreement.* https://www.blizzard.com/en-us/legal/fba4d00f-c7e4-4883-b8b9-1b4500a402ea/blizzard-end-user-license-agreement

Borghi, M. (2011). Chasing Copyright Infringement in the Streaming Landscape. *International Review of Intellectual Property and Competition Law, 42*(3), 316 -343.

Brusa, E. (2015). Professional Video Gaming: Piracy that Pays. *J Marshall Law Review, 49,* 217 – 270.

Caguioa, IAC, (2019). Recent Copyright Issues in Video Games, Esports and Streaming. *Ateneo LJ, 63,* 882.

Carlisle, S. (2015, April 2). *The Strange World of "Let's Play" Videos and the Copyright Problems They Create.* NOVA South-Eastern University. http://copyright.nova.edu/lets-play-videos/

Case C-110/15 *Microsoft Mobile Sales International Oy v Ministero per I beni e le attivita culturali* [2016] ECLI:EU:C:2016:717

Case C-355/12 *Nintendo Co Ltd v PC Box Srl* [2014] 1 WLUK 506, ECDR 6

Case C-355/12 *Nintendo Co Ltd v PC Box Srl* [2014] 1 WLUK 506, ECDR 6

Cass. 1re civ., June 25, 2009, *Lefranc c/ Sté SESAM,* pourvoi n°07-20387

Ceylan v Turkey App No 23556/94 (ECtHR, 8th July 1999)

Coogan, K. (2018). Let's Play: A Walkthrough of Quarter-Century-Old Copyright Precedent as Applied to Modern Video Games. *Fordham Intellectual Property, Media and Entertainment Law Journal, 28*(2), 381- 419.

Council Directive 2001/29/EC of the European Parliament and of the Council of 22 May 2001 on the harmonisation of certain aspects of copyright and related rights in the information society [2001] OJ L 167/10

Dyer, M. (2023, August 24). *Nintendo Copyright Claim Kills Metroid Fan Film on Kickstarter.* IGN. https://www.ign.com/articles/2013/08/23/nintendo-copyright-claim-kills-metroid-fan-film-on-kickstarter

Exceptions and Limitations to Copyright. (2017). European Audiovisual Observatory. https://rm.coe.int/168078348b

Farmaki, D. (2022). Copyright Protection of Video Games: a Comparative Study. *IELR, 5*(2), 107.

First Instance Court of Athens (ΠΠρΑθ) case 2221/2015

Frank, A. (2016, September 2). *Nintendo slaps Metroid 2 remake and 500-plus fangames with takedown orders.* Polygon. https://www.polygon.com/2016/9/2/12770344/nintendo-slaps-metroid-2-remake-and-500-plus-fangames-with-takedown-orders

Frank, A. (2019, February 12). *Five Years Ago, Twitch Plays Pokémon Changed Twitch Forever.* Polygon. https://www.polygon.com/2019/2/12/18221792/twitch-plays-pokemon-anniversary

Fredrik Neij and Peter Sunde Kolmisoppi (The Pirate Bay) v Sweden App No 40397/12 (ECtHR, 19 February 2013)

Geiger, C. and Izyumenko, E. (2019). Freedom of Expression as an External Limitation to Copyright Law in the EU: The Advocate General of the CJEU Shows the Way. *EIPR. 41*(3), 131.

Gesetz über Urheberrecht und verwandte Schutzrechte – Urheberrechtsgesetz 1965

Girasa, RJ. (2002). Click-Wrap, Shrink-Wrap, and Browse-Wrap Agreements: Judicial Collision with Consumer Expectations. *Ne J Legal Stud, 10*, 102.

Hagen, D. (2018). Fair Use, Fair Play: Video Game Performances and Let's Plays as Transformative Use. *Wash JL Tech & Arts, 13*, 245.

Harn Lee, Y. (2020). Copyright and Gaming. In T. Aplin (Ed.), *Research Handbook on Intellectual Property and Digital Technologies* (pp. 44-62). Edward Elgar Publishing Limited.

Jungar, E. (2016). Streaming Video Games: Copyright Infringement or Protected Speech? *Press Start*, 3(2), 22-47. https://press-start.gla.ac.uk/index.php/press-start/article/view/63

Kind, C. (2017). Forcing Players to Walk the Plank: Why End-User Licences Agreements Improperly Control Players' Rights regarding Microtransactions in Video Games. *Wm & Mary L Rev, 58,* 1365.

Larkey, M. (2015). Cooperative Play: Anticipating the Problem of Copyright Infringement in the New Business of Live Video Game Webcases. *Rutgers JL & Pub Pol'y, 13*, 52.

Ligman, K. (2013, October 21). *Developer Accused of Using Copyright Takedown to Censor Critic (Updated)*. Gamasutra. https://www.gamasutra.com/view/news/202810/Developer

Lu, T. (2018). Understanding Streaming and Copyright: A Comparison of the United States and European Regimes. *Journal of Business and Technology Law, 13*(2), 185 – 216.

Mackey, S. (2020, October 17), *Nintendo Takes Down Zelda Fan Game Trailers, Website.* Gamerant. https://gamerant.com/nintendo-zelda-missing-link-takedown/

Makeen, MF. (2020). Video Streaming and the Communication to the Public Right in the United States and European Union. In T. Aplin (Ed), *Research Handbook on Intellectual Property and Digital Technologies* (pp. 246-275). Edward Elgar Publishing Limited.

Marfo, N. (2019). Playing Fair: Youtube, Nintendo, and the Lost Balance of Online Fair Use. *Brook J Corp Fin & Com L, 13,* 465.

Matsui, S. (2016). Does it Have to be a Copyright Infringement: Live Game Streaming and Copyright. *Tex Intell Prop LJ, 24*, 215.

Microsoft. (2015). *Game Content Usage Rules.* https://www.xbox.com/en-US/developers/rules

Norowzian v Arks Ltd. (No 2) [2000] FSR 363

Nova Productions Ltd v Mazooma Games Ltd & Ors Rev 1 [2006] EWHC 24 (Ch)

Postel, C. (2017). Let's Play: YouTube and Twitch's Video Game Footage and a New Approach to Fair Use. *Hastings LJ, 68,* 1169.

Puddington, J. (2015). Fair Play: Economic Justifications for Applying Fair Use to the Online Streaming of Video Games. *BU J ScT & Tech L, 21,* 413.

Ramos, A. and others. (2013). *The Legal Status of Video Games. WIPO Report* 7. https://www.wipo.int/edocs/pubdocs/en/wipo_report_cr_vg.pdf.

Riot Games. *Riot Legal Jibber Jabber.* https://www.riotgames.com/en/legal

Skrebels, J. (2020, December 7). *Smash Bros, Splatoon and Other Fan Communities Clash With Nintendo.* IGN. https://sea.ign.com/news/166782/smash-bros-splatoon-and-other-fan-communities-clash-with-nintendo

Smlsalova, J. (2007). Shrink-Wrap/Click-Wrap Agreements and English Contract Law. *Common L Rev, 8*, 13.

Statista Research Department, (2023, November 8). *Lifetime unit sales of the Nintendo Switch console worldwide from March 2017 to September 2023.* Statista. https://www.statista.com/statistics/687059/nintendo-switch-unit-sales-worldwide/.

Steam. *Valve Video Policy.* https://store.steampowered.com/video_policy

Stephen, B. (2019, October 18). *Blizzard is Banning People in Its Hearthstone Twitch Chat for Spamming Pro-Hong Kong Statements.*

The Verge. https://www.theverge.com/2019/10/18/20921301/blizzard-bans-hearthstone-twitch-chat-pro-hong-kong

Taylor, TL. (2018). *Watch me Play: Twitch and the Rise of Game Live Streaming.* Princeton University Press.

Techniques (Anglia) Ltd. v Critchley Components Ltd. [1997] FSR 401

Ubisoft. *Video Policy.* https://www.ubisoft.com/en-us/videopolicy.html

Von Hannover v Germany (No 2) App No 40660/08 (ECtHR, 7 February 2012)

Gaming Their Way to Success: Esports and the Crucial Skills for Tomorrow's Workforce

By Tobias M. Scholz

The age-old admonition, "Stop playing video games and do something productive!" echoes through countless households, a refrain as familiar as it is outdated. As we navigate deeper into the digital era, the traditional paradigms of productivity are ripe for a seismic shift, challenging us to broaden our understanding of what constitutes meaningful engagement in our increasingly digital world.

Sim City: A Gateway to Urban Innovation

Imagine a child, absorbed in the world of Sim City, not just playing, but engaging in a sophisticated exercise of urban planning and management. This scenario transcends mere entertainment; it's a primer on managing urban complexities, resource allocation, and strategic planning. As cities grow more intricate, the skills honed in these virtual environments could well serve as the bedrock for future architects and city planners, offering them a visceral understanding of urban dynamics long before they set foot in a professional setting.

The Virtual Team Dynamics of World of Warcraft

Consider the teenager who leads a 25-member raid in World of Warcraft. Far from a simple pastime, this experience is a deep dive into leadership, team management, and strategic coordination. These are the very competencies that define success in the modern workplace, where managing diverse teams and driving them toward a unified goal is paramount. Through gaming, young leaders are already refining their skills in negotiation, team dynamics, and strategy, gaining a head start in the art of leadership long before their first job interview.

Counter-Strike: A Lesson in Strategic Thinking and Quick Decision-Making

The fast-paced world of Counter-Strike is not just about reflexes; it's a laboratory for strategic thought, risk analysis, and snap decision-making. In professions where time is of the essence—be it in marketing, analytics, or legal fields—the ability to make informed decisions swiftly is invaluable. Gamers are constantly training these skills, each session a microcosm of the high-stakes decision-making that defines many careers.

Beyond Games: A Journey Towards Personal Excellence

Exploring beyond the blockbuster titles, we find that every game, regardless of scale, offers lessons in perseverance, goal setting, and adaptation. Gaming is a microcosm of personal ambition, a space where players tackle challenges, set objectives, and adapt to new situations. This is not mere recreation; it's a training ground for life, where in-game achievements mirror the real-world capacity to overcome obstacles and adapt to change. Recognizing these virtual accomplishments as predictors of real-world success underscores the transformative potential of gaming.

The insights from the European Parliament, brought forth by Scholz and Nothelfer, are more than scholarly musings; they are a call to action. Global giants like BMW, Airbus, and DHL are on a quest for talent that thrives in the esports arena, recognizing that the skills developed in gaming—teamwork, strategic insight, adaptability—are directly applicable and highly sought after in the business world. In the competitive landscape of today's economy, these skills are not just advantageous; they are essential.

This ethos of continuous evolution is central to the esports mindset, fostering a culture where innovation is not just celebrated but expected.

The inherent gaming acumen possessed by many young individuals provides a foundational literacy in digital navigation. However, translating this natural proficiency into professional excellence requires a more structured approach. The University of Agder's pioneering bachelor's program in academic esports represents this bridge, offering a comprehensive curriculum that extends beyond gaming tactics to encompass project management, media production, and storytelling, ensuring that its graduates are well-rounded digital citizens, ready to tackle complex challenges in the business world.

This innovative program also emphasizes the importance of coding and technological fluency, preparing students not just to participate in but to shape the digital landscape. Additionally, the constantly evolving nature of esports instills a critical lesson in adaptability, preparing students for a future where change is the only constant.

The Rise of Company Esports: Blending Competition with Corporate Culture

Across Europe, the phenomenon of company esports is gaining momentum, marking a novel convergence of competitive gaming with corporate culture. This trend goes beyond simple entertainment, offering a unique platform for team building, brand promotion, and strategic partnerships within the esports ecosystem. Graduates from programs like the University of Agder's are perfectly positioned to lead these initiatives, leveraging their dual expertise in gaming and business to foster new forms of engagement and innovation within the corporate sector.

The future beckons with roles that blend gaming acumen with business savvy. Academic esports graduates might find themselves as community managers, nurturing the esports endeavors of their companies, while also serving as innovative strategists, injecting gaming-inspired insights into traditional business models. This hybrid approach reflects a broader trend of merging work and play, signaling a future where professional success is intertwined with digital fluency and gaming expertise.

Esports transcends mere gaming; it embodies a philosophy of perpetual adaptation and innovation. The academic esports program is not just a curriculum focused on gaming mechanics but a comprehensive education in resilience, strategic thinking, and adaptability. It teaches students that the future is not a fixed destination but a landscape that constantly shifts and evolves. Success in such a world demands more than just knowledge; it requires the agility to adapt, innovate, and lead change.

This ethos of continuous evolution is central to the esports mindset, fostering a culture where innovation is not just celebrated but expected. Students learn to view challenges not as obstacles but as opportunities for growth, a perspective that prepares them not only to navigate the future but to actively shape it.

The integration of gaming into academic curricula represents a paradigm shift in education, recognizing the value of gaming not as a diversion but as a potent tool for skill development. The academic esports programme stands as a testament to this shift, translating the passion and engagement of gaming into a structured framework for professional growth and development.

This approach challenges us to rethink our perceptions of gaming, viewing it not as time wasted but as time invested in developing the competencies and cognitive abilities that will define success in the digital age. It under-scores the need to embrace the potential of gaming as a means of preparing the next generation for the complexities of the future.

The Role of Gaming in Shaping Future Leaders

As we look to the future, the role of gaming in education and professional development is set to grow, with programs like academic esports leading the way. These initiatives are not just about harnessing the entertainment value of games but about leveraging the strategic, analytical, and collaborative skills that gaming nurtures.

In this context, gaming becomes a crucible for leadership, innovation, and resilience, qualities that are increasingly vital in our fast-paced, technology-driven world. By aligning gaming passions with academic rigor and professional training, we are preparing a new generation of leaders who are as comfortable navigating the complexities of the digital realm as they are in the physical world.

The fusion of gaming with professional development heralds a new era where the boundaries between work and play blur. In this landscape, the skills honed in virtual worlds become assets in the workplace, and the strategies of gaming inform real-world problem-solving and innovation.

This integration reflects a broader recognition of the diverse ways in which individuals learn and grow, championing an approach to education and professional development that is flexible, engaging, and aligned with the realities of the digital age. It represents a future where gaming is not just a part of our cultural landscape but a key pillar of our educational and professional infrastructures.

In conclusion, the journey from gaming to professional success is not a leap but a natural progression, facilitated by academic programs that recognize and cultivate the potential of esports. As we continue to explore the intersection of gaming and professional development, the message is clear: the skills of tomorrow are being played, practiced, and perfected today, in the virtual arenas of the gaming world. This realization not only challenges our traditional notions of productivity and education but also opens up exciting new pathways for personal and professional growth in the digital age.

Startup Culture Shouldn't Last Forever

By Cora Kennedy

In my talks with colleagues who are higher education researchers, many of them note that putting a positive spin on the data they collect about collegiate esports is a really difficult task. There is a growing mountain of evidence that collegiate is propped up more on promises and IOUs than any actual sound business practice, and that is only sustainable for so long. We are quickly heading on the path of a failed startup, and without positive and purposeful efforts towards change, collegiate esports could end up as just a blip on the history of academia. I don't want to see collegiate falter and die because, for the students who call it home, it is one of the most meaningful parts of college, and sometimes life, for them. I'm writing this piece as a reflection on where we stand now as an industry, where we falter and fail, and how we need to mold ourselves and grow beyond startup culture if we are to continue to grow ourselves into a staple in higher education.

It seems like almost every day there is some new controversy shaking the collegiate and/or professional esports space. From layoffs to infighting to fraud to cheating and so many more things, when you go beneath the surface of esports social media, with all its professional and well-done graphics and posts, the community itself is fraught with drama and a poorly determined understanding of what professionalism is.

Depending on where you check and how you define the true starting point of esports, whether it be Space Invaders competitions in the 80's or the more modern spin on it seen with StarCraft and others in the early 2000's, esports is 25+ years old. Furthermore, starting most notably with the now defunct Robert Morris University (Chicago) esports program in 2014, collegiate esports is nearing 10 years old from when it first started and nearly

six years out from when well established programs started. The ways in which we are still indelibly tied to internet culture baffles outsiders consistently. Why do we so willingly accept that collegiate esports has all the cultural signs of a failed startup? Why do we continue to stay rooted in our ways and refuse to do better? How can collegiate esports expect to be taken seriously by outside stakeholders, most notably the ones that monetarily and structurally allow us to exist at institutions, if we are genuinely an un-serious industry?

The upheaval and layoffs and massive financial instability that gaming and esports as a whole is seeing right now is not something that collegiate esports is immune to. While the failings of professional esports is far beyond the scope of this piece, collegiate is not the end-all be-all solution to the woes of the industry. Honestly, collegiate isn't even close to being as stable as some people think it is. We are plagued by problems that we identified upwards of five years ago or longer and still let persist. We are so overburdened by other things, or in many cases unprepared to address them, that we end up pushing issues off onto someone else or, if we do try to solve it, we create a committee to cover it that will proclaim itself as the new organizational group in collegiate, only to sputter out and die in two years.

Obligatory Credentials for Those Who Gatekeep

I realize that not every reader of this piece may know who I am, so I want to give a brief introduction to myself, my history with esports, and why I genuinely care so much about this space that I would dare criticize it so heavily for the sake of growth. So first off, hi, I'm Cora! I've been invested in esports ever since I started competing in Call of Duty: Black Ops 2 back in 2013 and, upon entering college in 2014, I started heavily following CS:GO, LoL, and basically every other game I could get my hands on. I watched and played so much CS:GO my first two years of college that the old CS:GO stream overlay is burned in on my TV from my dorm. In my later years of college, I started actively scrimming and competing in R6 and upon graduation with my math education degree, I started teaching high school. At that school I started an esports program the second day of new teacher training and ran that, along with a high school state league, for three years before coming to IWU to be the full time Director of Esports here. Since coming to IWU I have worked as the head TO of Venom, the world's first GC Valorant LAN (to my knowledge), created Aurora Series, and served on committees across partnerships, DEI, competition, and community engagement.

We absolutely need to understand and grow as a part of academia instead of insisting we are different enough to warrant special treatment.

In terms of esports, I've been there and done that. I've casted, produced, observed, coached, competed, TO'd, been upper management, done media, and pretty much anything else you can think of, oftentimes many of them concurrently. I am not saying I know everything about esports and gaming, and in fact there are a great many things I know that I don't know, but fuck me if I don't genuinely love and care about esports. I wouldn't be here, putting 80 hour weeks in for the past six years with long sleepless nights, an inability to ever disconnect, and my every waking thought filled with work, if I didn't truly care. The reason I feel compelled to give my qualifications is because I know that if I do not, many people will jump to gatekeep me and

prevent my opinions from being seen as valid because I'm perceived as not qualified enough to point out obvious flaws in our system. I know I need to prove myself, who I am, my qualifications, and why I "deserve" to be heard out in order for anyone to even read beyond this section.

I am writing this piece because I care, potentially too much, about collegiate esports. The amount of good that collegiate esports does cannot be understated. The genuine smiles on the faces of students when they see their team succeed or attend events or any cool marquee moment in their time in collegiate is what I live for. We send students to college where many may not have even sought it out before, we teach a whole host of soft skills, we help some students find meaning in their daily lives, we serve as a cornerstone of their life in a time where so much is changing, act as mentors, parental figures, and friends to those that need it the most, the list goes on and on. Collegiate esports does so many wonderful things for the students we serve, and we make such a positive difference in the lives of so many, but we need to get out of our own way.

This piece is borne out of my frustration with how collegiate esports is refusing to progress beyond accepting startup culture for what it is and patently alienating itself from academia for the sake of convenience. We don't have to constantly be at odds with ourselves, others, and our parent institutions. We absolutely need to understand and grow as a part of academia instead of insisting we are different enough to warrant special treatment. I am not saying everyone needs to have the experience of an educator or previous academic professional, but what I am saying is that we all need to actually learn what academia is like before we try to "revolutionize" it by refusing to listen. I will not be naming names or directly calling people/organizations out because that is counterproductive and only serves to hurt the message trying to be conveyed. What I want to be the end result of all of this is for people to look themselves in the mirror, objectively evaluate the program they run or are a part of, and commit to doing better. A revolution starts with a single brick, and together we can continue to make this space something we are proud of.

How Collegiate Esports is Stuck in Startup Culture

Someone shouldn't be able to ask me "did you hear about that controversy in esports last week" and I have to ask them to clarify which one they're talking about. This, along with many other things, are emblematic of the culture of a toxic tech startup in the dot-com bubble, or even now, and this section is dedicated to identifying how many of the ways toxic startups function mirror how collegiate esports functions as well. While many of these points mirror what exists in professional esports, that is not an acceptable excuse. We are educators, a part of academia! We should model professional conduct and behavior for our students and handle things like adults, not petulant children. We cannot let our culture be determined by people who won't, or can't, be us.

Ego Driven Culture

Bravado and esports go hand in hand, but it doesn't need to be that way. We have seemingly created, and encouraged, a culture where we value ego-based decision making over almost everything else. For good or for bad, esports, and by extension collegiate esports, lives on social media. In turn, we also die on social media. It is an almost daily occurrence that our perpetually online industry culture sees a new controversy pop out of nowhere on Twitter. Public callouts, vague tweets meant to ruffle someone's ego, direct accusations, and more all permeate the sphere of esports social media and many staff at collegiate programs find themselves feeding into it. Interspersed with inane, meaningless takes that are self-aggrandizing at best come posts from staff, full grown adults, that amount to nothing more than ego duels. Everyone wants to act like they have the moral high ground but all it ends up coming out as is obsessive infighting for little tangible gain.

While the corporate world is very much not free from drama, they mostly take care of it like competent and professional adults

whereas collegiate esports would rather turn to making a large public callout and let the court of public opinion take over. This almost obsessive rush to social media any time you feel wronged by a person or organization would be comical if it wasn't so frustratingly consistent. The lack of an ability to address things directly with someone and settle it like well reasoned adults just shows how far collegiate esports needs to go before it can be taken seriously in academia. The amount of drama in academia is monumental at times and as someone who worked as a researcher and has witnessed it live, it's childish yes. But it is not on public display for all to see and people generally resolve their differences like adults.

Furthermore, everything is somehow a contest in collegiate esports. Are we really that sucked into our own ego that we want to make every conversation about winning and losing? Yes, we are a fundamentally competitive ecosystem as we are founded around competition between institutions, but one of the greatest benefits I have always touted about academic esports is just how friendly this industry is. Every coach and director was always willing to talk with others and help each other out. My handbook for the high school team was a straight up rip (with permission) of the 2017–2018 Oswego High School esports handbook with some modifications to suit my situation.

We learn and grow together and this industry was built on the backs of helping each other for the sake of growth for all, so why are we so insistent on making everything into a contest? Social engagement statistics are meaningless, "winning" an argument online does nothing for you, so why are we hell bent on never admitting to shortcomings and doing better? Ego always gets in the way of progress when competition comes before collaboration. If the industry is still truly in its infancy like it is commonly purported to be (ignoring the projected $4.3bn market cap for 2024 — Statista), then why are we so unable to put our differences aside to help others?

Single Point of Failure

Another major red flag of any startup that is doomed to fail, that collegiate esports mirrors, is the tendency to have a single point of failure in an organization. All decisions have to go through one person and there are no checks and balances in place. This almost dictatorship level of control and a refusal to delegate often leads to organizations that will live and die by how willing the person in charge is to sacrifice their entire life for the organization. While having a competent and confident leader in place in an organization is essential to any group, if we function more as a cult of personality and less as a business, we are bound to fail. The same can be said of collegiate esports.

> *We cannot keep operating on handshake deals that only exist in writing in some Discord DM buried eons before in your messages with someone.*

Unfortunately, a problem that collegiate esports, and esports in general, is known for is somehow irresponsible people end up with control of all of the money. We are currently 45 days into 2024 at the time of writing and I have already seen three instances of felony-level embezzlement and fraud in esports, with one of these cases happening in academic esports. And all that we get out of it is an apology post that more or less summarizes to "whoops I did a crime, but I promise I won't do a crime in the future!". I know esports loves to brand itself as a home grown, grassroots community that loves to move fast, necessitating a lack of corporate structure and red tape, but please actually hire qualified and competent people if what you are dealing with involves financial and/or legal matters. Just because you are an organization or person who operates almost entirely online doesn't mean that committing fraud is any less real. We cannot keep accepting that our money disappears into Narnia every time we pay a fee for a league or tournament and the lack of timely payment, or sometimes payment at all, for most everything in esports is something I have been directly questioned about by my administration multiple times. If it gets bad enough that my admin ends up talking with me about this industry being poorly organized, that is concerning.

Bad Business Practices are Normal

I will concede that organizations without a lot of structure can move incredibly quickly, accomplishing a great deal of things in a short amount of time and esports was built on chasing our passions with this sort of vigor. However, the normalization and acceptance of genuinely bad business practices for the sake of convenience and "I don't know how to do it the right way" in collegiate esports has been drawing raised eyebrows since day one and still does. We cannot keep operating on handshake deals that only exist in writing in some Discord DM buried eons before in your messages with someone. If you were to get a job offer from a legitimate business, say the academic institution you work for, but they don't give you a contract or more or less anything else that says the details of your agreement, you would call the Department of Labor instantly. So why do we accept this in collegiate esports? It is really frustrating to go to ink a deal with someone with a formal contract and the other miscellaneous articles associated with a business or hiring deal only to be met with "I haven't ever had to do this before". This sort of red tape exists for a reason and it's not just to slow things down. It's to get proper authorization, understand the commitments all parties make, and to indemnify people in case of the worst. This cannot be a rare occurrence and we need to keep pushing for paperwork to be normalized.

Collegiate esports loves to bank on goodwill, utilizing promises over action and offering nothing more than an IOU for almost everything we do. Almost everyone in collegiate has some sort of story that ends with "and I was doing all of this...as a volunteer" and I myself have done many things at my own expense. My budget when I was running the high school team was genuinely my own credit card and every cent and more of my coaching stipend I was paid went directly back to the team. We so commonly accept working ourselves to the bone now for the promise of potentially being paid in the future that when I directly said I would pay all of my Aurora Series staff for the work they do, some of them sounded surprised. We shouldn't be ok with being taken advantage of for the sake of doing cool stuff. Know your worth and stand by it.

Furthermore, when it comes to money, collegiate esports loves to do everything digitally, much to the chagrin of university business offices everywhere. I had to fight tooth and nail to get a Paypal account for my team because I know that 99% of tournament organizers would only take payments and distribute funding that way. However, I ran the whole process through my administration and I tell them every time I use it because we cannot just circumvent proper practices with money because we want to. For many organizations in collegiate, they run it barely legally and often track funds and payments with only one person in charge of them, using a Google Form to see who needs to get paid, and without anyone with an accounting background involved.

If Everything is Urgent, Nothing is

When working for or with a larger esports organization beyond your own institution, volunteering your time for a cause you care about, a sense of false urgency creeps into all facets of the work. Volunteers and people who do things out of goodwill are the beating heart behind much of the progress and change in collegiate esports, but they so often get overwhelmed and have their role expanded far beyond what they signed up for. Broadly speaking, job titles tend to mean nothing in collegiate esports and the blending of duties on a moment's notice is a sign of how understaffed we are as an industry and how complacent we have become with this.

We all love bringing students into the fold and teaching them valuable skills in the industry like broadcasting, tournament organization, media, and all the other behind the scenes things that happen beyond just competition. As such, it is incredibly disheartening to see the student staff of most organizations in collegiate have a monumentally high turnover rate and need to be re-trained from scratch almost each semester. The students who step up and make our industry run, whether internally in our own programs or as a part of larger organizations, are invaluable and need to be protected at all costs. However, when their roles and scope of responsibilities are constantly shifting, I can't blame them for being overwhelmed when trying to balance their own schooling, their own esports program, their student work, and any semblance of a personal life they may have left.

I mentor many students outside of IWU and many of them share this same story, how everything has been billed as urgent to them and they barely have time to breathe and live their own life, leading to stress breakdowns and worse. Hustle culture is constant in our society, but we as staff members in collegiate esports are hired specifically to protect and help our students, so to see so many of the hired adults in the room blind to the open struggles of students is disheartening.

Refusing to be a Part of Academia

Beyond the ways in which collegiate esports culture mirrors that of a struggling startup, we are also often failing our mission of being part of academia as well. It is called "Collegiate Esports" for a reason, and while this industry employs many non-academics, that does not mean that we cannot think and act like academics. We cannot claim to be a part of academia, and reap the structural and financial benefits of being associated with an institution, while patently refusing to actually do most of what academia does. While the culture and practices of academia may not be perfect, and yes there are many ways in which they need to be fixed, it is a genuinely good and functional starting point for esports programs to build up from. We are not here to just do esports, and refusing to go beyond that is doing a disservice to your students, your program, your institution, and the industry as a whole.

What is Your Motivation for Being Here

The first question I ask whenever I talk to someone looking to get into collegiate esports as a staff member, whether they be a student leader, esports professional, or an outsider entirely, is "why do you want to be here?" If their answer isn't something along the lines of "for the students", I do my best to counsel them away from leadership roles in collegiate. Working at a university, and especially in a student facing position like being part of an esports program staff, necessitates that people genuinely care about their students beyond just what they can accomplish as a player. The first principal I worked under, Doug Sczinski, would always ask me one question when I proposed a new idea to him: "is it good for the students?" If I could say yes and explain why, he would agree to my idea almost without hesitation. Beliefs like that, that all our decisions need to be rooted in being good for the students, is what carries me forward every day and is why I put the happiness and wellbeing of my students above almost anything else.

I now ask myself "is this good for students beyond just them as an esports player?" whenever I can. Broadly speaking, you don't get into academia for the pay, and in fact almost every list and survey I can find frankly refuses to discuss pay because it is widely known that educators are not being paid well. Pay is the last thing on anybody's mind because being able to make an impact and help students grow in a crucial time in their life always comes first for any good educator, so to see someone not value the students at all is disheartening.

So why do we still have people in collegiate esports who value winning over the sanity and happiness of their students? Are the results of some random match or potential championship even worth sacrificing everything for? We have seen how poorly this sort of mindset, as well as the mismanagement of player wellbeing, goes in the professional space, most notably with the struggles and failings of Evil Geniuses and their former player Danny, so why do we allow programs who cycle through players like crazy to still exist? Collegiate esports cannot continue to prop up and celebrate the successes of programs who run on a "winning first" mindset if it comes at the cost of their students. We are actively moving away from our mission as educators, and given we work in academia we are all educators whether we know it or not, by abandoning community building, student support, and advocacy for our students for the sake of prize money and some internet fame.

Caring about students can take many forms too, and many of them aren't exactly cheery ones. Celebrating successes with students is just as meaningful as being there for struggles, and as the eminent "adult" in the room as a collegiate staff member, it is your job to help students feel at home in your program and institution as best you possibly can. A thing commonly talked about in student affairs administration in higher ed is how impactful just your presence can be. Showing up in campus spaces that are not necessarily your own to support or join in with your students such as sporting events, arts performances, or even just grabbing a meal with them in the campus dining center, can change their perspective greatly and make an impact they may not even realize.

Being present for students also means being there when they struggle though. It is well understood that college can be one of the most stressful times in a student's life up until that point, and many of them are facing life struggles outside of college that make the pressures of school and competition even worse. When their mental health is at an all time low, students may look for any trusted adult around them to help, and if you make yourself available to them and build trust, that adult can be you. I cannot count the number of late night calls students have made to me to just talk them off a metaphorical ledge. While it's not my job, I couldn't live with myself if I didn't. Referring them to resources and helping them where you can and are able to are hidden parts of actually caring about your students that very few things prepare you for, but you have to be ready when they happen.

Lack of Professional Development

Professional development can take on a great many forms, but at its base level, it's a training that helps you be better at your job … that's it. So the lack of meaningful and useful professional development training and tools in collegiate esports is frankly appalling given how long the space has existed. Some do exist, such as NAECAD and smaller panel series, but the low turnout at these sorts of things is frustrating as well. The people who go to these trainings tend to be very new to the space, and as such training is geared towards them. This leaves a gap where higher level content does not exist and your development as a professional stalls unless you are intrinsically motivated to seek it out or create it yourself.

> *We have a responsibility to model professional and productive conduct inside our departments, in our institutions, on social media, and with other colleagues in the industry.*

Professional development in collegiate esports as it currently stands mostly consists of small, one-on-one conversations with people you trust, but this can also create an echo chamber wherein new content and ideas are dismissed for not already being an idea one of the in-crowd has. Meanwhile in academia, the training never stops and there are an abundance of resources at all levels and all contents and you are expected to attend a minimum number of certified professional development seminars per year in order to retain your teaching license. While higher education is a bit less regulated in this regard, professional development is still an expectation and you are seen as a failing professional for not being a participant.

Given the broad lack of professional development specifically for collegiate esports, the next best thing is to train yourself as a higher ed professional. If we as an industry are going to keep hiring folks who don't have an educational background because they know esports (a practice that has its merits), then we need to train them up to be higher education professionals. Below are some that I have been through or heard good things about:

- Green Dot training around bystander recognition and intervention.
- Any and ALL campus training that is offered to staff.
- Most anything NASPA hosts as many of us are in student affairs.
- It would also be beneficial to keep up with the Chronicle of Higher Education and Inside Higher Ed to understand trends in the space and know more about higher ed as a whole.
- Talk with your direct supervisor, they will undoubtedly know many PD opportunities.

Modeling Professionalism

We are the proverbial "adults" in the room for our students, and as such a lot of our behaviors will rub off on them or they will learn lessons from them. We have a responsibility to model professional and productive conduct inside our departments, in our institutions, on social media, and with other colleagues in the industry. Given this, it has been increasingly frustrating to see how collegiate esports has been trending towards more and more unprofessional communication and interactions. Like I mentioned earlier, ego seems to supersede all logical thinking when it comes to social media in esports, and engaging in this teaches students that "hehe funny numbers go up" justifies being unprofessional and overall detrimental to the image of our industry.

No other part of academia struggles this much with a negative social media presence and it is embarrassing to have to explain this week's newest drama to my supervisor because he follows our program and saw more esports drama in his "for you" tab on Twitter. Genuinely, learn from your colleagues in higher education. Have you ever noticed how most folks in higher education do not care one bit about their social media clout and just love what they do? We all set examples for our students in how we talk about other programs privately too, and generally clamping down on language and conversations isn't limiting free speech, it's modeling professionalism. You set an example every day for your students, make it a good one.

Leaving Marginalized People by the Wayside

Time and time again I have seen, and been told directly, how students from marginalized populations in terms of the institution, or in terms of esports, feel like a fly on the wall in their own program and it's disheartening to hear every time. I have directly seen how some staff members in collegiate esports do not pay attention or help students who do not share an identity with them, and that fundamentally fails the mission of academia. Being a member of academia means that you are there to serve the students, all of them, and intentionally failing to do so shows a refusal to understand the mission of higher education.

Students from marginalized communities are not just a problem for the Office of Diversity and Inclusion on your campus, and in fact falls on you as a staff member because those students are under your care. If students are differently abled, it is your responsibility to enable them to succeed with technology and other such measures. I have seen firsthand from another director the impact that getting an adaptive controller can have on the positive outcomes of a student and I genuinely wish every other person in this space thought like they did.

Being in academia means working with everyone, and it is your responsibility to create a welcoming environment by your words and actions in order to do this. Avoid tokenizing students (see my piece on this here), don't set their value solely on their competitive outcomes (see my piece on this here), and understand how a program's culture comes from you as a staff leader (see my piece on this here). I am not perfect, and I am not trying to claim that my way of doing things is

the objective right way to do things. However, I want this whole piece, and especially this section, to spark thought within you about the students you serve and how you can better serve them.

Realism and Enacting Positive Change

I understand that a majority of this piece has been fairly negative and admonishing, but I needed to sufficiently and properly explain the shortcomings of the system(s) we currently have and how collegiate esports falls short of what it proclaims itself to be. This is by no means an exhaustive list (future publications may come expanding on some of these topics), but I want it to spark thoughts and help others understand what they want to change and how. Introspection and a realistic reflection on where we stand now is the only way we can take steps forward for the betterment of the space for the sake of the students that call it home. In the end, it's all about students, and like my former principal said, the first thought behind everything we do must be if it's good for the students. While the solutions I propose below are not complete and do not fully cover every situation, I want them to be a guiding thought process that can help all of us be realistic about where we are now and how we can elevate ourselves.

Understand Your Core Values

When doing research for this, I did some genuinely searching on what a toxic startup culture looked like (see above sections) and how to remedy it and almost every piece I found directly or indirectly talked about starting with setting core values, understanding them, and living by them. So genuinely, stop for a moment and outline what your core values are right now for yourself, your program and your institution (you can look at your institution's strategic plan for this generally). Then, make a second list of what you want these values to be if you are not already there. When creating a values list, think about what motivates you as a person and why you even care to be here. I will stop right now and say if it is for the paycheck and not the students, please leave collegiate esports, nobody will miss you. Once you have that, start living that out and modeling that for all students to see.

Talk with your colleagues, your staff, your student leaders, and anyone else who will listen and just talk about what you love about what you do and why you do it. Talking about values you genuinely believe in and follow through on will almost never come off as preachy and generally comes off as just genuine. Culture comes from the top, and so do values, and setting core values that guide your decision making process and everything that you do will make a world of difference.

Burnout is the Only Endgame Right Now

Virtually every collegiate esports director I talk to says that they are burned out. Coaches say that they are burned out, student workers say they are burned out, players say they are burned out, everyone is burned out. Esports is an industry that preys on passion and preaches hustle culture above all else because if you outwork your opponent, you supposedly have a better chance of succeeding. This industry is purpose-built to take advantage of people and burn them out. There is a distinctly non-zero number of staff in collegiate esports who consider self-harm and suicidal ideation every school year because of the stresses of their job, something that is a clear warning sign that this industry is destined to chew up people at a record rate.

You know your limits, you learn what works and what doesn't, and you learn more about the population you work with and how you can more effectively work with them.

A conversation I see people starting to have is "what happens once all the good people leave?" and honestly, I don't have a good answer. Collegiate esports is seeing a slow but consistent exodus of staff from programs because they are burnt out and can't take it anymore and finally take that step for themselves, but what happens next? How do we recover our continuity of knowledge, subject matter experts, and people who are willing to work themselves to death for this space if they all leave?

Thoughts like this are never far from my mind as many people I have talked with have all said something along the lines of "I want out of esports now" for burnout related reasons, and I can't blame them. We all need to be vigilant as a community to help others through burnout as well as spot it in ourselves. We get vacation time, sick time, and sometimes mental health days that we can all use and should be actively using. Balancing work and life is a constant struggle as a working adult, but any steps we can take towards modeling what a healthy balance looks like for our students is a positive one. So please, take some time to outline a reasonable weekly schedule for you, compensating your time when you work late and adjusting your schedule as needed and allowed in order to not work overtime as much as you can. Outline vacation time, plan things for yourself, and do your best to take care of yourself. Burnout is the only endgame right now, and that cannot continue to be the case if we want to continue keeping our veterans around and not scare off our new staff.

Learning From Missteps

One of the hardest things for me to realize as a new educator was that my degree was just a piece of paper. Much of the learning I did in my education classes was under highly idealized situations and applied to very select populations. The reason education at all levels prioritizes experience over degree level in many cases is because experience changes everything. You know your limits, you learn what works and what doesn't, and you learn more about the population you work with and how you can more effectively work with them. Along with this comes an understanding of where you fall short. Knowing what you don't know is just as important as knowledge in the first place, and being able to ask for help and learn from your mistakes in collegiate esports separates people who are here for the long run from those who just want their name on a liquipedia page somewhere. Your administrators and supervisors are genuinely experienced people who, in all likelihoods, know a lot more than you about a ton of things. While they may not have experience with the specific issues you may be facing in esports, listening to their experience and understanding the comparisons you can make to your own situation will go a very long way.

Truly Embody a Higher Education Professional

Improving as a higher education professional starts with genuine, purposeful introspection. If you want to keep getting into ego-fueled petty slap fights on social media over things that could be better settled with a direct conversation as opposed to garnering public favor, then that's ok. But please, get out of collegiate esports then, you're an embarrassment as a professional and modeling awful behavior for every student who looks up to you. Being a professional means being able to swallow your pride, your petty sense of justice, and having respectful, professional, and well reasoned conversations with others. If you want to improve the space and are passionate about it, great!! But don't do that by demeaning and putting down others.

This point will always ring true: higher education professionals do not (broadly speaking) act like how collegiate esports people act like. Furthermore, we cannot chalk that up to "that's esports baby!" and move on. If we are going to embed ourselves as a core part of a student's experience in their time in higher education, we need to actually act like it.

Constant infighting, petty vague tweets, and gatekeeping non-endemics only serves to alienate us from higher education and draw further ire from administration. Actually, be a higher education professional and look to your administration and colleagues across campus for what to do and how to get there. You aren't doing this alone if you don't want to, but isolating yourself for the sake of being excused from professionalism is one quick way to get there.

Conclusion

Collegiate esports is no longer in the infant stages as we can still claim. Many well established programs are approaching over five years of age, millions in scholarship money is being thrown around, and the travel budget for many teams exceeds my salary. Given all of this, we cannot keep excusing and allowing the industry to retain the culture of a failed startup, fueled by ego and empty promises, and we absolutely have to do better. If we want to be a part of higher education in the long run, we need to get over ourselves, our petting infighting, our refusal to adapt as higher education professionals, our shoddy business practices, all of it. We need to start modeling what being a genuine professional looks like for our colleagues and students and stop accepting the excuse of "esports is still new, we are allowed to be different". Yes we are different, no we should not be using this to excuse open, felony-level, fraud and other such massive missteps. We can do better and I am deeply frustrated by colleagues in collegiate esports who keep leaning on the old ways for the sake of retaining an ever dwindling semblance of power. If we burn out all the people that truly care about students over profit and praise, who is left then?

CS:GO to Valorant: Informal Reflections on an Ongoing Auto-Netnographic Journey in Esports

By Brian McCauley

Consumer journeys in esports are dynamic as consumers engage in a variety of differing experiences within the same consumption field (Huston et al, 2022). The following account is an informal reflection on my own consumer journey of starting to play online esports titles during the pandemic as part of an auto-netnographic study. As a lifelong gamer that has been to a multitude of esports events and interviewed literally hundreds of community members I considered myself an *authentic* esports researcher. But you don't have to have been a player or a gamer to be a legitimate researcher of esports. For many of my ongoing research projects, I actively seek out collaborators who don't have that background in order to bring neutral perspectives and a balanced view to analyses. It's not that I am a more 'authentic' researcher after engaging with both CS:GO and Valorant for the previous four years. Instead what I have gotten is a more nuanced understanding of what esports is for the majority of the audience. There are aspects of esports I could never have appreciated fully without engaging as a player. What I present here are the aspects of esports that were fully realized for me through the act of play.

The three defining characteristics of esports are that it is human, digital and competitive (Scholz, & Nothelfer, 2022) and so esports has been around since digital gaming began. In fact, the first game invented by physicists in 1958, 'Tennis for Two', was multiplayer and could be characterized as such. So having gamed across almost every available platform over the last (almost) forty years, I've engaged in a lot of esports, before the concept was even defined. What is possibly my first time playing video games actually exists in an old video from a family get together on my uncle's farm. As my uncle wanders through the event filming, he captures five year old me playing on the Spectrum against my cousin, Rory. We were playing Match Day, a soccer simulator on the Spectrum which was released in 1984 and both of us were entranced. And so began a lifetime of engaging in esports through playing games against my friends. The defining game of my teen and early adult years was Pro Evolution Football or 'Pro Evo' as we called it across several generations of consoles. While EA's franchise has since superseded Konami's in terms of global appreciation, it was the evenings spent playing PES while drinking cheap beers with friends that perhaps defined my early adulthood. There were of course other 90's games that truly delivered an authentic esports experience. You have to be a certain age to remember the jolt of fear experienced as someone dropped a coin in the Street Fighter II arcade machine to challenge you as you played. If they beat you, then game over, as was the sacrifice of ten pence that could have been spent on a tasty treat. These were real stakes for a ten year old and modern children will never have to choose between playing and candy. Those born digital instead exist in a world where gaming is mainstream and esports is increasingly a part of their social identity (Cestino et al., 2023).

Yet gaming has always been part of my identity, before it was cool and mainstream. Like many Generation Xers, the esports aspect of it lapsed as adulthood took over. For many, single player games become the easiest route to gaming as leisure. Work, schedules, relationships, family and a myriad of adult complexities conspire to make gaming a treat enjoyed only through sacrificing other responsibilities. Modern esports as we know it, started its mainstream rise in 2014 when Amazon acquired Twitch (Scholz, 2019). Around then I was a university researcher in Vietnam, indulging in single player Playstation 4 games through an internet connection that could be best described as 'patchy'. It was actually through a study on gaming culture in Vietnam (see: McCauley et al., 2020a) that the prevalence of esports became apparent. Esports was a key thread running through all of the findings in that paper and it was when I moved to Sweden and Jönköping, the 'City of DreamHack' that I truly became engaged as an esports researcher. The city then hosted DreamHack twice a year and also had one of the first Kappa Bars, a bar dedicated to gaming and esports where I met many of my first friends in Sweden. It was at Kappa and DreamHack that I first experienced esports as community, spectacle and identity. I was meeting people whose passion, knowledge and commitment was at another level to mine. This ongoing and immersive learning experience was a catalyst for my role in the Esports Research Network and also resulted in the paper on regional esports actors (see: McCauley, Tierney & Tokbaeva, 2020b). What many academics don't like to admit is what they don't know while I'll happily profess my ignorance so I can learn more. There is so much that I don't know and indeed can't know. What I (and other researchers) have is a different, often unique, perspective, one that is informed through collating and analyzing the experiences of others. Despite my engagement with esports starting before many of my younger friends were born, I was still a 'noob' when it came to playing modern esports. Perhaps the only good thing to come out of the Covid 19 pandemic for me personally was that I got the opportunity to enjoy esports as a player, consumer and member of the community.

Sweden never really experienced lockdown like other countries. But working from home was advised so I found myself at home with my work laptop which was inherently better performing than my aging and battered Asus.

On a whim I decided to download CS:GO as one part diversion and one part curiosity around the experience. I had already experienced and enjoyed live CS:GO tournaments including the 2019 Cologne Major where ERN was founded. I had sat through live streams at Kappa Bar as patient friends had explained to me (the 'esports professor') the intricacies of weapons, maps and tactics. I had watched over the shoulders of 'JUSTICE' (Jönköping University Student Team In Competitive Esports) as they competed live in the LAN lanes at several DreamHacks. I had been told many times by esports friends that I should forget console FPS games and join the 'Master Race' of PC gamers in order to play 'properly'. So amid the pressures of the pandemic, I found myself playing CS:GO casual mode through my wireless connection on a laptop that could just about handle it. And it was brilliant. Over four months, I completed a total of 300 hours in casual mode until my friend Anton helped me build a low cost gaming PC and I was ready to try CS:GO in its proper 5 vs 5 esports mode. I started to keep a diary of my experiences that officially began on the 22nd of September 2020 when I played my first competitive game, solo queuing on the CS:GO matchmaking services.

Those born digital instead exist in a world where gaming is mainstream and esports is increasingly a part of their social identity.

For methodology I stuck to the works of Robert Kozinets and approached this as an auto-netographic study (Kozinets & Kedzior, 2009). Ethnographic methods and approaches are unique to each researcher and the context being investigated (Kozinets, 2015, 2020) with auto-netnography is defined as an "approach to netnography that highlights the role of the netnographer's own experiences of his or her own online experiences" (Kozinets & Kedzior, 2009, p. 12). It's about applying a technocultural lens to explain the increasing pervasiveness of digitality within society, written from a less formal first-person perspective (Kozinets, 2020). In our increasingly digital world I agree with him that "netnography should be at the vanguard of service experience studies of new immersive technology contexts" (Kozinets 2022 p 105). More details of my approach can be read in the paper I published through this study (see: McCauley, 2023) but in essence I was following the approach of Emma Witowski. In her seminal work, published in Games and Culture, Witowski described how her playing experience in Counter Strike has advantaged her. "As a playing researcher, I have played both CS 1.6 and CSS in LAN settings as well as online for several years. Playing has offered a visceral experience of the field of play that the players contend with; a sense of how timing and teamwork sits in the body; an experience of focus, accuracy, and body control; as well as a feel for the technologies in play" (Witowski, 2012 p352). Between May 2020 and January 2022 I completed and documented over 2000 hours of play in CS:GO. Adding to this, between October 31st 2021 and April 16th 2023, I played Valorant by Riot Games for a total of 1081 hours through 1320 competitive Games and 655 unrated games. Since I stopped documenting my play experiences and at the time of writing I have played a further 471 hours. So in total I have completed in excess of 3500 hours of play across a period of four years. It's an average of fifteen hours a week spread over that period but that does include the around a year and a half of the pandemic where socializing physically wasn't an option (if I can offer that in defense).

My approach to documentation included screenshotting every match outcomes, purchase or unusual experience while reflecting on games, interactions, training and emotions experienced. In total my CS:GO diaries exceed 350,000 words while my Valorant diaries are approx 155,000 words with approximately ten thousand screenshots between both. It's a lot of data and it's going to require a lot of work to articulate it fully through peer reviewed research papers. My paper on smurfing (McCauley, 2023) only scratched the surfaces of my experiences as a consumer

and an esports/marketing academic. Within esports, incoming players are 'new consumers' that are socialised within online consumption collectives through a network of practices that can be both constructive and destructive (Huston et al., 2023). The value of my experiences as a 'new' consumer are not constrained to marketing or business arenas but instead reflect the interdisciplinary nature and potential of esports (Brock, 2023). The following are some of my reflections on becoming a more 'authentic esports researcher'. Auto-netnographic approaches to understanding consumption of esports through the act of play have value for researchers as "it allows a more nuanced appreciation of complex phenomena experiences" (McCauley, 2023, p 9). In no particular order the following represent some facets of the context that were made tangible to me through active engagement with playing esports FPS titles.

Skills, Learning and Mastery

Esports titles are different from normal gaming in that ongoing engagement with esports titles requires a mastery of a variety of skills (Witowski, 2012). Yet measuring and indexing these skills as performance indicators is complicated. Clear indicators such as final game score or a player's kill death ratio may not fully measure a player's contribution in CS:GO (Sharpe et al., 2023). Great players have quick reactions ,great mouse control and accuracy combined with game sense and communication skills (Sharpe et al., 2023). Becoming a better player takes time and effort. I love that esports science is increasingly pointing to a focused and planned approach to improvement as opposed to the grind of playing ten hours a day. But you still have to spend time immersed in the game to develop your game sense which is 'knowing what to do in a certain situation, from prior experience or understanding the timings of the game perfectly' (Sharpe et al., 2023). I have put the time and effort into becoming a better player at both CS:GO and Valorant through playing, training and researching. Yes, I am a better player than when I started but still I'm a lower skilled CS:GO player based on my past rank (see: McCauley, 2023). I did briefly reach the higher skilled rank of Gold Nova four based on previous categorizations (Toth et al., 2021) but calling myself higher skilled as an esports player is not something I can do with a straight face. My highest rank achieved through solo queuing in Valorant is Gold 2 but the majority of my time has been spent in the bottom 50% of the player base.

While playing CS:GO I spent time training and tracking my training performances in my diaries. The key thing I learned from that experience within that particular game was the importance of spray training. I spent hours trying to control the bullet spray of various guns through countering the spray pattern until it became automatic. If I could go back and do it again I would have started with this as the key aspect to master before playing. I listened to podcasts and news while I did it so that it wasn't so much 'wasted time'. I looked up videos and made notes on a range of precise smoke grenades and flashbangs for each specific map. I found a video that claimed thirty minutes a day of aim training for a month could make others think you're cheating because of how good your aim would be. Spoiler alert, it didn't. What got me to the Gold Nova four rank was finding and joining a group of four German friends playing together as a team. We played the specific map 'Nuke' together and through communication and teamwork strung together a series of victories that allowed me to rank up.

Soft skills such as communication, teamwork and leadership are inherently sharpened through competitive play that involves problem solving and strategizing.

When I started playing Valorant, I had spent time 'mastering' the FPS mechanics of the keyboard and mouse through CS:GO. So I had a head start entering the game compared to my previous experience. I had played a couple of games during an online games conference but I made sure to have a full clear day when starting to play the game as research. In simple terms, Valorant is CS:GO layered with Blizzard's Overwatch so the basics of the game were familiar to me. The unique characteristics of each agent however required a new learning curve, both in terms of using them but also responding to them as opposition across a variety of maps that augmented the use of individual abilities. Optimally successful teams have a complimentary team structure and coordinate their abilities through clear communication and strategies. Unfortunately at the lower ranks it is more a case of trying to fumble your way through responses to what your teammates do, with many of them unwilling to use their mic and communicate.

Limitations on every published study resulting from my auto-netnographic journey will have to include that the experience was limited by my (lack of) skill. I'm not necessarily a bad player but I'm certainly not a good player and I'm fine with the label 'lower skilled' at both Valorant and CS:GO. I realize that I could spend twenty minutes a day aim training and could research 'lineups' for specific agents on specific maps. But that's 'work' I don't need as someone approaching 43 years of age with work and life commitments. But now at least I do understand the effort required to engage in playing esports at all levels. And the skills that come with play cannot be understated.

Over the last month I've watched my partner's son, Zaia, move from Roblox on his tablet to beating 'Ori and the Blind Forest' on my Xbox. Through completing the game he had to develop new ways of strategizing that were unavailable to him through the simplicity of Roblox games. We have started to play the co-operative game, 'It Takes Two' and after only a few hours of play, he is now spotting things before me and our progress through the game has accelerated. He's almost eight so maybe there's a bit of time left before I introduce him to esports titles such as CS2 or League of Legends. But my own experiences of play have left me optimistic that engaging with esports can level up a host of crucial skills relevant for the modern world. Soft skills such as communication, teamwork and leadership are inherently sharpened through competitive play that involves problem solving and strategizing. Similar to traditional physical sports, esports can be used as a platform to develop a range of skills (Scholz, & Nothelfer, 2022). The 2022 EU resolution on video games and esports recognizes that more esports should be used in education to help develop young people. But as I've learned through my experiences there are also challenges to fully realizing this.

People and the Emotional Rollercoaster of Competitive Play

Playing esports titles can be an intense experience, no matter what level you play at. One of the motivations to smurf articulated to me was the sheer effort and pressure of playing at the higher ranks of a game (McCauley, 2023). But my experiences have allowed me to understand that this pressure can happen at all levels as you're dealing with a wide variety of people. Hedlund (2021) identified that only 28 % of players play truly competitively with the majority engaging for more casual reasons. My favorite quote that explains the reality of matchmaking in esports is as "some kid in his room that just presses the play button" (McCauley, 2023). When you join a matchmaking server and press the play button, you join a team of random strangers that have different motivations, expectations and capabilities. Optimally this leads to 'friended strangers' (Karluhati, 2020), those who you become friends with through play. I've talked to a lot of people at the DreamHack LAN events, and have ongoing studies on LAN events from the perspectives of organizers and attendees. What I always loved was when people explained to me they were meeting in real life for the first time but had played together online for years. Playing CS:GO during the pandemic was a brilliant social outlet for me. I added a diverse range of people as friends on Steam during that period and actively played with them. This experience allowed me insights on the legitimacy of relationships formed through gaming. The best experiences in either CS:GO or Valorant are while playing with positive communicative teammates who don't get upset or frustrated during games.

Conversely the randomness of matchmaking and the perceived anonymity of online play can lead to negative experiences through other people. Through my experiences in both games, I have observed that smurfing, cheating and griefing is much more prevalent in CS:GO than Valorant. Yet the experiences in both games are inherently based on those you play with and against. I actively had to learn to regulate my emotions during games and not respond to negative actors. It's more difficult than one may imagine, with most games reflecting the intensity of traditional sports without the physical proximity of your teammates or opposition. It's hard to stay calm when a game is finely poised during the last round and your random teammate decides to throw the game as an act of malice. I'm a middle aged man who has lived and worked on several continents, accumulating a lot of experiences that most people will not. Yet even I find it hard to play well when a 15 year old teammate is getting verbally aggressive due to a perceived mistake by me. It's often the perfect storm of internet anonymity and *perceived* high stakes outcomes, which can be enhanced through a variety of external pressures such as a pandemic or teenage angst. This experience has allowed me to fully appreciate the value of how grassroots esports actors can structure environments and pass on positive values (McCauley et al., 2020; Cestino et al., 2023). I'm not a teenager who feels powerless within a life that is dictated by higher powers (parents) while the world seemingly swirls in chaos. And for that I am grateful. Everytime someone uses 'gay' or a variation as a slur or in a derogatory way, my mind immediately goes to how impactful that would be for a young person struggling with their sexual identity. Being told "you're shit" or to "delete the game" is not pleasant for me, or indeed anyone. But I can imagine it's worse for a shy fourteen year old introvert who wants to make friends or the top fragging female player being told that, just because she used her mic and identified herself as a 'girl'. Like any and all digital environments, esports can be a platform to experience sexism, racism and general toxicity. A fully sustainable esports future needs to be socially sustainable (Nyström et al., 2022). And there's a lot of ongoing efforts to achieve this, every member of the community can play a part.

Representation & Evolution of Games

The approaches of both CS:GO and Valorant have allowed me to understand a lot of what can be done to address issues within gaming communities. The matchmaking platform for CS:GO has always been a wild west of randomness when it comes to players. My diaries are replete with examples of cheaters or toxic experiences. When people get serious about CS:GO they move to a platform with anti-cheat software such as Faceit. I tried it for a while but it came with a different form of toxicity through pressure by teammates to perform and win. Riot Games on the other hand require their anti cheat 'Vanguard' be installed in order to play on the main game server. Essentially through starting to play both games, you will experience a lot more cheaters on CS:GO although many don't like the perceived invasive nature of the Vanguard software. But what truly stands out for me in terms of how publishers can improve the player experience is through Valorant's approach to representation and their reporting functions.

Statistics vary on the player bases for both games in terms of demographics such as gender. Somewhere between 5 – 20% of CS:GO players are female while estimates on Valorant are between 30 - 40%. While females represent fully 50% of all gamers this is not reflected in esports with many playing alternate genres to online multiplayer esport titles. The internet is not the best place to be female with 20% of UK Generation Z males recently expressing admiration for the grotesque ponderings of a certain mister Andrew Tate. Video games have traditionally been viewed as a 'male' leisure pursuit (e.g. GamerGate) and its seemingly still gate kept well in esports by males enjoying the anonymity of online gaming. If you're being cynical then you have to think that it's in the game publisher's interest to tap into that 50% of gamers. Actually from a business perspective, that's a no-brainer. But what Valorant does

so well is provide representation through choice of agents. Half the agents you can choose from are female and from my perspective many of them are essential to a well functioning team. And they are not overly sexualised unlike the purple haired female skin I used in CS:GO that sounded worryingly sexual when they spoke. It's hard for the white cis straight male from a middle class background to understand a lack of representation in the media. But it does matter and playing Valorant while talking to female teammates about their experiences has helped me understand this. I still get occasional male teammates being weird or inappropriate when they realize our teammate is a female when they speak. Similarly you occasionally get teammates from 'conservative religious' backgrounds that like to preach that they hate homosexuals. Apart from verbally picking them apart in a calm logical manner, you can also report their behavior through the easy to use function provided in game. There is positive reinforcement through messages from Riot confirming that the offending player was penalized. Usually they lose access to their main account for a period of time but the simple confirmation that it happened is enough to positively reinforce my behavior and as Riot says 'help keep the community safe'.

A fully sustainable esports future needs to be socially sustainable.

There is a lot more that needs to be done at all levels of the esports ecosystem. Educating young people on how to play and deal with others is better than letting them model behavior from random teammates they come across online. The key actors here from my perspective are the publishers who should/could make more effort to reduce negative experiences and keep people playing their games. After all, that is where the revenue comes from.

Identity and the Value of Virtual Goods

If something is free then you are the product. Over 3500 total hours of play, I would estimate that I have spent approximately 700 euros on virtual skins and passes for both games (note: my own money). Essentially around 1 euro for every five hours of play. That's actually not bad value per hour compared to what else I could have spent it on. But if you had told me that I would spend that before I started to play, I would have dismissed the suggestion out of hand. For anyone who hasn't played, this may be the most difficult aspect to understand of the consumer's journey. Not because it's real money for items that are virtual, but instead how these virtual items and the game itself become a part of your identity. I start every marketing communications class I teach with the example of how diamonds are intrinsically worthless so engagement rings were a marketing ploy. But value is ultimately personal and linked to what you can afford. The pandemic certainly left me with some extra 'entertainment' money but the pandemic also meant that playing became a bigger part of my identity overall. You are what you eat, but also as gamers, you are what you play. And also identify with who you play with. I managed to excitedly tell former NIP legend Potti about how I reached Gold Nova 4 without realizing who he was. He's a nice guy though and seemed genuinely pleased for me. We are part of the same tribe even if our skill levels are comparative to me entering a mixed martial arts competition for eight year olds.

And when you begin to identify as a player of the game, then skins and cosmetics begin to make sense. In CS:GO I could customize my guns through stickers and by naming them. I bought and renamed specific guns in order to give them to my CS:GO friends when they finally left Silver ranks to join the hallowed ranks of Gold. I gave away my most expensive skin 'Cassie'(named after my cat) to Siggie of Para Esports. I even got to enjoy the fact that my skin actually *killed* Potti through Siggie in a charity game at DreamHack. But mostly I enjoyed the skins for myself as part of what defined me in the game. At least three guns had 'I'm too old for this' stickers while I renamed my AWP skin to 'You Will Miss' so any enemy picking it up might have a moment of doubt. With

CS:GO you can also re-sell your skins so if I ever get around to it, I do theoretically have some extra savings I can cash in. But that's the thing, I'm no longer a CS:GO player as I now identify as a Valorant player.

CS:GO was escapism and socializing during the pandemic but Valorant fulfills a different role in my life. In CS:GO I could meet a lot of people around my age but Valorant trends younger towards Generation Z. It's simple escapism that gets my mind off other things rather than a social outlet. But as a gamer, Valorant defines me as it's what I mostly play. Similarly my agents of choice define how I play (Breach/Killjoy/Brimstone mains). And still I enjoy purchasing virtual items as weapon skins. Research on CS:GO suggested that weapon skins do not impact performance but has suggested it may boost confidence (Stahl & Rusk, 2020). Valorant's approach is different with individual weapon skins having distinct sounds. For myself and others I have talked to, this can make some guns 'feel' more accurate through sound. Could be a worthwhile research topic on its own, as this may indeed improve your performance. Weapon skins also have special effect 'finishers' that occur with the last kill of the round to really add a moment of joy to victory.

What my unique position as a researcher who engages with esports has afforded me is the opportunity to possess a RIOT gun buddy. Gun buddies are little trinkets that hang from your weapon to add a little unique flair (similar to stickers in CS:GO). The RIOT gun buddy is a unique rare buddy that can only be granted to a player by a RIOT employee (thanks Graham). It's sometimes granted by a RIOT employee who wants to reward positive play in a game but more commonly pro players, streamers and influencers have them. When others notice it, they ask if I'm a 'Riot Dev' or a streamer and often ask for one. I've had members of the opposition team try to add me as a friend after they notice it. While I have to admit it did give my inner child's ego somewhat of a thrill to be in possession of one, the reality is that it provided me with a form of legitimacy in-game. So if asked where I got it, I would reply because I was a 'professor specializing in esports' which could lead to some interesting discussions. I still use the gun buddy because it also seems to reduce the potential toxicity of teammates. Games felt tangibly less serene during a period when I removed it for a couple of weeks. Asking shoutcaster Mitch McBride about this effect on Discord he replied "Oh 100%, if you have it on people often assume you can ban them [as in know somebody who can] so they nicen up". So my official stance on using my buddy is not 'ego boost' but instead as a symbolic shield that can deflect toxicity.

Conclusion

The reflections here are only a snapshot of what I've learned through active engagement with esports play. The volume of data still to be framed, analyzed and written up is actually somewhat intimidating. Sometimes I used a voice transcription software to make live notes during a game which truly captures the emotional trip that a single game can elucidate. But while I mostly played in my free time, it was still a form of work. It's only since I stopped keeping diaries that I can truly use esports play as a form of full relaxation. There are a number of times recorded in my diaries where I observe that I should have muted someone early on but for the 'sake of research' I kept listening to the detriment of my own peace of mind. Ultimately the experience has been a positive one as have the majority of interpersonal exchanges. Most people playing games online are doing it for the right reasons and negative experiences may simply be the result of someone having a bad day. I now understand a lot more about the communities around the games I play while also understanding the perspectives of those within the esports ecosystems. With so many layers of practices, rituals and memes around each of the multitude of esports titles, there is a need for a multitude of auto-netnographic studies to unpack it all. Such studies can be of value from almost any academic discipline with bonus points for interdisciplinary studies that tap into how esports can act as a future lab for the digital society.

I can supply some tips for gaming researchers looking to follow my path in playing as research. First tap into your social capital. I had a multitude of esports actors and academics I could reach out to so I could clarify how I perceived experiences through ongoing dialogues with them. Also I've played with many of these connections including through games that allowed me to contextualize my specific experiences within the wider FPS genre. People were happy to spend a few hours guiding me through the experience of Overwatch on PC or helping me attempt Apex Legends on the XBox. Just a note that if you enjoy console/controller based FPS games, then you should not switch to the PC keyboard/mouse format. It's impossible to return to aim assisted inaccuracy after you experience the precision of a mouse to shoot.

Next up, the concept of swatting is a real thing. Probably not the best idea to let a mischievous random teenager know who you are exactly even if it's just to avoid toxic comments on your public facing profiles. If you're actually worse than me and truly struggle with your performance then you can always put dedicated effort in to improve. Conversely, a paper on your experiences as a truly awful player would be a fascinating read. There's no shame in not being good at games. This paper probably makes me the only person scientifically 'proven' to not be good at two games. Brian McCauley is not very good at CS:GO (McCauley, 2023) acts as a great ice breaker for any presentation. Next course that I teach will also include this paper as part of introducing myself so that I can introduce myself as bad at two games.

You can also use your experiences as a better way to connect with a variety of gaming and esports stakeholders. It's a shared culture and in the era of liquid modernity it's gaming that can connect us. I actually co-wrote a book chapter on the Black Mirror episode Playtest which looked at how modern society is more 'liquid' and people lack the societal anchors of previous generations (See: Macey & McCauley, 2021). The EU resolution on games and esports even recognizes how games can be a crucial part of forming a common European identity. I don't attend events as a researcher, I primarily attend as someone who loves gaming culture and is genuinely curious about the different facets. Every paper I have ever read that uses the term 'computer games' as opposed to video games, makes me question if the authors actually do understand the wonderful world I'm lucky enough to engage with through my work.

I'll finish with a statement that only low elo Valorant players can truly understand. I just want to end on a sentiment that has been felt and stated in some form a lot within the Valorant play experience. Instalock Reynas are the worst!

References

Brock, T. (2023). Ontology and interdisciplinary research in esports. *Sport, Ethics and Philosophy*, 1-17.

Hedlund, D.P. (2021). A typology of esport players. *Journal of Global Sport Management, 8*(2), 460–477. https://doi.org/10.1080/24704067.2021.1871858

Huston, C., Gracia B Cruz, A., & Zoppos, E. (2022). Dimensionalizing esports consumption: Alternative journeys to professional play. *Journal of Consumer Culture, 22*(2), 456-475.

Huston, C. Y., Cruz, A. G. B., & Zoppos, E. (2023). Welcome to esports, you suck: understanding new consumer socialisation within a toxic consumption collective. *Journal of Marketing Management*, 1-26.

Karhulahti, V.-M. (2020). *Esport play: Anticipation, attachment, and addiction in psycholudic development*. Bloomsbury Publishing USA.

Kozinets, R. V. (2022). Immersive netnography: a novel method for service experience research in virtual reality, augmented reality and metaverse contexts. *Journal of Service Management, 34*(1), 100-125.

Kozinets, R. V. (2015). *Netnography: redefined*. Sage.

Kozinets, R.V. (2020). Netnography today, a call to evolve, embrace, energize, and electrify. In R.V. Kozinets & G. Rossella (Eds.), *Netnography unlimited: Understanding technoculture using qualitative social media research* (pp. 3–24). Routledge.

Kozinets, R.V., & Kedzior, R. (2009). I, Avatar: Auto-netnographic research in virtual worlds. In N.T. Wood & M.R. Solomon (Eds.), *Virtual social identity and consumer behavior* (pp. 3–19). Routledge

Macey, J., & McCauley, B. (2021). Mind Games. *Reading» Black Mirror «: Insights into Technology and the Post-Media Condition, 75*, 69.

Macey, J., & McCauley, B. (2021). Mind Games. *Reading» Black Mirror «: Insights into Technology and the Post-Media Condition, 75*, 69.

McCauley, B., Nguyen, T. H. T., McDonald, M., & Wearing, S. (2020a). Digital gaming culture in Vietnam: an exploratory study. *Leisure Studies, 39*(3), 372-386.

McCauley, B., Tierney, K., & Tokbaeva, D. (2020b). Shaping a regional offline eSports market: Understanding how Jönköping, the 'City of DreamHack', takes URL to IRL. *International Journal on Media Management, 22*(1), 30-48.

McCauley, B. (2023). An Auto-netnographic Approach to Understanding Alternate Gaming Accounts: How Smurfing Impacts the Prosumer Experience in Counter-Strike: Global Offensive. *Journal of Electronic Gaming and Esports, 1*(1).

Scholz, T. M. (2019). *eSports is Business* (Vol. 15). Springer International Publishing.

Sharpe, B. T., Besombes, N., Welsh, M. R., & Birch, P. D. (2023). Indexing esport performance. *Journal of Electronic Gaming and Esports, 1*(1).

Ståhl, M., & Rusk, F. (2020). Player customization, competence and team discourse: Exploring player identity (co) construction in Counter-Strike: Global Offensive. *Game Studies, 20*(4).

Toth, A. J., Ramsbottom, N., Constantin, C., Milliet, A., & Campbell, M. J. (2021). The effect of expertise, training and neurostimulation on sensory-motor skill in esports. *Computers in Human Behavior, 121*, 106782.

Witkowski, E. (2012). On the digital playing field: How we "do sport" with networked computer games. *Games and Culture*, *7*(5), 349-374.

Exploring Women's Experiences in Collegiate Esports Leadership

By By Kim S. Johnson, Jesus H. Trespalacios, Brett Shelton, Chareen Snelson

It has multiple names, but esports is defined as collaborative video game competitions (Darvin et al., 2020). Historically, esports began early in arcade play in the 1980s (Borowy & Jin, 2013). Around the same time that esports gained popularity in the United States, it picked up steam in South Korea (Kim et al., 2020). Esports now realize explosive growth at all levels of competition and in all industry sectors (Darvin et al., 2020). As a result, it is a topic that has become increasingly popular with researchers (Reitman et al., 2020).

As there is in business (Northouse, 2013), higher education administration (Cantu-Lee, 2013; Lu, 2020), and collegiate athletic administration (Samuel, 2020), a leadership gender gap exists in collegiate esports as well. Although researchers have conducted studies on some aspects of esports, including issues involving gender, player and spectator experiences, definitions, history, and status as a sport (Castillo, 2019; Cullen, 2018; Malvone, 2020; Ruotsalainen & Friman, 2018), the role of collegiate varsity coaches and directors has not been the focus of an esports study. Therefore, we know little about women's experiences leading collegiate varsity esports programs. Learning about these women's experiences in leadership roles is essential as they are role models and mentors for other women. Their experiences may provide insight into how the leadership gender gap may be tightened or closed or how we may negate or supersede stereotypes. Women serving as esports program leaders are involved in teaching, leading, and managing players and programs in a high-tech atmosphere. It is likely that these women coaching or directing esports did not come into the position as players first, although some might have (Salo, 2017). Women in this role work in a male-dominated culture, and they have learned some things about how to navigate it. This study provides a stage for these women who are collegiate varsity esports leaders allowing us to understand the essence of their experience through themes they have in common.

Giving voice to these women may illuminate problems they have encountered during their careers or provide solutions to issues that many women confront on the path to serving in leadership. Sharing these experiences may help educate men working in these environments on how they may support women seeking to break barriers to positions of authority. Women need support from other women as well. These stories may show women how they can better assist each other. Providing a platform for these women to share their experiences may also motivate or inspire others seeking to break barriers leading to more significant opportunities. Thus, the purpose of this descriptive (transcendental) phenomenological study was to explore and describe the essence of women's lived experiences in their role in leading collegiate varsity esports programs at institutions of higher education. Leading collegiate varsity esports programs involves coaching or directing university-sanctioned esports teams or programs. The research question, "What are the lived experiences of women serving as leaders of collegiate esports programs?" was the basis for this study.

Esports

Esports is just one name for this activity, also known as "electronic sports, cybersports, gaming, competitive computer gaming, virtual sports" (Jenny et al., 2017, p. 1), and professional gaming (McTee, 2014). There is no single definition of esports that everyone subscribes to (Freeman & Wohn, 2017).

Wagner's (2006) widely cited definition reads, "esports is an area of sports activities in which people develop and train mental or physical abilities in the use of information and communication technologies" (p. 3). In their discussion of previous definitions, Darvin et al. (2020) called it "competitive video gaming competitions that take place in person and/or in an interactive online environment" (p. 36), and Reitman et al. (2020) also cite Hamari and Sjoblom's (2017) definition, "a form of sports where the primary aspects of the sport are facilitated by electronic systems; the input of players and teams as well as the output of the eSports system are mediated by human computer interfaces" (p. 213). Freeman and Wohn (2017) discussed these competitions in virtual worlds, where teams must complete collaborative tasks at high speed. Railsback and Caporusso (2019) stated that "electronic sports (eSports) is a novel type of competition and spectator entertainment that pits individuals or teams playing video games in front of a large crowd attending the show in person or remotely" (p. 1). According to Ruvalcaba et al. (2018), "esports reconceptualizes sports as a combination of competition, ability, and digital technology" (p. 1). Simply put, "E-sports commonly refer to an organized and competitive approach to playing computer games" (Witkowski, 2012, p. 350). There is a complexity to esports because it is new and an aggregate of technology, society, economics, and sport (Jin, 2010).

The various definitions are similar in that they revolve around esports' technical, organized, competitive, and game aspects. Differences in the definitions arise when adding a level of complexity by including the mention of training, location - virtual worlds, interactive online environment, and the addition of remote or in-person viewers.

As esports has grown in popularity, esports research has also increased, though it is still early in the game (Darvin et al., 2017; Kim et al., 2020; Reitman et al., 2020; Salo, 2017). Esports literature doubled in quantity in 2012, and growth continues to be steady (Reitman et al., 2020). Esports research covers various disciplines such as sports sci-

ence, psychology, business, sports management, law, gender studies, and technology (Reitman et al., 2020). Many esports studies provide a definition of esports, a brief history of esports, a discussion of whether esports is a sport, compare it to traditional sports, and discuss the types of games that make up esports (Funk et al., 2017).

A problem exists at all levels of athletic administration as women are underrepresented in interscholastic sport leadership and intercollegiate sport.

Several studies examine the role of esports in developing highly desirable and transferable soft skills such as communication, teamwork, collaboration, and problem-solving (Castillo, 2019; Richard et al., 2019; Rothwell & Shaffer, 2019; Wagner, 2006). Common themes of recent studies discuss male dominance in esports, the lack of women players, and the toxicity of the computer gaming culture as explorations involving esports shift to examining esports communities and culture (Castillo, 2019; Lopez-Fernandez et al., 2019; Reitman et al., 2020; Ruotsalainen & Friman, 2018; Witkowski, 2014). While researchers may examine players' experiences, other researchers may focus on the affairs of the viewers (Ruotsalainen & Friman, 2018). Studying the experiences of those in esports leadership and, specifically, women in esports leadership has not attracted much attention from researchers.

Women in Sports Leadership

A problem exists at all levels of athletic administration as women are underrepresented in interscholastic sport leadership (Massengale, 2009) and intercollegiate sport (Acosta and Carpenter, 2014). Researchers have found the barriers in this field (Gray, 2020) are obstacles similar to those seen in "media, business, and politics" (Lu, 2020, p. 6). Some of those barriers are "gender stereotypes" in leadership (Eagly & Carli, 2007, p.94), shortage of mentoring and networking opportunities (Kellerman & Rhodes, 2007), family and work balance, pay discrimination, "the old boys club" (Schneider et al., 2010, p. 16), lack of respect (Stangl &Kane, 1991), intense scrutiny (Samuel, 2020) "glass ceiling" (Eagly & Carli, 2007, p. 6), "homologous reproduction" (Stangl & Kane, 1991, p. 47), and "Queen Bee Syndrome" (Derks et al., 2011, p. 1243). "Queen Bee Syndrome" is when a woman serving in leadership does not wish to support other women trying to make their way into leadership positions (Derks et al., 2011, p. 1243). Additionally, barriers that women face may be structural, those outside of a person's control, such as discrimination. Discrimination may hinder access by denying a person access to resources or a position, or discrimination may show as mistreatment of people (Cunningham, 2021). Other barriers may be individual, such as a person's mindset that may keep them from excelling (Gray, 2020).

One might assume that the underrepresentation of women should not exist in athletics due to the passing of Title IX. Surprisingly, the number of female collegiate athletic directors plummeted after the enactment of Title IX in 1972, followed by implementation in 1978 (Samuel, 2020). Though this enactment has been a positive for women athletes, it has not been an improvement across the board for the most part. More sports are available for women now, and many more are playing collegiate sports (Acosta & Carpenter, 2014). However, there is a profound deficit in a career in coaching or directing athletics (Whisenhunt et al., 2005, Samuel, 2020; Semonova, 2020).

Before Title IX, women directed 90% of women's athletic programs (Acosta & Carpenter, 2014), and women coached most women's teams. When the government implemented Title IX in 1978, schools merged men's and women's athletic departments in most cases, and the leadership position usually went to the male athletic director (Acosta & Carpenter, 2014). In some football-related instances, athletic directors may be retired football coaches due to the weight given to revenue-producing athletic programs (Kies, 2014).

The number of women serving as athletic directors is deficient – in 2012, that percentage was 22.3% (Acosta & Carpenter, 2014). Looking at the figures for Division I Athletic Directors, in 2014, only 10% were women. Even more dismal, 11.3% of colleges have no women in athletic administration (Acosta & Carpenter, 2014). The number of women coaching women's sports has also diminished, leading to fewer women coaching in the future. Fewer women serving in collegiate sports leadership is an unfortunate, unforeseen effect of intentionally developing something to improve women's situations. Women athletes are more likely to see coaching as an employment option if they played for a woman coach than a male coach (Everhart & Chelladuari, 1998).

The lack of women leaders in politics, business, higher education, and athletic administration speaks to the essential nature of studies focusing on women's leadership, emphasizing those conducted by women (Lu, 2020). Research studies focusing on women athletic directors at the collegiate level in the U.S. have been light, at least up through 2015. However, more literature exists on women leading professional athletic programs in Europe (Kies, 2015). More women sharing their experiences in collegiate sports leadership will keep the issue from falling by the wayside (Inglis et al., 2000). Though not a substitute for in-person mentorship (Bower et al., 2009), perhaps women researchers helping women leaders share their stories through such studies will affect change. These researchers describe the successes and difficulties of role models and describe leadership opportunities for women in business, higher education administration, collegiate athletics administration (Kies, 2015; Samuel, 2020), or even collegiate esports.

Methods

Methodological Framework

The chosen theoretical framework for this descriptive (transcendental) phenomenological study was phenomenology. Though there are multiple types of phenomenology, the two most prevalent philosophies are those of Edmund Husserl and his student, Martin Heidegger. Husserl is known as the father of phenomenology (Peoples, 2021). Peoples (2021) stated that phenomenological philosophy is the primary theoretical framework for guiding a phenomenological research study. Peoples (2021) explained that Husserl's phenomenology, also known as transcendental or descriptive phenomenology, demands that phenomenological philosophy is the only framework for this type of study. In contrast, Martin Heidegger's phenomenology, a departure from Husserl's form known as hermeneutic or interpretive phenomenology, allows for a secondary framework as a lens for viewing the data (Peoples, 2021). Therefore, depending on the variety of phenomenology chosen, other theoretical frameworks may be used secondarily as a lens for viewing the experience.

Though variations of phenomenological studies exist, the descriptive (transcendental) phenomenological philosophy and methodology guide this study for several reasons. First, the descriptive (transcendental) form of phenomenology is appropriate for human science in education (Cartwright et al., 2018) and educational technology (Cilesiz, 2009, 2010; Valentine et al., 2018), and it is a relevant approach to studying groups who may be underrepresented (Cartwright et al., 2018). In addition, researchers using Husserl's version of phenomenology benefit from detailed data analysis procedures outlined in Moustakas (1994).

One might assume that the underrepresentation of women should not exist in athletics due to the passing of Title IX.

Due to the selection of Husserl's approach to phenomenology, a single framework was applied to this inquiry – appropriately, that of phenomenological philosophy. As there are no studies pinpointing women in collegiate esports leadership, this study was exploratory and should not be boxed in or tethered down by expectations leveraged by additional frameworks (Peoples, 2021). Therefore, data emerged naturally from the conversations with participants, followed by careful and thoughtful analysis (Seidman, 2019), which was instrumental in achieving "a pure essence of the phenomenon," as Husserl ascribes (Peoples, 2021, p. 30).

Selection of Participants

Information about this study was sent to the National Association for Collegiate Esports (NACE) organization for distribution to its members to generate an initial pool of participants. This information included an invitation to women coaches or directors of collegiate esports programs inviting them to participate in the study. Interested parties may respond to the invitation through email. In addition, invitations were emailed directly to women identified through the NACE member database or an online search that met the participant criteria. Once potential participants were identified, they received detailed information about the study via email. Because participants lived anywhere in the country, interviews were via Zoom web conferencing conducted from a studio at work.

Seven participants were a criterion sample - they met specific criteria. In this case, they were women who were leaders in collegiate varsity esports programs at various institutions of higher learning across the nation, serving as coaches, directors, or coordinators. Each of these women had experience with the phenomenon of leading a collegiate varsity esports program. The recommended number of participants for phenomenological studies varies; however, typically, the number falls between "3 to 4 participants to 10 to 15" (Creswell and Poth, 2018). Sufficiency, one of the traditional data collection criteria, may be met through as few as five participants (Seidman, 2019). For this study, the minimum number of five participants came from the low end of the ranges cited by Seidman. Eight is the approximate number of participants for the upper end of the participant range – though that remains fluid - keeping in mind the importance of manageable data management by limiting the number of participants and at the same time aiming to meet the primary goal of data saturation (Seidman, 2019; Peoples, 2021). According to Peoples (2021), data saturation is more critical in qualitative studies than adhering strictly to a projected number of participants. Seidman (2019) pointed out that in-depth interviews can be highly fruitful. Since there were three in-depth interviews with each participant, the extra time spent with each participant may have led to saturation with fewer participants than in studies with only one discussion per participant (Fusch & Ness, 2015).

Data Collection

Following Seidman's (2019) phenomenological interviewing methodology, data was collected through three semi-structured interviews with each participant over four weeks. Seidman explained:

"The first interview establishes the context of the participants' experience. The second allows participants to reconstruct the details of their experience within the context in which it occurs. And the third encourages the participants to reflect on the meaning their experience holds for them." (p. 21)

The first interview sessions centered on the personal history or historical context that prefaced the participants' experiences in collegiate esports leadership. A second interview with each participant focused on their actual experiences as leaders of collegiate esports programs. With intentionality, participants described their memories or "mental representations" of the actual experiences (Jacobs, 2019) of leading a collegiate esports program. The third interview session targeted their work as leaders of collegiate esports programs and how it was meaningful to them. The last session was also top of mind allowing for probing or follow-up questions and clarification if needed. Collected data

reached saturation with seven participants as no new themes emerged (Peoples, 2021).

The three separate interviews with each of the seven participants were conducted via web conferencing using the Zoom application from a private studio at work. Participants scheduled the sessions at their convenience and attended the sessions from their choice of location. The interviews were conducted primarily in the mornings and early afternoons. Participants had the choice of whether or not to use their cameras during the interviews. One participant chose to keep her camera off. Before each session, preconceptions were purposely noted in the reflection journal and bracketed or set aside. The first two sessions with each participant were approximately 45 minutes in length. The third sessions were 20-30 minutes in length. The Zoom application made audio and video recordings available. In addition, an audio recorder provided backup. Transcripts were generated from the audio files using Office 365 dictation and then checked and edited for accuracy. Each participant received edited transcripts for their records, providing an opportunity for further input.

The interviews were semi-structured in that each of the three interviews had a particular theme centered on lived experiences - not perceptions, not opinions – only experiences. To avoid sharing perceptions and beliefs, participants should "reconstruct the experience" or "tell a story," and the researcher should "ask for concrete details" (Seidman, 2019, p. 93-95). Participants received interview protocols listing each discussion's theme and general questions. The first interview uncovered how the participant got involved in esports in the context of their personal history. How did they find themselves in this type of work? A second interview built upon this unique history served to record experiences - the day-to-day details - of what an esports leader does. Finally, a third interview delved into each participant's meaning of these experiences.

Data Analysis

First, the process of phenomenological reduction that began with bracketing continues with examining each participant's experience statements or horizons. Each horizon will have an equal value from the onset (Moustakas, 1994). Invariant constituents, also known as horizons or statements, describe a portion of the experience and can be labeled (Moustakas, 1994). The comments or horizons which are insignificant – those things that are repetitious, unclear, or are perceptions or opinions, or do not apply to the phenomenon are set aside (Moustakas, 1994; Yüksel & Yıldırım, 2015). Next, sort significant statements according to themes as "phenomenology tends to look at data thematically to extract essences and essentials of participant meanings" (Moustakas, 1994; Miles et al., 2020, p. 21). There may be overarching themes related to the primary focus of each interview session, such as historical context, daily experiences, and meaning. More descriptive themes may be nested within these higher-level themes or other themes added to this level during analysis. As the list of themes emerges, participants' statements are coded to the themes, essentially grouping them within the core themes (Moustakas, 1994).

Taking a second look at the invariant constituents and themes and ensuring they are explicit in the complete interview transcriptions and compatible is a recommended validation process. If the statements and themes do not pass the validation test, they should be removed (Moustakas, 1994). The phenomenological reduction phase concludes by forming in-depth textural descriptions of the themes and horizons for each participant based on the perspective of their experiences as leaders of collegiate esports programs. Descriptions included examples in the original phrasing from the interview transcripts (Moustakas, 1994). A synthesis of participants' individual textural descriptions yielded a composite textural description (Moustakas, 1994).

Next, the goal of imaginative variation is to "seek possible meanings" and "uncover(ing) essences" (Moustakas, 1994, p. 97-98; Yüksel & Yıldırım, 2015). Reflect on each of the participant's descriptions of their experiences while viewing them through varying "perspectives, imagination, positions, roles, or functions" to generate a structural description for each of the participants (Moustakas, 1994, p. 97-98; Yüksel & Yıldırım, 2015). That is to look for the experience's underlying structure, or as Moustakas (1994) questions, "how did the experience of the phenomenon come to be what it is" (p. 98)? Moustakas (1994) suggested considering structures such as "time, space, bodily concerns, materiality, causality, relation to self, or relation to others" concerning the phenomenon (p. 99).

First interviews with participants that focused on personal history and provided context for their current work were helpful during this process of discerning the "how" of the experience (Moustakas, 1994). Writing individual structural descriptions for each participant led to the generation of a composite structural description. Data analysis concluded with a "synthesis of meanings and essences" (Moustakas, 1994, p. 100). The participants' meanings and essences held in common are where the overall essence of the phenomenon appears (Cilesiz, 2010). Husserl (1931, p. 43 as cited in Moustakas, 1994) describes essence as "that which is common or universal, the condition or quality without which a thing would not be what it is" (p.100). Upon completing the analysis, the result is a rich, transparent composite textural-structural description that expresses the essence of women's experience in collegiate esports leadership as the fruit of this study (Creswell and Poth, 2018).

Validity

Creswell and Poth (2018) suggested several validation strategies to employ throughout the project, such as asking a "valid phenomenological question" and analyzing genuine experiences as opposed to perceptions and opinions (p. 272). In addition, this study sits on the foundation of phenomenological philosophy. Reflexivity and bracketing through journaling separated the researcher's position from the participants' experiences throughout the interviewing and analysis process (Creswell & Poth, 2018, Moustakas, 1994, Peoples, 2021). Since the interview process included three meetings, there was a chance to build a working relationship with participants, further validating the project (Seidman, 2019).

Another key was to use questioning strategies for phenomenological study validation and evaluation criteria (van Manen, 2014). Once interview transcriptions were available, participants received copies of their transcriptions to review. Participants had the chance to edit the transcription as desired before data analysis begins. Allowing participants to review and edit the transcripts was a form of member checking, offering further validation (Cilesiz, 2010; Seidman, 2019). Finally, several "Big Tent" strategies lead to high-quality qualitative research. These strategies from Tracy (2010) included: ensuring the topic is "worthy of study, has rich rigor, sincerity, credibility, resonance, is a significant contribution, is ethical, and provides meaningful coherence" (p. 840).

Results and Discussion

The phenomenon investigated in this study was the women's lived experiences in their role in leading collegiate varsity esports programs at institutions of higher education. As a thematic array may be used as a visual summary of analysis (Miles et al., 2020), the thematic array displayed in Figure 1 illustrates the relationships between the interview topics and themes and the overall essence of being a woman leading a collegiate esports program. Personal history affects our current work and how we see it as meaningful and both are structures that uphold our current work experience and along with that experience make up the essence of the experience. The construction of each participant's individual textural description was associated with these six themes: managing tasks, managing facilities, managing people, interfacing with various groups of people, women in leadership, and the work environment.

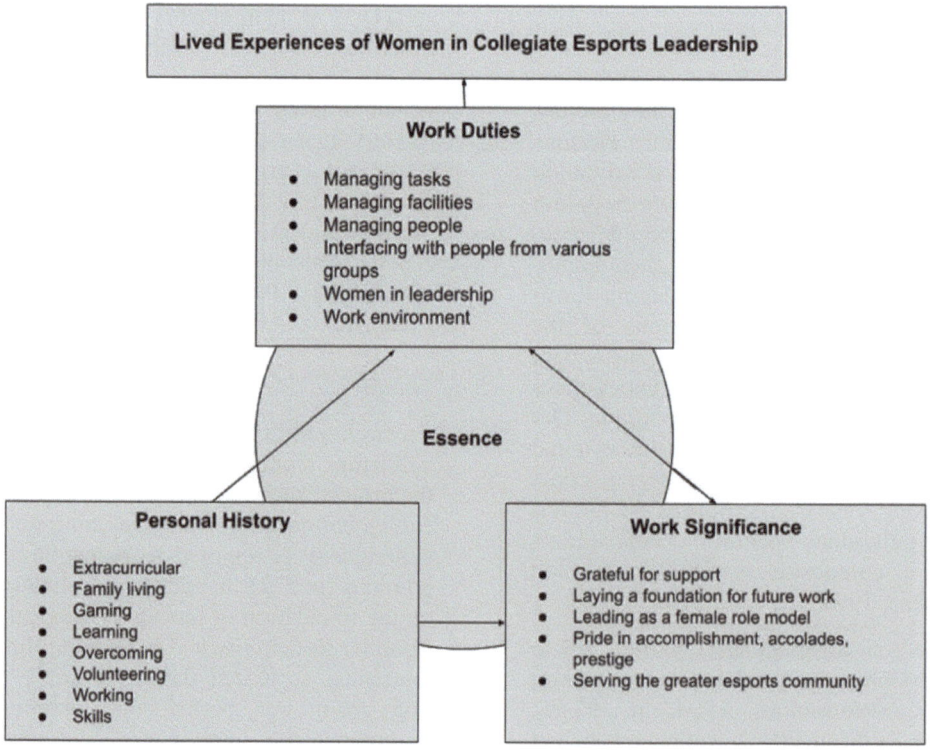

Figure 1 Thematic array: Lived experiences of women in collegiate esports leadership

Managing Tasks

Women who are leaders of collegiate esports programs' lived experiences include overseeing various managerial tasks that involve marketing, scheduling, planning, budgeting, and policies and procedures. One participant stated, "I am the person, you know, typically answering all channels of social media and phone calls, emails, making the website as well, and just making sure that we have a plan for the campaigns that …go out." Each of these tasks is multi-faceted. For instance, marketing includes promoting the brand, the teams, events, and tryouts. Scheduling involves scheduling competitive matches, scrims, practices, tournaments, tryouts, co-sponsored events, and meetings. Planning includes setting short-term and long-term goals for all aspects of the program and planning special events. Budgeting may be simple for a smaller program but very complex for a larger program. Formal or informal policies and procedures must be created or adopted and are vital to every facet of the program. For instance, another participant stated,

I really have a hard time with esports because I do not get a schedule ahead of time. It is very all over the place where people are like, hey, we need to reschedule - like my League team is still trying to reschedule tonight, and that is absolutely driving me crazy. Like why did we not work on this four days ago? I would rather have it worked out and then move forward.

All participants described experiences with managing tasks such as scheduling, planning, tryouts, tracking eligibility, fundraising, and policies and procedures. They also described "recruitment, budget, and marketing responsibilities" (Stevens, 2020, p. vi). Marketing issues, registration for events, and communicating with sponsors are duties that may fall to the team or program manager (Lipovaya et al., 2018) or director or head coach. These tasks are similar to those used for running an athletic program housing multiple sports or a small business with several lines, as each esports program has various teams. Streaming is another task that directors and coaches must manage as they struggle to keep up with the streaming schedule as demand for streaming esports continues to grow (Rothwell & Shaffer, 2019). Some programs reside in an athletic program that provides an established system. Other programs live in IT, student development, or an academic department (Shelton & Haskell, 2018), where a system may need to be built or revised for managing an esports program.

Managing Facilities

Women who lead collegiate esports programs' lived experiences include managing esports facilities, ranging from a competitive space, a practice space, and maybe a casual gaming space. Some programs repurpose computer labs for their esports space. Some facilities are arenas built specifically for esports competition. Often, there is a nearby practice space and possibly an additional space for casual gamers for which esports leaders are responsible. For instance, one participant mentioned,

Yes, so we have a door that separates it out, and so we have TVs and …couches and stuff in that room. And then people can sit down and watch on the TV while we have noise-canceling headphones and a door separating the two. And then the varsity players will be playing in this space while the casters are casting. It is pretty close by.

For smaller programs, the competitive space may be available to casual gamers when not in use. Managing facilities includes scheduling the facilities for competition, practice, casual use, and special events. Leaders oversee the maintenance of hardware and software on gaming computers. They may take care of it themselves, have someone from IT assist, or pay for gaming management software to take care of these needs. Leaders must maintain policies for public health, whether that has to do with spacing, sanitizing, or masks, as in 2020. They may use signed agreements, ID entry, and security cameras to control access and security. Leaders must solve any issues that arise in the facilities. Esports facilities are busy on nights and weekends, so leaders are often present. Related to this situation,

We have cameras set up, so if I think that anything is an issue or something along those lines, then ...I can check with campus safety, and we can figure it out. But other than that, because there is always something going on in the evening, usually a manager is there. ...we cannot watch the space 24/7, but usually, people respect it, 'cause you know we are providing free stuff for people to play on ...there has never been a case of theft or anything along those lines just because like there is, there is no point. There is no point to it. So, people are usually very, very respectful regarding that. We are aware it is a community space.

All participants shared their experiences managing esports facilities, whether small or large, competitive or casual. Railsback and Caporusso (2019) described esports as "a novel type of competition and spectator entertainment that pits individuals or teams playing video games in front of a large crowd attending the show in person or remotely" (p. 1). Venues ranged from simple computer labs to esports arenas for fan support and equipped for broadcasting matches (Castillo, 2019; Funk et al., 2017). Coaches and directors schedule the space, maintain health policies, and deal with any issues. They mentioned streaming some or all of their matches, so the facilities also have a broadcast area to manage. Management includes keeping games, software, and hardware up to date as this sport entirely relies on technology (Kaytoue et al., 2012). Some participants describe the rapid growth and facing a shortage of space and computers for students, making scheduling facilities more difficult.

Managing People

Women leaders of collegiate esports programs' lived experiences include managing students, paid and volunteer staff, and coaches involved in the program. Students may be competitive players, club members, or casual gamers. Leaders must hire staff members and coaches and, at times, let them go. Leaders rely on good communication skills to teach, train, motivate, and inspire each group of people and set expectations. They must schedule players and workers and

ensure everyone is present and does their job. One of the participants described an example of this situation,

They have never competed in a college event before, so I have to be there on their first and then to get them started because they have no idea what to expect. They do not know how to log into the game to meet with their opponent in the chat box. It is like those are things that that - it is a new experience, and that is what I am there for.

Organization skills are essential, especially with large numbers of players and workers. Some players are on scholarship, and some are not. Leaders must keep up with how their students are doing academically and make decisions about eligibility. Some workers receive compensation, and some are volunteers. There may be work studies and interns. Managing such a variety of people adds to the challenge. The leader must help to settle disputes that arise between players or workers. For instance,

Exactly, we have a really large group of students, so right now, I have about 50 to 60 who are across our competitive teams. Probably like 50. And then we have our club, which is about 100. It is climbing ...this is just the start of a new esports club on campus, but in our server, on our campus, we have just recently hit several hundred members.

As discussed in the literature, some duties of the esports coach include evaluating opponents, developing strategies, and encouraging the team (Lipovaya et al., 2018) before, during, and after the match. Most of the head coaches and directors hired part-time coaches or professional players as needed for coaching specific games. That may include preparing the teams physically and mentally (Kim et al., 2020; Railsback & Caporusso, 2019). Most players are males, and though there are some females participating, there is a lack of female team members at every level of competitive esports (Borowy & Gin, 2013; Darvin et al., 2020).

Interfacing with Various People Groups

Leaders rely on communication, networking, and interpersonal skills as they navigate communication among various groups. Contact may be in person or online through web conferencing or social media. Is esports a sport? In esports research, whether esports is a sport is frequently discussed (Malvone, 2020). At least one participant spoke to this aspect directly, and most of them indirectly, as day in and day out, they fulfill the role of esports advocate on their campuses and in their communities, sharing why it is vital to engagement, recruitment, and retention. For instance, looking at relationships with other clubs, one participant mentioned, "I do work ancillary with other clubs…so I have done some workshops with them… you know whoever happens to…want to reach out and talk esports or …lean into stuff that may work with us and their goals."

Approval, funding, programming, staffing, recruiting, and success of the esports program may rely on successfully sharing their vision with these groups. Leaders advocate for esports among faculty, staff, administration, donors, sponsors, and the community as one of their duties includes communicating with stakeholders (Näsström & Arvérus, 2019). They may collaborate on special events with other departments or clubs, and meet with current or future donors and sponsors about additional funding. Interaction with other teams or league officials may occur during tournaments and with other coaches and directors at conferences. Leaders have mentors in and out of esports that they lean on for support and advice. For instance, "I do a lot of the administrative …talking to people, so we have budgeting and things and talking to IT, talking to HR to hire people like the student worker, getting …paying stuff with payroll."

There are also interactions with the esports community – leagues, teams, and other program leaders. The National Association for Collegiate Esports (NACE) is a league for the collegiate varsity level (Andre et al., 2020; Shelton & Haskell, 2018). University members may expect support in developing varsity programs, including help with scheduling, discounts on gear, and consultations with experts. Most participants mentioned the importance of their experiences with mentors in and out of collegiate esports and expressed an appreciation for other women leading collegiate esports programs. Queen Bee Syndrome is not a problem in this circle as the women genuinely support one another (Derks et al., 2011, p. 1243). Many participants in this study have visited or plan to visit local high schools to share information about their programs.

Women in Leadership

Women leaders of collegiate esports programs' lived experiences include leading by building, serving, influencing, and inspiring others locally and in the greater esports community. For example, one participant stated, "A lot of the media requests that I get are to specifically talk about being a woman in esports. Like if it is a panel, it is usually women in esports. It is never …we want you to talk on a panel because your team is really successful." Some leaders are constructing their programs from the beginning, some are taking over very new programs, and some may be working with more established programs – though esports is still very new overall. Being a woman in this position – part of the 10%, can be a driver for success.

> *As rapid growth and frequent changes are commonplace in esports, these participants are constantly adjusting.*

Some leaders offer consultations to schools trying to start programs. For instance, "I started the program from scratch…and managed competitive teams, budgeting, program structure, all of the things you can think of." They serve on boards, are invited to participate in discussion panels, and speak on podcasts, offering their knowledge, expertise, and hard work to benefit the greater esports community. They desire to represent women well and receive recognition for their work. As they perform their work in the public eye on campus or outside their school, they inspire young women and draw them to the gaming community, making it more inviting. "I have to …advocate for esports and why it is important and how are we engaging the students …I am an advocate. I am an educator to make sure that people understand the importance of what we are doing."

Some participants provide assistance, resources, or mentoring to high schools just starting esports programs. The number of high schools offering competitive esports is increasing (Tseng, 2020). With advances in technology and participation in traditional youth sports waning, competitive esports help to fill the gap (Malvone, 2020). Several participants relayed that being a woman in this leadership position was a draw for females as it made the space more inviting. One should not underestimate women's gaming skills and overall technical prowess (Choi et al., 2019; Cullen, 2018). Many young women play games, and perhaps one day, more of them will represent their schools on esports teams (Castillo, 2019).

Work Environment

Women who are collegiate esports program leaders' lived experiences include wearing many hats for long and unusual hours in a creative, rapidly-growing, fast-paced, and understaffed environment. Typical days are not typical. The schedule can be erratic and may include work on nights and weekends. Because the programs are snowballing, staffing may fall short and leave directors or coaches with extended hours, and additional facilities may be required. For instance,

I prefer it that way because we know that esports is kind of like a little bit of a weird schedule. It is a lot of after-hours and weekend stuff, so I do not want to …take up too much of their daytime hours outside of those meetings and the assignments that they need to do in those hours.

Leaders accomplish various tasks and manage multiple groups of people and facilities, as mentioned in the abovementioned themes. They try to keep up with the creative side of esports marketing with content creation, streaming, and social media. Esports as a whole is fast-paced. Leaders must keep up with new rules, multiple leagues, and games' popularity shifts. For collegiate esports directors and head coaches, peers are mainly males in their twenties and thirties. Players are mainly males as well. Esports is so new that it is uncharted territory. There is no guidebook, so coaches and directors write it as they go. About these situations, one participant stated,

Our league rules for NACE change daily sometimes, and so trying to stay on top of that. …people always ask the question, where do you want to be in five years, or where do you think esports will be in five years? And you cannot equate to that. It is where will esports be in three months? In five months, in one - even one year? You cannot tell. New leagues pop up all the time. New rules are set, and so just trying to stay on top of that is a job itself.

As rapid growth and frequent changes are commonplace in esports, these participants are constantly adjusting. Esports as an industry has experienced expeditious growth (Malvone, 2020; McTee, 2014)) during the past ten years (Darvin et al., 2020). Coaches and directors describe frequent game schedule changes and league rule changes. Changes in the popularity of games may mean changes in teams. They work long and varied hours juggling tasks. Many colleagues are young as this career path is new, and most are male. All of the participants stated that the majority of their players are males. Esports is complex partly because of its newness, and participants pointed out that there is no guide on how to do this work. Further, esports is a conglomeration of technology, society, economics, and sport (Jin, 2010).

Conclusions, Limitations, and Future Research

The participants' experiences shared in this study significantly extend the literature on esports, specifically about women serving in collegiate esports leadership. In addition to themes from their actual work experiences, the study also highlighted themes rising from their personal context and work significance

(Seidman, 2019). Therefore, esports literature is also extended in areas related to these themes. As the study covered much ground, pinpointing several takeaways may be helpful. The following list displays some key takeaways.

- Women in leadership positions are role models that attract and influence young women.
- Leading a collegiate esports program is exciting, challenging, and satisfying.
- Leading a collegiate esports program requires knowledge of gaming or esports and managerial, organizational, interpersonal, and technical skills.
- Women leaders of collegiate esports programs do not allow discomfort that might come from being in the 10% to prevent them from leading, serving, and achieving.
- Having experienced or witnessed toxicity, women who lead collegiate esports programs are determined to build a welcoming, inclusive, and toxicity-free gaming environment.
- Leading a collegiate esports program does not require prior experience competing in collegiate or professional esports or being a specific game expert.

A limitation of this study was that the sample is seven participants. The number of women in collegiate esports leadership is not large, and not everyone invited to participate in the study responded to the invitation or agreed to participate. Though the sample size is somewhat smaller, data reached saturation as no new themes were needed (Peoples, 2021). The findings of this study are particular to this group of women at this specific time (Moustakas, 1994). Though the results may seem typical, they cannot be generalized across the population of women in collegiate esports leadership.

In phenomenology, the horizon is the current situation, and "the horizon cannot be bracketed"; therefore, some revelations may become apparent later (Peoples, 2021, pp. 82-83). One recommendation for future research based on the findings of this study would be to repeat the process with this group of women in two to three years. Findings in the literature described that esports is experiencing rapid growth within programs and as a whole as more programs come on board. The work environment theme from the second interviews revealed the rugged, fast-paced, and draining schedule for esports coaches and directors. Most of them were putting in a lot of time and effort in their positions as they were building the foundations of new or newer programs and thinking that things would ease up some as the programs became more established. It would be helpful to see whether that was the case - if they could take more time off and lead a more balanced life after the program became more established.

Another recommendation for research that sprung from the findings of this study from the work environment theme would be to explore the compensation for collegiate esports coaches and directors as one participant spoke of how it is a topic of discussion among leaders and about the gravity of the situation. In the literature, there was a mention of esports' profitability; however, there was no discussion of collegiate coaches' and directors' salaries. A final recommendation arises from a limitation of this study as it is a phenomenology. With phenomenology, only experiences are examined, not opinions or perceptions. Perhaps, researchers would consider conducting a cross-case study with this group or a similar group reviewing the perceptions of women leading an esports program.

References

Acosta, R.V., & Carpenter L.J. (2014). Women in intercollegiate sport. A longitudinal, national study, thirty-seven year update, 1977 – 2014. https://files.eric.ed.gov/fulltext/ED570882.pdf

Andre, T.L., Walsh, S.M., Valladao, S., & Cox, D. (2020). Physiological and perceptual response to a live collegiate esports tournament, *International Journal of Exercise Science,* *13*(6), 1418-1429.

https://www.ncbi.nlm.nih.gov/pmc/articles/PMC7523907/

Borowy, M., & Jin, D. Y. (2013). Pioneering eSport: The experience economy and marketing of early 1980s arcade gaming contests. *International Journal of Communication, 7*, 2254-2274. https://ijoc.org/index.php/ijoc/article/view/2296/999

Cantu-Lee, A. J. (2013). The transformation of a higher education change agent: Women in digital administration (Publication No. 27961879) [Doctoral dissertation, Texas A&M University, Kingsville]. ProQuest Dissertations and Theses Publishing.

Cartwright, A.D., Avent, H.J. R., Munsey, R.B., & Lloyd, H. J. (2018). Interview experiences and diversity concerns of counselor education faculty from underrepresented groups. *Counselor Education & Supervision, 57*(2), 132–146.

Castillo, C. I. (2019). Building heroes. [Undergraduate honors thesis, University of Colorado Boulder]. https://scholar.colorado.edu/concern/undergraduate_honors_theses/v979v345q

Choi, Y., Slaker, J. S., & Ahmad, N. (2019). Deep strike: Playing gender in the world of Overwatch and the case of Geguri. *Feminist Media Studies, 20*(8), 1128-1143.

Cilesiz, S. (2009). Educational computer use in leisure contexts: A phenomenological study of adolescents' experiences at internet cafés. *American Educational Research Journal, 46*(1), 232–274.

Creswell, J.W., & Poth, C.N. (2018). *Qualitative inquiry and research design: Choosing among five approaches* (4th ed). SAGE.

Cullen, A.L.L. (2018). I play to win: Geguri as a (post)feminist icon in esports. *Feminist Media Studies, 18*(5), 948-52.

Cunningham, G.B., Wicker, P., & Walker, N.A. (2021). Editorial: Gender and Racial Bias in Sport Organizations. *Front. Sociol, 6*,

Darvin, L., Vooris, R., & Mahoney, T. (2020). The playing experiences of esport participants: An analysis of treatment discrimination and hostility in esport environments. *Journal of Athlete Development and Experience, 2*(1).

Derks, B., Van Laar, C., Ellemers, N., & de Groot, K. (2011). Gender-bias primes elicit queen-bee responses among senior policewomen. *Psychological Science, 22*(10), 1243–1249.

Eagly, A. H., & Carli, L. L. (2007). *Through the labyrinth: The truth about how women become leaders.* Harvard Business School Press.

Everhart, C. B., & Chelladurai, P. (1998). Gender differences in preferences for coaching as an occupation: The role of self-efficacy, valence, and perceived barriers. *Research Quarterly for Exercise and Sport, 69*(2), 188-200.

Freeman, G., & Wohn, D.Y. (2017). Esports as an emerging research context at CHI: Diverse perspectives on definitions. In *CHI EA '17: Proceedings of the 2017 CHI Conference Extended Abstracts on Human Factors in Computing Systems,* (pp. 1601–1608). Association for Computing Machinary.

Funk, D.C., Pizzo, A.D., & Baker, B. (2017). eSport management: Embracing eSport education and research opportunities. *Sport Management Review, 21*, 7-13.

Fusch, P.I., & Ness, L.R. (2015). Are we there yet? Data saturation in qualitative research. *The Qualitative Report, 20*(9), 1408-1416.

Gray, E. (2020). Barriers to senior leadership positions for women in sport management: Perceptions of undergraduate students and insights from their professors. [Master's thesis, University of Western Ontario]. Electronic Thesis and Dissertation Repository. https://ir.lib.uwo.ca/etd/7098

Hamari, J., & Sjöblom, M. (2017). What is eSports and why do people watch it? *Internet Res., 27*(2), 211-232.

Jacob, P. (2019). Intentionality. *The Stanford Encyclopedia of Philosophy.* Edward N. Zalta (ed.). https://plato.stanford.edu/archives/win2019/entries/intentionality/

Jenny, S.E., Manning, R.D., Keiper, M.C., & Olrich, T.W. (2017). Virtual(ly) athletes: Where eSports fit within the definition of "sport" *Quest, 69*(1), 1–18.

Inglis, S., Danylchuk, K.E., & Pastore, D.L. (2000). Multiple realities of women's work experiences in coaching and athletic management. *Women in Sport & Physical Activity Journal, 9*(2), 1-26.

Jin, D. Y. (2010). *Korea's online gaming empire.* MIT Press.

Kellerman, B., & Rhode, D. L. (2007). Women at the Top: The Pipeline Reconsidered. Longman, K.A. and S. R. Madsen (Eds.), *Women and Leadership in Higher Education* (pp. 23-40). IAP.

Kies, A.L. (2014). *Division I collegiate women athletic directors' perceptions of sexism and career experiences.* [Doctoral dissertation, University of Wisconsin Milwaukee]. UWM Digital Commons. https://dc.uwm.edu/etd/564

Kim, Y.H., Nauright, J., & Suveatwatanakul, C. (2020). The rise of E-Sports and potential for Post-COVID continued growth. *Sport in Society, 23*(11), 1861–1871.

Lipovaya, V., Lima, Y., Grillo, P., Barbosa, C. E., De Souza, J. M., & De Castro Moura Duarte, F. J. (2018). Coordination, communication, and competition in eSports: A comparative analysis of teams in two action games. *ECSCW 2018 - Proceedings of the 16th European Conference on Computer Supported Cooperative Work -Exploratory Papers, 2(1).* European Society for Socially Embedded Technologies. https://dl.eusset.eu/handle/20.500.12015/3122

Lopez-Fernandez, O., Williams, A. J., Griffiths, M. D., & Kuss, D. J. (2019). Female gaming, gaming addiction, and the role of women within gaming culture: A narrative literature review. *Frontiers in Psychiatry, 10*, 1-14.

Lu, X. (2020). The barriers, facilitators, and solutions for women in educational leadership roles in a Chinese university. *International Journal of Chinese Education, 9*(1), 5-24,

Massengale, D. (2009). The Underrepresentation of women in interscholastic sport leadership: A qualitative study on the effects of role incongruity. UNLV Theses, Dissertations, Professional Papers, and Capstones. 64.

McTee, M. (2014). E-Sports: More than just a fad. *Oklahoma Journal of Law and Technology, 10*(1), http://digitalcommons.law.ou.edu/okjolt/vol10/iss1/3

Malvone, N. (2020). Esports Game Changers Impact Society Following the Path of Traditional Sports", *International Journal of Business Management and Commerce, 5*(2), 30–37. http://ijbmcnet.com/images/Vol5No2/4.pdf

Miles, M.B., Huberman, A.M., & Saldana, J. (2020). *Qualitative data analysis: A methods sourcebook* (4th ed.). SAGE.

Moustakas, C. (1994). *Phenomenological research methods.* SAGE.

Näsström, O. and Arvérus, S. (2019). *Managing performance in virtual teams: A multiple case study of esport organizations.* [Unpublished bachelor's thesis, Jonkoping University]. http://urn.kb.se/resolve?urn=urn:nbn:se:hj:diva-44297

Northouse, P.G. (2013). *Leadership: Theory and Practice* (6th ed.). SAGE.

Peoples, K. (2021). *How to write a phenomenological dissertation: A step-by-step guide.* SAGE.

Railsback, D., & Caporusso, N. (2019). Investigating the human factors in eSports performance. In T. Z. Ahram (Ed.), *Advances in Human Factors in Wearable Technologies and Game Design. AHFE 2018. Advances in Intelligent Systems and Computing, vol 795.* (pp. 325-334). Springer.

Richard, G. T., McKinley, Z. A., & Ashley, R. W. (2019). Collegiate Esports as Learning Ecologies: Investigating collaboration, reflection and cognition during competitions. *Transactions of the Digital Games Research Association, 4*(3), 1-41.

Rothwell, G., & Shaffer, M. (2019). eSports in K-12 and Post-Secondary Schools. *Education Sciences,* 9(2), https://doi.org/10.3390/educsci9020105

Reitman, J.G., Anderson-Coto, M.J., Wu, M., Lee, J.S., & Steinkuehler, C. (2020). Esports research: A literature review. *Games and Culture, 15*(1), 32–50.

Ruotsalainen, M., & Friman, U. (2018). There are no women and they all play mercy: Understanding and explaining (the lack of) women's presence in esports and competitive gaming. D*iGRA Nordic '18: Proceedings of 2018 International DiGRA Nordic Conference.* http://www.digra.org/wp-content/uploads/digital-library/DiGRA_Nordic_2018_paper_31.pdf

Ruvalcaba, O., Shulze, J., Kim, A., Berzenski, S. R., & Otten, M.P. (2018). Women's experiences in eSports: Gendered differences in peer and spectator feedback during competitive video game play. *Journal of Sport and Social Issues, 42*(4), 295–311.

Salo, M. (2017). Career transitions of eSports athletes: A proposal for a research framework. *International Journal of Gaming and Computer-Mediated Simulations*, *9*(2), pp. 22–32.

Samuel, D. (2020). *Female Division I athletics directors and credibility in a historically male-dominated location: a feminist rhetorical analysis*. (Publication No. 27958226) [Doctoral dissertation, New Mexico State University]. ProQuest Dissertations and Theses Publishing

Schneider, R. C., Stier, W., Henry, T. J., & Wilding, G. E. (2010). Senior woman administrators' perceptions of factors leading to discrimination of women in intercollegiate athletic departments. *Journal of Issues in Intercollegiate Athletics*, *3*, 16-34.

Stangl, J. M., & Kane, M. J. (03/1991). Structural variables that offer explanatory power for the underrepresentation of women coaches since Title IX: The case of homologous reproduction. *Sociology of Sport Journal*, *8*(1), 47-60.

Seidman, I. (2019). *Interviewing as qualitative research: A guide for researchers in education and the social sciences* (5th ed.). Teachers College Press.

Shelton, B. E. & Haskell, C. (2018). *College esports: What you need to know*. Baxajaunak Technology.

Stevens, H.M. (2020). *Coaching the coach: Identifying intercollegiate coaches' attitudes toward needs for leadership development*. (Publication No. 27997628) [Doctoral dissertation, Widener University]. ProQuest Dissertations Publishing.

Tracy, S.J. (2010). Qualitative quality: Eight "big-tent" criteria for excellent qualitative research. *Qualitative Inquiry*, *16*(10), 837-851.

Tseng, Y. (2020). The principles of esports engagement: A universal code of conduct. *Journal of Intellectual Property Law*, 27(2). https://digitalcommons.law.uga.edu/jipl/vol27/iss2/3/

Valentine, K. D., Kopcha, T. J. & Vagle, M. D. (2018). Phenomenological Methodologies in the Field of Educational Communications and Technology. *TechTrends, 62*, 462–472.

van Manen, M. (2014). *Phenomenology of practice: Meaning-giving methods in phenomenological research and writing*. Left Coast Press.

Wagner, M. G. (2006). On the Scientific Relevance of eSports. *Proceedings of the 2006 International Conference on Internet Computing and Conference on Computer Game Development*. 437- 442. https://www.researchgate.net/publication/220968200_On_the_Scientific_Relevance_of_eSports

Witkowski, E. (2012). On the digital playing field: How we "do sport" with networked computer games. *Games and Culture*, *7*(5), 349–374.

Yüksel, P., & Yıldırım, S. (2015). Theoretical frameworks, methods, and procedures for conducting phenomenological studies in educational settings. *Turkish Online Journal of Qualitative Inquiry,* 6(1), 1-20.